Advance Praise for

Health Care Choices in the Boston Area

"*Health Care Choices in the Boston Area* as a resource for consumers will contribute greatly to achieving our goal of patients as partners in health care."

Francis X. Van Houten, MD
President, Massachusetts Medical Society

"It's critical for consumers to have as much information as possible in order to access the present health care system. *Health Care Choices in the Boston Area* is an inclusive source of vital information and excellent resources. This book is an invaluable guide for medical consumers and professionals."

Linda DeBenedictis
President, New England Patients' Rights Group

First Lady Hillary Rodham Clinton
On the companion to *Health Care Choices in the Boston Area*:

"*Health Care Choices for Today's Consumer* is a comprehensive guide to help you and your family ensure that you receive the best and most affordable health care. It comes to you from Families USA, an organization that is a thoughtful and effective advocate for the American health care consumer."

"*Health Care Choices in the Boston Area* is an important publication, long overdue. It provides older people the opportunity to be so well-informed they can make their own health care decisions. I am certain the *Health Care Choices* books will be best sellers."

Elsie Frank
President, Massachusetts Association of Older Americans

"*Health Care Choices in the Boston Area* is an important resource for all of us who are helping people find the health care services they need. It will be indispensable in helping us guide people through the maze called a health care system. *Health Care Choices in the Boston Area* should be in the office of every social worker, social service agency, and health center in the commonwealth."

Rob Restuccia
Executive Director, Health Care for All

"*Health Care Choices in the Boston Area* offers the kind of provider-specific information that should prove particularly helpful to consumers. You will find it useful in meeting your health needs and those of your family."

The Honorable Paul E. Tsongas
Former U.S. Senator

"*Health Care Choices in the Boston Area* finally fills the information gap consumers have long experienced in making their health care decisions. Starting where Families USA's *Health Care Choices for Today's Consumer* leaves off, it provides Boston-area consumers with the specifics we've all needed but haven't had available."

Alan Solomont
President and CEO, ADS Group;
Past President, Massachusetts Association of Nursing Homes

"*Health Care Choices in the Boston Area* should be must reading for consumers. With people young and old facing important, complex decisions about health care for themselves and their families, this book provides timely, valuable information about the resources available in metropolitan Boston and costs as well. With chapters written by people of unusual integrity, this book is both wise and readable."

Evelyn F. Murphy
Former Lieutenant Governor of Massachusetts

HEALTH CARE CHOICES

IN THE BOSTON AREA

Guide to Quality & Cost

Edited by
Marc S. Miller
Martha S. Grover
Philippe Villers

Families USA
Washington, DC

Warning: The instructions and advice presented in this book are in no way intended as a substitute for medical counseling.

Published in the United States of America by
Families USA Foundation, 1334 G St., NW,
Washington, DC 20005

Distributed to bookstores by
Independent Publishers Group, Chicago, IL (800)888-4741

Design, layout, and original artwork by Hobbamock Design
Production by Anne Read
Marketing by Lee Phenner Communications

Grateful acknowledgment is made for permission to use the following materials:
Choice in Dying, Inc., for health care proxy and living will forms.
Center for the Study of Services for materials on eye care and dental care.

To order additional copies of *Health Care Choices in the Boston Area,* use the order form at the end of this book, call (800)699-6960, or check in local stores.

For information on bulk orders, contact Families USA, Health Care Choices, (617)338-6035, ext. 302.

Printed on recycled paper.
Manufactured in the United States of America
ISBN 1-879326-24-8
10 9 8 7 6 5 4 3 2 1

Table of Contents

Acknowledgments

Literally countless people contributed to *Health Care Choices in the Boston Area.* In particular, the members of the advisory board for the *Health Care Choices* project contributed far beyond their "official" roles. Our thanks to J. Larry Brown, Michael Crump, Thomas Delbanco, MD, Barbara Ferrer, Norbert Goldfield, MD, Suzanne Mercure, Joseph Restuccia, DrPH, Richard Rockefeller, MD, Richard Rowe, Michael Segal, Rina Spence, and Harriet Tolpin. Of this number, Richard Rowe deserves special mention: he contributed the initial *idea* that Families USA Foundation issue a consumer's guide to health care.

The chapters in *Health Care Choices in the Boston Area* draw on material in the companion book, *Health Care Choices for Today's Consumer,* the authoritative and comprehensive guide to the U.S. health care system. We thank the authors who contributed to that volume: George J. Annas (Consumer Rights and Death With Dignity); Cindy Brach and Gail Robinson (Mental Health); Nicolás Carballeira (Alternative Health Care); Peggy Denker (Long Term Care); Lou Glass and Mal Schechter (Elders As Health Care Consumers); Robert Krughoff (Eye Care and Dental Care); Nancy Lessin and Laurie Stillman (Workplace Illness and Injury); June Mendelson (Specialists); Ron Pollack (Unreformed Health Care); Joseph Restuccia, Alan Labonte, and Jeffrey Gelb (Hospitals); Martha Taggart (Women As Health Care Consumers); Harriet Tolpin (Primary Care); Nancy Turnbull (Health Insurance); Nora Wells (Parents As Health Care Consumers); and Anne P. Werner and James P. Firman (Home Care).

Our colleagues at Families USA Foundation stole time from the intense demands of their jobs to assist the *Health Care Choices* project, especially Executive Director Ron Pollack and Kate Villers, director of the Massachusetts office. In addition, Rena Murman, Phyllis Torda, Susan Sherry, Natalie Seto, Michelle Weiner, Arnold Bennett, Peggy Denker, and Barbara Campbell contributed, as did many others at Families USA, including board members Robert Kuttner, who played a major role in fleshing out the original concept, Robert Crittendon, and Velvet Miller. Our apologies for not naming the entire organization.

Interns have been indispensable. Thanks to Doreen Balbuena, Sherrylyn Cotaco, David Cuttino, Joshua Dyckman, Shulamit Lewin, Kathryn McKinney, Nonkosi Mzamane, Jason Reblando, Deepika Reddy, and Magda Elise Schaler.

Many other individuals, organizations, and companies contributed time and expertise to *Health Care Choices in the Boston Area.* In roughly alphabetical order, they are: Myron Allukian, Boston Department of Health and Hospitals; Michael Bailit, Massachusetts Healthcare Purchasers Group; Charles Bell, Joel Gurin, and Rhoda Karpatkin, Consumers Union; James Bentley and Peter Kralovic, American Hospital Association; Robert Blendon and John Benson, Harvard School of Public Health; Nancy Bolduc, Dolores Mitchell, and Charles Slavin, Massachusetts Group Insurance Commission; Boston Women's Health Book Collective; Stan Butler, Gay and Lesbian Advocates and Defenders; Frank Coldiron and Andrew Dreyfus, Massachusetts Hospital Association; Thomas Crossman, Jean Delahanty, Lou Friedman, Paula Griswold, Scott Osborne, Kevin Pryor, and Amy Simms, Massachusetts Rate Setting Commission; Phil Kerth, Barbara Masters, Nancy Navin, and Matt Siegel, Massachusetts Division of Insurance; Linda DeBenedictis and Ann Mueller, New England Patients' Rights Group; John Delfs, New England Deaconess Hospital; Cathy Dunham, Robert Wood Johnson Foundation; Maria Durham; Susan Edgman-Levitan, Margaret Gerteis, and Jan Walker, Picker-Commonwealth Program for Patient-Centered Care; Roz Feldberg, Massachusetts Nurses Association; Carol Greenfield and Ken Phillips, New England Employees Benefits Council; Judith Hall; the staff of Health Care for All, especially Cathy Anderson, Marcia Hams, Meizhu Lui, Michael Miller, Kim Shellenberger, Rob Restuccia, and Mary Yeaton; James Hunt, Massachusetts League of Community Health Centers; Karen Ignani, Nina Lane, Sue Palsbo, and Susan Pisano, Group Health Association of America; Jeffrey Kichen, Massachusetts Medical Association; Martha Kleinerman, Dorothy Lohmann, Louise Osborn, and Alice Verhoeven, Planned Parenthood Clinic of Greater Boston; Robert Krughoff, *Checkbook* magazine; Shirley LaBerteaux; Janet Leigh and Virginia Sullivan, Massachusetts Department of Public Health; Julie Mallozzi; John May and Margaret Fearey, Massachusetts Association of HMOs; Jeanne McGee; Susan McTier, Medirisk, Inc.; Ken Melansen, Vinfen Corporation; Andrea Monderer and Rebecca Morse, Women's Educational and Industrial Union; New England HEDIS Coalition; Al Norman, Mass Home Care; Margaret O'Kane and Linda Shelton, National Committee for Quality Assurance; Pat McDonald and Patrick O'Reilly, Massachusetts Peer Review Organization; Lee Phenner; Barbara Popper, Children in Hospitals; Alan Raymond, Harvard Community Health Plan; Anne Read; Gail Ross, Lichtman, Trister, Singer, and Ross; Martin Schneider, *Health Pages* magazine; Terry Shannon, Agency for Health Care Policy and Research; Loretta Sherblom; Gary Snyderman and Doug Steel, Joint Commission for the Accreditation of Health Care Organizations; Elliot Stone, Massachusetts Health Data Consortium; Deborah Thomson, Massachusetts Law Reform Institute; Manny Weiner, Massachusetts Senior Action Council; Karen Wong, Hobbamock Design; Richard Wurman; Gina Yarbrough, Massachusetts Mental Health Legal Advisors Committee; Joan Yesner; and Arnold Zide.

Marc S. Miller *Martha S. Grover* *Philippe Villers*

Foreword

By Senator Edward M. Kennedy

Within 20 miles of downtown Boston lie some of the country's finest medical resources—prestigious teaching hospitals, high-quality community hospitals, world-renowned physicians and other health professionals, an outstanding network of community health centers, and a broad variety of health maintenance organizations and other managed-care programs. Model government programs offer services to many who would otherwise be left out. These superb medical institutions and health care professionals are capable of providing the best quality care in the world to every resident of the metropolitan area.

Unfortunately, the presence of superb health professionals, facilities, and programs does not mean that everyone in this area receives the best care available. Often, the best and worst care exist side by side in the same community. Genuine reform, both in Massachusetts and across the United States, is needed to redress the unnecessary failings and inequities of the current health care system. It should be the goal of government to insist that quality health care is accessible and affordable for every citizen, so that no family need fear that a personal medical crisis will force it into poverty or put adequate and timely care out of reach.

Even under health reform, a great deal will remain up to individuals and their families. In the end, citizens themselves must make many key health decisions. If employers offer more than one health insurance plan or if individuals are buying health insurance on their own, they must decide which plan makes the most sense. Every family must decide for itself which physician and hospital best meet their needs, and which health plan offers the choices they want at a price they can afford.

Health Care Choices in the Boston Area and its companion, *Health Care Choices for Today's Consumer,* provide useful assistance to every family facing these difficult choices. In practice, the health care system can be confusing to almost everyone. People face many challenges in finding a primary care doctor or a dentist, deciding among health plans or insurance options, knowing what to expect from a hospital stay, and familiarizing themselves with public or private programs that are available.

Health Care Choices in the Boston Area is a valuable resource for everyone. It spans a wide range of essential issues, from primary care to mental health to long term care to hospices. It tells how to take advantage of the variety of opportunities open to people in the Boston area and provides information on meeting a wide range of special needs. For those who lack or lose their health insurance, it tells about various options for finding coverage that fits the circumstances of their families.

Good health care will most often be available to those who know where to turn to find it. In providing this information, the Families USA Foundation is providing an important service to the people of Boston and is helping to make better health care available to all.

HEALTH CARE CHOICES

IN THE BOSTON AREA

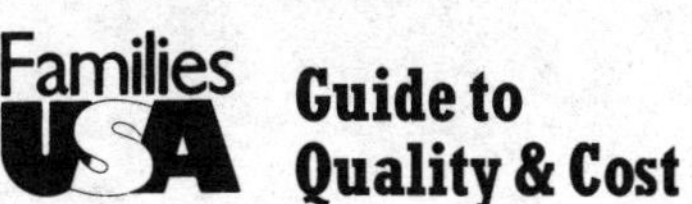

A Message from Families USA

By Katherine S. Villers

Late in 1993, Families USA Foundation embarked on a new and, for us, unusual venture. Long committed to the reform of America's health and long term care systems, we decided to augment our advocacy programs with a direct service to Americans confused by the maze of opportunities for—and barriers to—getting high-quality health care. You hold the result in your hands: *Health Care Choices in the Boston Area* is the first in a series of consumer guides for cities across the United States. We have also just released a companion guide, *Health Care Choices for Today's Consumer*, a 350-page national sourcebook that shows you—in depth and step by step—how to get the best care no matter where you live. Read together, these two *Health Care Choices* books answer basic, critical questions that almost all of us face as we encounter today's revolution in the U.S. health care system.

When the project began, national health care reform, if not imminent, held a reasonable chance of enactment in 1994, and we tried hard to win that battle. But Families USA also knew that consumers would benefit from the *Health Care Choices* series regardless of what Congress might do that year. Today, even as the federal government continues to discuss health care reform, all of us must adapt to bewildering changes in how we encounter the health care system. Across the Boston area, hospitals are merging, as are health-plans; managed care is coming to dominate the insurance market; and regulations and laws are changing constantly, sometimes for the better, sometimes not. Meanwhile, employers are shifting the health care options they offer to their workers.

Consumers say they are more bewildered than ever. That's where *Health Care Choices in the Boston Area* comes in. Along with *Health Care Choices for Today's Consumer*, it can help you in several ways. First, its pages can guide you to more

---

Katherine S. Villers and her husband Philippe Villers founded Families USA Foundation in 1981. She is a member of its board of directors and directs the Massachusetts office of the foundation.

informed choices and give you tools to advocate on your own behalf. Moreover, these books can act as a powerful incentive for health care providers to serve you and your neighbors better. We expect that future editions of *Health Care Choices in the Boston Area* will report that providers and policymakers—in response to pressure from consumers like you and supported by the publicity of seeing their records appearing in print—are meeting your needs even better than they do today. And we invite you to send us your comments on *Health Care Choices in the Boston Area* to help us make that next edition an even more effective tool for consumers.

I am proud that the first local edition of *Health Care Choices* appears here in eastern Massachusetts, where I live and work. This area offers perhaps the best health care in the nation, if not the world—if you know how to use it *and* have the resources to do so. Just as important, local consumer organizations and communities, the state government, and health care providers themselves appear committed to making health care for all a right, not just a privilege. We hope that *Health Care Choices in the Boston Area* will play a strong role in making that possibility a reality.

Chapter 1 Health Insurance

By Nancy Turnbull

Choosing a health plan is one of the first and most important steps you'll take to ensure that you and your family will receive high-quality health care now and in the years to come. Although it's difficult to predict your future needs, it's always best to decide on your coverage while you are healthy.

Along with data presented in *Health Care Choices* and information from health plan representatives or your employer's benefits manager, you can investigate a number of other sources when choosing health insurance. These include your friends, coworkers, and current health care providers. What do they think of particular plans? Use the questions below to help you in your research. Some questions apply only to certain types of plans; others are important only to certain families. Think about what's most relevant to your own situation and your potential health care needs.

Nancy Turnbull is an instructor in health policy and management at Harvard School of Public Health. As former first deputy commissioner of insurance at the Massachusetts Division of Insurance, her responsibilities included regulating HMOs and other health plans. She also worked for the Blue Cross/Blue Shield system for five years.

• How easy is it to change your primary care doctor if you're dissatisfied?

• Are you likely to need any services listed in the "exclusions" section of the benefits description? What will this cost you?

• What is the procedure for getting second opinions?

• Is there a limit on your out-of-pocket copayments?

• Is there a lifetime limit on what the plan will pay for your health care?

• With which hospitals is the plan affiliated? Are they nearby? Are certain ones only available to you for a limited range of conditions or services?

• Are your current medications covered? What pharmacies must you use? Are they convenient? What are the copayments for prescriptions, and do they vary based on the drugs?

• What medical equipment is covered? Under what circumstances?

• What health-education and wellness programs are provided and at what cost?

• Are the hours and location of the plan's facilities convenient? Are lab and other tests conducted in a convenient location? Is parking or public transportation available?

• How long does it take to schedule an initial routine check-up?

• Will you most often see a doctor, a nurse practitioner, or a physician's assistant?

• Does the staff appear friendly, helpful, compassionate, patient?

• How is emergency care provided?

Your Choice

To help you decide about your health insurance, beginning on Page 52, the editors of *Health Care Choices* present information about the major health insurance plans in the Boston metropolitan area. Much of this information is what you *don't* get from the promotional literature and enrollee handbooks the health plans provide.

Keep in mind that what may be a good health plan for one person might not be good for another. Thus, *Health Care Choices* doesn't rank the quality of health plans or presume to say which one or which type is best for you.

• What is the procedure when you need a specialist? Is it clearly explained?

• How does the plan pick its doctors?

• What services for long term care are covered? What are the limits on such services? Are services in the home, such as nursing care and home health aides, covered?

Pay special attention to complaints and compliments from people about their health plans. You want to hear the opinions of those who have had reason to make use of their health plan for more than just an annual check-up. This will indicate deficiencies that might affect your care in the future. Check into what actions a plan may have taken to correct shortcomings reported to you by friends, the media, or other sources you consult for advice and information.

Read the Fine Print

After you join a plan—and before, if possible—read the *member contract* carefully. Note that the contract usually differs from the member handbook, which may not fully describe benefits, referral procedures, and requirements for filing claims.

You can usually get a copy of the member contract from the plan itself. If you get your insurance through your employer, the benefits office where you work can also supply a copy. If you have questions about the contract language, which is often difficult to comprehend, ask a health plan representative or benefits person.

The Types of Health Plan

In choosing a health plan, one of your basic decisions usually centers on what kind of plan would best serve the situation of you and your family. Three major types of plan are available in Massachusetts: health maintenance organizations (HMOs), traditional indemnity plans, and preferred provider organizations (PPOs)—although few plans fit totally into one category.

• *Health Maintenance Organization (HMO):* Members choose a primary care doctor who manages their health care and must approve referrals to specialists. Members receive physician and hospital services from a list of "affiliated network providers" who contract with the HMO. Members file no claim forms. HMOs are required to have programs to monitor and assure quality. Out-of-pocket costs tend to be lower than other types of plan. All Massachusetts HMOs cover preventive care, such as annual checkups, health screens, and immunizations. Many have introduced point-of-service (POS) options that allow members to see unaffiliated providers—that is, "go outside the network"—for some services, although at a higher cost. Over two million people in Massachusetts belong to HMOs. That's 35 percent of the residents, the highest proportion in the nation.

- *Traditional indemnity insurance:* Members can choose any physician or hospital, and they can see specialists without prior approval or referral. Members usually pay a deductible before insurance coverage begins and file claims to get reimbursed for medical services. No requirements about quality assurance apply to indemnity plans. Members' out-of-pocket costs vary, and the plans generally don't cover preventive care.
- *Preferred Provider Organization (PPO):* Members can choose any physician or hospital; cost and coverage incentives encourage—but do not require—them to use providers affiliated with the plan. Members usually file claims for care received out of the network. Members usually pay a deductible before insurance coverage begins and must get approval for some services. PPOs may engage in some quality monitoring. Out-of-pocket costs tend to be moderate in the network and higher out of the network. Preventive care and prescriptions are sometimes covered.

One type of health plan sounds like a regular PPO but differs significantly from the point of view of consumers.

Financial Incentives and Doctors

A complex question about the quality of care you'll receive centers on how a health plan pays its primary care physicians. Financial incentives on physicians could lead a doctor to undertreat or overtreat you. To date, data comparing the actual effect of differing incentives is inconclusive, but it promises to become important in the near future as a way of predicting which health plans and which types of plan better meet the needs of their members.

Wellness

Health Care Choices asked local health insurers about their wellness and health promotion efforts and found that almost every HMO and PPO features a "wellness program." Among the offerings are classes in smoking cessation and to help you lose weight, discounts to health clubs, free health newsletters, work-site health education, stress-prevention programs, and nutrition classes.

Wellness is part of the "health maintenance" orientation of these plans. On the other hand, heavy marketing of wellness programs is also an effort to attract healthier members—who cost the plan less to insure. In addition, many of these classes are available only for a fee.

These "contract PPOs" are companies that assemble networks of physicians and other clinicians and contract with insurance companies, unions, or some large employers to form Preferred Provider Organizations without carrying the financial risk for claims made by the members. Such plans in Massachusetts include the Preferred Plan of Massachusetts, Private Healthcare Systems, Affordable Medical Networks, Cost Care, and Health Care Value Management. These companies are not listed in *Health Care Choices* because they are not insurers, open to individual subscribers, or subject to regulations pertaining to financial stability and mandated benefits.

Individual (Non-Group) Insurance

Many people who are unemployed, self-employed, or lack insurance through their employer buy a policy on their own. The options in such cases are probably more expensive and offer more limited coverage than for group plans obtained through an employer, a union, or an association to which you belong. The insurer will usually require you to provide detailed information about your present health and your medical history. It may use this information to set your premiums, limit your coverage for preexisting conditions, or simply deny you insurance.

That said, here are your major options for obtaining a policy on your own for you and your family.

• Two Boston-area HMOs, Harvard Community Health Plan and Fallon Community Health Plan, offer "direct" enrollment policies for individuals and families. Applicants must complete medical history forms, and the plans may reject you based on this information. The policies do not cover prescriptions.

▼ **FOR MORE INFORMATION**
on these plans, turn to Page 52.

• Blue Cross/Blue Shield of Massachusetts, as the "insurer of last resort" in the state, must accept all individual applicants regardless of their health. However, these individual policies are expensive, may require up to a 240-day waiting period, and may limit or exclude coverage for preexisting conditions for up to three years. For more information, contact Non-Group Customer Service Center, Blue Cross/Blue Shield of Massachusetts, P.O. Box 9140, North Quincy 02171-9140 (617)956-3934 or (800)822-2700.

• The Massachusetts Business Association, 135 Wood Road, Braintree 02184 (617)848-4950 or (800)696-8167, provides information on insurance policies for self-employed people or companies with 25 or fewer employees. If you have a small business, the Massachusetts Small Business Group Reform law limits the ability of insurers to exclude you from coverage and places limits on premium increases. Insurance companies such as Guardian and Principal offer indemnity policies to groups of as few as one person. Preexisting conditions can be covered if you've been continuously covered by a group health plan, and you cannot be rejected for health reasons if you qualify as a small business. Association plans offer HMOs and lower rates but can exclude individuals for health reasons. Two other organizations to contact are the Small Business Service Bureau at (508)756-8513 and the Consolidateed Group Trust at (800)451-8000.

• Your local Chamber of Commerce may have information on professional groups offering insurance to chamber members.

• If you decide to look into other options for indemnity

insurance, a local insurance agent can help you explore the range of products and possible eligibility for group coverage through professional organizations. An agent may also have information on short-term policies and can help file claims.

• If you are age 50 or over and a member of the American Association of Retired Persons, several types of insurance are open to you with guaranteed acceptance. For more information, contact AARP at (800)523-5800.

Domestic Partner Health Benefits

A few employers extend health insurance benefits to domestic partners—couples who consider themselves family but either choose not to marry or are legally prevented from doing so because they are lesbian or gay.

Some Massachusetts companies that offer benefits to domestic partners are Boston Oil Consumers Alliance, Children's Hospital, City of Cambridge, Clark University, Harvard University, Lotus Development Corporation, Massachusetts Institute of Technology, Northeastern University, Stride Rite, Wellesley College, and WGBH.

Government Assistance

A variety of state and federal programs are available for people with low incomes or disabilities and for people who lack insurance for other reasons:

The Children's Medical Security Plan offers affordable health insurance for any child under age 13. It assists families with incomes too high to qualify for Medicaid but who can't obtain private health insurance for their children—for example, self-employed people, part-time employees, and people who work at companies that don't offer health insurance at all or that exclude their employees' dependents.

The plan pays for sick visits, routine checkups, immunizations, eye exams, $100 worth of prescription drugs each year, emergency care, up to 13 mental health visits each year, and other benefits. It doesn't cover such services as hospital care and physical therapy. Premium rates vary, ranging from no charge to $74.49 per child a month, depending on the size of your family and your household income. There are no copayments for preventive care and minimal copayments for illness and injury visits and prescriptions. For more information, contact John Hancock Mutual Life Insurance Co., (800)909-2677.

The Caring for Children Foundation, a non-government program offered by Blue Cross/Blue Shield of Massachusetts, provides free health benefits (checkups, immunizations, and emergency treatment) for unmarried children ages 13 to 18 in low-income families. Due to enrollment limits, there may be a waiting list. For more information, call (617)832-4849 or (800)221-2259.

CenterCare operates through various community health centers and offers care to uninsured people with family income below certain limits. Copayments may apply for some services. There are a limited number of spaces for CenterCare members, so you may be denied enrollment or put on a waiting list. For more information, call the Massachusetts Department of Medical Security, (617)727-8300 or (800)238-0990.

CommonHealth, administered by the Department of Public Welfare, provides health insurance to working disabled adults and disabled children in families that do not qualify for Medicaid. It covers most of the same services as Medicaid. There is no income limit, but the premium schedule is based on income. For more information, call (800)662-9996.

The Free Care Pool provides inpatient care and services through participating hospitals and community health centers at no charge to people who qualify. Each hospital or health center covers different services under the pool. The hospital services of a private physician are covered only if the hospital actually employs the physician. Care is free or subsidized, depending on the patient's income. Apply for benefits at hospitals. Because the application process is long, apply before admission if at all possible. And to avoid the surprise of unexpected bills, find out ahead of time which services are covered and which aren't. For more information, contact the Massachusetts Department of Medical Security, (617)727-8300 or (800)238-0990.

Healthy Start offers insurance coverage for pregnant, low-income, uninsured women and teens, including undocumented residents who are not eligible for Medicaid. It covers prenatal care, labor and delivery, one postpartum visit, and one pediatric examination for the newborn baby. For more information, contact the Department of Public Health, (800)531-2229.

The Kaileigh Mulligan Home Care for Disabled Children provides medical services to children under 18 who are disabled according to Social Security Administration guidelines and need ongoing medical services that can be provided more cheaply in the home than in an institution. Eligibility is determined by medical guidelines and the assets of the child without regard to parental income. For more information, call (617)348-5530 or (800)841-2900.

Medicaid, also known as MassHealth, is a state/federal program that pays for outpatient, inpatient, and long term care for the poor, elderly, and disabled. It covers a broad range of services, including checkups, immunizations, medications, hospital services, mental health services, speech and physical therapy, medical equipment, and transportation to and from medical appointments. Apply at your local Department of Public Welfare offices. For more information, contact the Division of Medical Assistance, (800)841-2900. People in need of nursing home care should apply to a long term care unit office at (617)242-8855 or (800)322-1448, or write to the Long Term Care Eligibility Officer, 529 Main St., Charlestown 02129.

Free Prescriptions

If you have problems paying for prescriptions, a new program may provide some relief. A number of pharmaceutical manufacturers provide necessary medicines free of charge. To qualify, you cannot have insurance that covers drugs. You must be low-income, but there are no uniform guidelines; many drug companies decide who to help on a case-by-case basis.

To obtain free prescriptions, ask your doctor to help you access the program. He or she can call the Pharmaceutical Manufacturer's Help Line, (800)762-4636, for eligibility information.

▼ FOR MORE INFORMATION
on elders and Medicaid, turn to Chapter 6.

The Medical Security Plan provides free health insurance to people who are receiving unemployment benefits. Coverage continues until 28 days after you receive the last unemployment check. Get information at unemployment offices or call (800)914-4455.

▼ FOR MORE INFORMATION
on Medicare and Medicare supplemental insurance, turn to Chapter 6. Medicare is the federal health insurance program for people over 65, the disabled, and people with end-stage renal disease.

Massachusetts Laws and Regulations

The Massachusetts Division of Insurance oversees the financial solvency of all insurance companies doing business in the commonwealth. It ensures that each company has the financing to pay the current and projected claims of its policyholders.

The Division of Insurance is also responsible for ensuring that all health insurers comply with state regulations that require all health plans to cover certain benefits. These "mandated benefits" include preventive care for children up to age six, treatment for mental and nervous conditions and alcoholism, prenatal care and childbirth, cardiac rehabilitation, home care services, mammography, certain "off-label" drug treatments for cancer and HIV/AIDS, diagnosis and treatment of infertility, and more. (These benefit requirements and other state laws do not apply to those large employers that "self-insure," meaning that they carry the financial risk for their own employees' insurance claims and may use insurance companies only to administer claims or supply provider networks.)

HMOs in Massachusetts submit quarterly reports and premium rate filings to the Division of Insurance. PPOs are less regulated, although they submit annual reports to the division on financial matters, enrollment figures, and the number and types of health care providers with whom they contract. The

HMO and PPO reports and filings are open to the public. Much less information is available to the public on traditional indemnity insurers, which do not have to submit specific product information to the division. Blue Cross/Blue Shield of Massachusetts, a nonprofit company, is the only indemnity insurer that must provide data to the division.

College Student Insurance

All students in Massachusetts enrolled at least three-quarters time in an institution of higher education must have health insurance. The school must offer health plans to qualifying students and should inform students about the application process. Some schools may allow students to be covered through a comparable plan, such as under a parent's policy. The Department of Medical Security ensures that plans cover a minimum level of benefits at a reasonable cost. For more information, call the department at (617)727-8300 or (800)238-0990.

Complaint and Grievance Procedures

Health plans generally handle member complaints similarly to one another. The enrollee handbook should clearly explain the exact procedure. However, this is not true for all plans—be cautious about any plan that lacks established procedures.

Typically, the first step is to call the plan's member-services department. If you're still not satisfied, submit a written complaint. Most plans specify the maximum amount of time they'll take to respond to written complaints. It's usually 30 days. A formal appeals process follows if you choose to pursue your complaint further. This

Discrimination Is Illegal

Health insurers in Massachusetts cannot discriminate against enrollees or applicants for health insurance based on race, religion, sexual orientation, income, geographic residence, or HIV status. If you feel you have been discriminated against, contact the Division of Insurance Consumer Services Section at (617)521-7777.

often ends with a hearing before a health plan-controlled grievance committee—which can make it hard for you to get a fair hearing.

Another place to go for assistance is your employer's benefits manager or human-resources department. Depending on the type of grievance, you might also enlist the support of your physician or other health care provider. He or she can help document your need for services or care. The Massachusetts Board of Registration in Medicine handles complaints about care provided by physicians.

▼ FOR MORE INFORMATION

on the Board of Registration in Medicine, turn to Chapter 2.

If you are dissatisfied with your health plan's response to a grievance, contact the Massachusetts Division of Insurance. Its Consumer Helpline addresses concerns and questions about all kinds of insurance. Most complaints need to be submitted to the division in writing or by visiting their offices. Consumer complaints to the division may involve delays in reimbursement from an insurance company or denial of coverage. The division will investigate the complaint and take action to resolve the problem if it finds that the company is violating state laws or regulations. Call the Division of Insurance Consumer Services Section at (617)521-7777.

Write It Down

Keep copies of any correspondence or claim forms regarding your complaint. Take notes on all phone conversations, indicating the people with whom you speak and when.

You can also consult a consumer advocate, such as Health Care for All or the Attorney General's Bureau of Regulated Industries (see Page 17). These offices are familiar with Massachusetts laws and regulations and can assist you with complaints about health insurance or getting access to services.

A final option in extreme cases is to "go public." If you have tried other approaches, a phone call from an elected official or even attention from the media can often persuade a health plan to reconsider paying for services it previously denied.

Resources

Boston Mayor's Health Line
1010 Massachusetts Ave.
Boston 02118
(617)534-5050 or (800)847-0710
Call for information on Medicaid, the Children's Medical Security Plan, the Free Care Pool, and other state programs. This office also makes referrals for prenatal care, private insurance, and to other health agencies. The staff can speak Creole, French, Portuguese, and Spanish, and other translators are available through the AT&T Language Line.

Disability Law Center
11 Beacon St.
Boston 02108
(617)723-8455
Call for assistance regarding disability rights, insurance coverage, insurance discrimination, coverage of disability-related health care, and access to health care.

Health Care For All
30 Winter St.
Boston 02108
(617)350-7279
Consumer Helpline: (800)272-4232 or (617)350-6207
Call with questions or problems about your health insurance or getting access to health services or state programs, including the Free Care Pool.

Insurance Library of Boston
Saval Insurance Education Center
156 State St.
Boston 02109
(617)227-2087
Call or visit the library for literature, informational services, and classes on insurance. Open to members only (individual membership is $75); non-members can visit once for free.

Massachusetts Division of Insurance
Consumer Services Section
470 Atlantic Ave.
Boston 02210
(617)521-7794
Consumer Helpline: (617)521-7777
Call for a list of insurance companies licensed in the state or to make an appointment to look at the filings and reports for HMOs, PPOs, and Blue Cross/Blue Shield of Massachusetts. Call the Helpline with complaints about insurance claims, delays in payment, or denial of coverage. The division also provides information about the financial standing of insurance companies in Massachusetts.

Massachusetts Department of Medical Security
One Ashburton Place
Boston 02108
(617)727-8300 or (800)238-0990
DMS ensures that hospitals follow eligibility criteria for the Free Care Pool, a program for residents entitled to free or reduced care at any Massachusetts hospital or health center. Call with questions about this program or for assistance with access to health insurance programs and eligibility requirements.

Massachusetts Law Reform Institute
69 Canal St.
Boston 02114
(617)742-9250
Call for assistance with access to Medicaid and other state health programs, or with legal questions about health insurance.

Office of the Attorney General of Massachusetts
Bureau of Regulated Industries
131 Tremont St.
Boston 02111
(617)727-2200, ext. 3322
Call with complaints about insurance, such as denial of claims or coverage or an employer who fails to make premium payments.

The Consumer Voice: What You Say

By the Staff of *Health Care Choices*

Health Care Choices went to the original source—you, the consumer—to find out about your health insurance. In cooperation with several local employers and health plans, we received survey information and comments from over 500 of you on local HMOs, PPOs, and indemnity insurers.

A strong word of caution: the *Health Care Choices* survey is not scientific and does not indicate the quality of individual health plans. Rather, we present it as an incentive: we strongly invite academic researchers, government agencies, coalitions, and the plans themselves to follow up on this preliminary survey with scientific studies whose results on both individual plans and health insurers as a whole *would be open to the public.* Based on such studies, health plans could improve the quality of their services, and consumers could make more informed decisions about their health insurance.

The *Health Care Choices* survey provides two types of information for you to consider:

- Potential areas to watch for—and watch out for—as you choose and use a health plan, based on answers to 20 questions we asked members about their perceptions of the quality of care they receive, the ease of using their health plan, and their satisfaction with the plan as a whole.
- Written comments on the specific experiences of individuals.

The Survey Responses

Judging by the positive responses to survey questions, consumers appear generally satisfied with their health plans. In particular, they report that they are pleased with their doctors, the lack of excessive paperwork, and the convenience of the plan. Consumers are less likely to say they are satisfied with specialists' familiarity with patient medical records and the helpfulness of member-services departments. They are also less satisfied with the overall benefits and coverage, which are often decided by a person's employer rather than his or her health plan.

On the other hand, the most telling information in a survey

often comes from negative comments—from people who mildly or strongly state a negative opinion. Somewhat reassuring for consumers is that the fewest complaints arise on questions directly related to medical care: contacts with medical staff, overall satisfaction with doctors, and the willingness of medical staff to listen to patients. In contrast, the greatest dissatisfaction arises in connection with what could be called the operations and structure of health plans—that is, how they interact with members. Consumers most often disagree with the statement, "I am satisfied with the available benefits." Similarly, dissatisfaction is high on how well health plans explain member benefits.

For consumers, policymakers, and health plans, this potential area of dissatisfaction is important because most people make little use of their health plan most of the time. Heavy users of services have far more experience with the failures of health care providers than do average consumers. According to the *Health Care Choices* survey, patients with two to five visits in the past year to health care providers seem less pleased than people who saw providers once or not at all. However, overall satisfaction appears to rise among more frequent users of health care services, people who made more than five visits in the past year.

The implications of these results parallel those on member services in general. A "threshold" of experience may be involved as consumers learn to make use of a health plan through direct experience. If more scientific studies bear out this conclusion, health plans would be well advised to better educate new and continuing members about available benefits and how to use them. Even more important, plans could make services simpler to receive, while policymakers could insist that health plans not only provide comprehensive benefits but also actively encourage people to use the available services to improve their families' health.

Your Comments

Following are a few of the hundreds of comments you and your neighbors made about health plans in the Boston area. Take these statements as a sign that you can receive high-quality care easily—and also that you must be prepared to encounter and overcome real difficulties. The comments are unedited, except for correcting punctuation and spelling and removing the names of health plans.

• The referral process is quite grueling and time-consuming. I don't feel that Plan A's customer service is always as knowledgeable as it should be.

• I would like the choice to buy drugs from my neighborhood drugstore rather than being dictated to buy from a large national chain.

• I would very much like to have dental insurance.

• I had outpatient surgery twice this past year. Doctors were great! I got to choose doctors. I had almost no paperwork to be concerned about, which allowed me the ability to focus completely on my health and how I was cared for. Only once did I have a problem with referrals. However, after talking with a Plan A representative, the matter was cleared up quickly and accurately. High marks for this HMO!

• Before our company switched to Plan B, I was covered by Plan F, which was excellent. I have found with Plan B there is always some reason why a claim is not paid. I have spent countless hours on the phone (generally on hold) trying to get claims resolved. In no instance has my claim ultimately not been paid, but the time wasted is enormous.

• Plan B stinks! Doctors will not accept it. I'd rather pay more and get better coverage. You feel like a second-rate person when they tell you they do not take Plan B.

• The one glaring exception to generally satisfactory coverage is mental health benefits. The current plan is biased against employees' mental health and discourages them from becoming mentally healthy.

• My family and I have had several claims for covered services rejected. These claims were quickly handled by my employer's Human Resource Department. It seems to me that some claims are rejected just to see if the subscriber might pay it!

• My plan is excellent. Not one complaint!

• I would really like to have the nicotine patch covered by my insurance.

• Would like to see coverage for partners of gay/lesbians.

• We have been members of Plan C for years and overall it has served us well through two children, one major surgery, and one major hospitalization. I like having all my services under one roof.

• They are great at preventive medicine. However, if there is a problem, you really have to fight to insist on better care.

• Overall, the plan is convenient. However, I feel I need to know more about myself medically in order to get a diagnosis from a physician.

• My doctor seemed preoccupied during recent visits. Nurse practitioners, however, answered my questions more thoroughly. Overall, I was treated as if my concerns weren't taken seriously.

• I'm about to marry and would like to cover my husband. Because of the cost of the "family plan," which does not allow for a reduction in cost for childless couples, I cannot. I am very upset about this.

• I have requested a female private physician, but none are available (all booked up).

• More professional staff of color needed ASAP! Mental health services from professionals of color are quite limited. It seems that you have to be in crisis to see a therapist of your own gender and race.

• Very difficult to maintain confidentiality of medical records. So many [people] have access to them. Annual physical exams are too short, too rushed, and too truncated.

• Add coverage for smoking cessation.

• I recently changed my primary care physician. I was not satisfied with his level of service, but my new physician is excellent.

• My major complaint is that in seven years with Plan C, I have had six different primary care physicians. Turnover is too high.

• My primary care provider is quite good, and I feel our relationship is excellent. However, the referral process and the referral circle at my hospital has not proven competent. My records were lost at one point, and the referrals were also lost.

• Previously I spent years with Plan C. I was short-changed for the full time. Plan C denied or deflected problems and categorized them as typical ailments when in fact my family had several serious problems. I regret my time with them. We have physical scars as a result of their substandard attention. We rarely saw a physician in two years for a family of four.

• Overall, I'm pleased with the plan. However, I've had to fight hard to get some bills paid and have ended up on collections lists with service providers—that's a big hassle.

• I will never choose Plan D again!!!

• Plan D is excellent. I would never switch.

• The plan keeps changing hospitals it uses, and this is confusing (and dangerous!).

• I have an HMO plan, and my son is very sick with cancer. Because of all the treatments he needs, it gets very confusing when referrals are needed.

• The information packets for open enrollment are seldom enough to make an intelligent decision. Cost information is usually not available or current. Plan E does a poor job on prenatal care.

• I really like the personal attention I get when I call with a question. They have good follow-up and have resolved problems in billings from doctors. I'm very satisfied.

• Good plan overall. Finding a doctor was tough because I was new to the area and had no references to go by. I got lucky and have had no problems with any primary care physician.

• I had a problem with a referral/specialist physician this year. I didn't like his method of treatment and didn't think he was thorough. As a result I got a second opinion outside the system. I submitted a reimbursement form to Plan F and talked to my primary care physician, and received total reimbursement for my second opinion. It was good to know my primary care physician backed me on my decision to go outside the system.

Chapter 2 Primary Care

By Harriet Tolpin

Primary care is your appropriate first contact with the health care system. It also constitutes your regular source of care on an ongoing basis.

Primary care aims both to prevent premature death or disability and to enhance your ability to function well and maintain a high quality of life. It focuses on you as a whole person, not on specific diseases or illnesses, and it also works to keep you healthy while detecting and treating problems that do arise. And usually it is your primary care provider who should coordinate and manage all of your health care, including care from specialists, social-service agencies, and others.

Primary care lowers your health care bills by detecting an illness early and initiating treatment before it becomes more serious and costly to manage. For example, a nurse practitioner's familiarity with you could alert her or him to heart disease that runs in your family or to stress in your life that might affect

---

Harriet Tolpin, PhD, is Dean of the Graduate School for Health Studies and Professor of Economics at Simmons College and Clinical Professor in the Department of Community Health at Tufts University School of Medicine.

your health. Familiarity may also lessen the need for tests at each visit and for each condition.

Who Provides Primary Care?

Primary care services are generally offered through private practices, outpatient clinics, HMOs, community health centers, and other community sites such as workplaces and schools. At least three types of providers may deliver primary care in those settings:

- Physicians, especially family practitioners and internists;
- Physician assistants; *and*
- Advanced practice nurses (nurse practitioners and certified nurse-midwives).

Family practitioners generally receive the broadest training among primary care providers. They look at medical, social, and psychological factors affecting health and can manage the entire range of other primary care services, including immunizations, physical exams, medication, and routine pregnancies. Family practitioners can care for everyone in your family and recognize problems that arise from the family system. They can deliver care over the years, working with you from infancy to adulthood through old age.

The Elements of Primary Care

Primary care providers take responsibility for:

- Promoting and maintaining your good health;
- Preventing disease and disability;
- Detecting and treating common health problems;
- Educating and counseling you and your family; *and*
- Referring you to other providers when appropriate.

However, family practitioners won't have comprehensive knowledge of all specific health problems, in part because they must know something about everything. Any given practitioner will be more comfortable with certain conditions than with others, although precise weaknesses and strengths of this nature relate more to the knowledge, experience, interests, and skill of the person than to the field of family medicine.

Primary Care Teams

Strongly consider getting primary care from an interdisciplinary team comprised of physicians, physician assistants, and nurse practitioners. Additional team members can reflect your individual situation: if you're an older person, for example, the team might include a nutritionist and a social worker.

The team approach enhances your opportunities for receiving integrated medical, nursing, and social services. You can find and request teams in many of the settings in which primary care services are provided—HMOs, community health centers, and private practices.

Internists have more training than family practitioners in certain types of problems, such as heart disease. They are also more likely to provide total management for adults during a hospitalization. However, among primary care providers, internists tend to order more tests than family practitioners. And an internist may be less comfortable with the full gamut of health concerns and the factors that contribute to them.

Physician assistants provide diagnostic and therapeutic medical services. PAs always practice under a physician's direction or supervision. They take health histories, perform comprehensive physical exams and minor surgery, order and perform routine diagnostic tests, develop diagnostic and management plans, treat common illnesses, counsel patients on preventive health, and facilitate referrals to local health care and social-service agencies. PAs are nationally certified with training as generalists; some specialize through work experience, but they do not receive certification in a given field. PAs can prescribe certain medications.

Nurse practitioners and *certified nurse-midwives* can handle much of primary and preventive care—usually at a lower cost than doctors.

Nurse practitioners are the major non-physician providers of primary care. Their practice includes assessing patients' general physical condition, diagnosing and treating common acute illnesses and injuries, educating patients in ways to promote health and prevent disease, and coordinating care. NPs train as generalists but some specialize in caring for particular groups: newborns, children, women, adults, employees, families, or elders. Nurse practitioners provide care independently or in collaboration with physicians and can prescribe most medications.

Certified nurse-midwives provide primary care for pregnant women. They offer prenatal and gynecological care, deliver babies in homes, hospitals, and birthing centers, and care for a mother in the months after she gives birth. CNMs refer complicated cases to physicians, consult with physicians, or work jointly with physicians. They also provide family-planning services to women and postnatal care to normal newborns and infants.

In addition, several other types of health care providers offer primary care. For example, many women receive primary care from obstetricians and gynecologists. Pediatricians provide primary care for children. And some geriatricians deliver primary care to seniors.

▼ FOR MORE INFORMATION

on parents as health care consumers, turn to chapter 4; on women as health care consumers, turn to chapter 5; and on elders as health care consumers, turn to chapter 6.

Community Health Centers

Community health centers play a major role in primary care, especially, but not exclusively, for the poor and the uninsured. Also known as neighborhood health centers, neighborhood clinics, and primary care centers, these organizations have strong local roots and serve communities by furnishing accessible and affordable health care.

Primary care at community health centers is often provided by an interdisciplinary team—to the benefit of patients. In addition, the centers often offer excellent services that address language, cultural, financial, transportation, and other barriers that make it hard for some people to get good health care. Most centers are affiliated with nearby hospitals.

In general, community health centers focus on underserved groups, such as teenagers, people who live in rural or inner-city areas, and so on. For example, Boston's Fenway Community Health Center is one of a handful of centers in the country that treats primarily lesbians and gay men, including a large number of people with AIDS. South Cove Community Health Center, located in Boston's Chinatown, has become a center for Asian Americans throughout the metropolitan area, while Neponset Health Center, in Dorchester, reaches out to immigrants from Vietnam.

Serving the Community

The services of community health centers are open to everyone, regardless of income or insurance. Many middle-class consumers find that health centers excel at delivering high-quality, affordable care for the entire family.

Established in 1970, the East Boston Neighborhood Health Center has a national reputation for offering a high standard of primary care to some 60,000 people living north of the Callahan Tunnel. On staff are 40 full-time primary care physicians, with another 70 doctors on the medical staff. The center's emergency services are especially important, because the tunnel limits the ability of residents of East Boston and nearby communities to reach Boston's major hospitals quickly for acute care.

▼ **FOR A DIRECTORY**

of community health centers in the Boston area and information on several hundred primary care providers who are accepting new patients, turn to the listings that begin on Page 73.

Choosing a Primary Care Provider

In most cases, step one in selecting a primary care provider is to examine your health insurance. Does it restrict your choice in any way? For example, does your plan pay for the services of nurse practitioners and certified nurse midwives? HMOs, other health insurers, and public programs such as Medicare and Medicaid determine which providers are eligible for reimbursement and for what specific services.

If you belong to a managed-care plan, you'll probably choose a provider from a list of affiliated practitioners. The member-services department will give you information on the plan's primary care providers to help you decide. While this information often includes a provider's training and availability, it may not cover many other facts you really want to know—for example, the provider's skill, knowledge, and "track record." In any case, state any preferences you have about such characteristics as a provider's age, gender, and training—and be willing to exercise your option to change providers.

No matter how you pay for primary care, there are many questions you should consider. Start by finding out if a provider is accepting new patients. If so, find out more. Talk to your friends, look in the library for medical directories and other reference materials, and call each provider's office. Gather information from other consumers who use—or have used—particular primary care providers.

At this stage, it's likely that one or more providers will stand out in your mind. Now proceed to get answers to all the questions that are important to you:

• Does he or she deliver *primary care*? For adults? For children? For both? Does he or she treat the whole family (if that's what you want)?

• Does she or he focus on areas of particular relevance to your health concerns and those of your family, such as women's health, adolescent health, or elder care?

• What is his or her training?

• Is this a group or an individual practice? How likely is it that you'll see the provider you want in a group or team practice? Can you decide whom to see? Can you benefit from the team perspective?

• With which hospitals is the provider affiliated?

• Is the practice easily accessible? Are evening or weekend appointments available? Does the provider make house calls if you can't get to the office?

• Can you readily get advice on the telephone, both before scheduling an appointment and for follow-up advice?

• Does the office provide other services that may be important to you, such as language translators, referral relationships with social-service agencies, and arrangements for watching children who accompany a parent on a visit?

• What is the provider's reputation with other physicians? With patients?

When you narrow your list to one name, make an appointment. Use this visit to decide if you feel that you can establish a comfortable relationship of trust and mutual respect with this individual. Remember, you're not only looking for some-

Where to Look

In most communities, a number of health professionals offer primary care. Don't feel compelled to accept the first person you contact.

To compile a roster of potential primary care providers:

◆ Ask friends, colleagues, and any medical personnel you know who they use.

◆ Call the Massachusetts Medical Society at (800)322-2303 and ask for the names of primary care providers in your community.

◆ Contact local hospitals, medical schools, and nursing programs, which will identify providers on their staffs or in affiliated group practices.

◆ Contact a referral service, whether a local nonprofit agency listed in the yellow pages or a hospital-based service such as Ask-A-Nurse, (800)544-2424.

◆ Consult publications such as the *American Medical Directory* and *Folio's Medical Directory of Massachusetts*. These are available in many public libraries. To order a copy of *Folio's Medical Directory of Massachusetts* ($52, plus tax and shipping), call Folio's Medical Directories of New England, (800)223-2333.

◆ Contact the Massachusetts Coalition of Nurse Practitioners at (617)575-1565.

◆ Beginning on Page 73, *Health Care Choices* lists several hundred primary care physicians in the Boston metropolitan area who are accepting new patients, as well as all community health centers.

one to provide high-quality health care but for a partner and a strong advocate in the health care system. (If they can afford it, some people try out two or three providers. The point is to find a person you *want* to work with, rather than one who will merely suffice.)

A visit helps you judge the atmosphere of the office, even if you don't arrange for a regular appointment or full physical examination. Does the office appear well-organized and efficient? Is the staff friendly on the phone and in person? Do interactions among the staff and between staff and patients seem smooth? If the answers are yes, you have a better chance of receiving quality care. And your health will benefit from good record keeping, shorter waiting times, and enough time with caregivers.

If you schedule a regular appointment, note the following: Does the primary care provider take enough time to learn about you and your family, or does she or he act rushed and impatient? Does the initial health assessment include questions about your lifestyle and your health habits? Does the provider's philosophy toward medical care include a strong commitment to prevention? Does the primary care provider encourage you to ask questions, and are your questions answered satisfactorily? Does the primary care provider share information with you that is relevant to your current and future health? Does he or she explain the reasons for all tests and treatments? Are you given options? Does the provider seem to prefer to teach or to give orders? Does the provider welcome your efforts to participate in all decisions about your health care? Does the provider offer you a copy of your medical record?

Specialists and Your Primary Care Provider

From cardiologists to oncologists, psychiatrists to surgeons, we often turn to specialists when we need specialized care. Some of the most difficult medical decisions center on this type of care: When should you see a specialist? What kind of specialist is best for you? How can you pay for the high cost of specialized medicine?

Your primary care provider is your key to answering such questions. She or he can provide information about your options and continue to help monitor the adequacy of your care. Work closely with your primary care provider in seeking a specialist. Indicate the qualities you desire. The primary care provider typically knows the backgrounds of specialists he or she recommends and can provide you with important information.

What Kind of Practice?

Physicians practice alone, in groups, and on the staff of health plans or other organizations.

Multispecialty group practices, in particular, have several advantages over individual practices. Care tends to be better coordinated, more of your needs will be met at a single location, and information is more easily shared—and tests less often repeated—than when referrals occur among isolated practitioners. On the other hand, multispecialty practices can be hectic, information about you can fall between the cracks, and more people have access to your medical record, which may threaten confidentiality.

Most doctors in solo and group private practices participate in one or more managed-care networks. Such organizations rely heavily on primary care providers to manage and coordinate their patients' care.

"Staff model" HMOs, such as Harvard Community Health Plan, typically have facilities that resemble large multispecialty group practices or community health centers. Because many of these facilities also handle diagnostic services—such as laboratory tests and X-rays—and minor surgeries, they provide "one stop" health care for patients. They often have nurse practitioners on staff who collaborate with physicians, as do many individual and group private practices.

Choosing a Specialist

The distinctions among the multitude of medical specialties often make little sense from your perspective. For example, three types of specialists focus on the age of the patient—pediatricians for children, adolescent-medicine physicians for teenagers, and gerontologists for older people—while obstetricians and gynecologists treat only women. Many more specialties focus on parts of the body, such as the heart or the lungs. Surgeons constitute a particularly large and broad group; most specialize even further, dealing with only one organ or area of the body.

Choosing specialty care may seem an overwhelming challenge. Do you choose a provider appropriate to your age or gender? Or one who specializes in a particular part of the body? How do you find proper treatment? And how do you get the right amount of treatment—neither too much nor too little?

As you face these and other choices, your primary care provider is an invaluable asset. For one thing, most people lack the training fully to determine their own medical needs. Second, some specialists will make an appointment with you only if you have a referral from a primary care provider. Finally, specialists focus on a narrower field of knowledge than do primary care physicians. Because many parts of your body are related to one another, an illness in one part often affects the rest of you.

What to Look for in a Specialist

Good specialists—like good primary care providers—devote the time it takes to respond to all your concerns, explaining diagnoses and the choices inherent in treatment plans. You should share the decision-making with the specialist and also consult your primary care provider about important decisions.

The Referral

If you agree with your primary care provider on the need to see a specialist, she or he will refer you to an appropriate provider. At this point, make sure you understand why you need to see a specialist, why that type of specialist, why that person, and what the specialist will look for. Ask your primary care provider about dangers, cost, time, options—and what happens if you disagree with the specialist's recommendation. You might also ask if your primary care provider has ties to this specialist. Such ties may exist if your primary care provider belongs to a group practice of which the specialist is also a member and may enhance the exchange of important information.

Ties certainly exist if you belong to a health maintenance organization or other form of managed-care health plan, where the primary care provider acts as a gatekeeper and makes referrals to a selected panel of specialists within the plan. These managed-care plans are more likely than traditional health insurers to monitor physicians' recommendations and your choice of procedures and treatments. And only rarely will a physician in a managed-care plan refer you to a specialist outside the plan's network, although he or she may do so if you require highly specialized care. You can expect your primary care provider to be your advocate in convincing the plan of your need for specialized care.

Know Your Insurance

Find out what types of specialty care your insurance covers, including restrictions on who provides it. Glossy brochures extolling the benefits of health insurance seldom include a frank discussion of referrals "out-of-plan." Ask before joining a new plan.

Few people have a problem getting a referral to a specialist when the primary care provider considers it *medically* necessary. But physicians and patients don't always agree on what is necessary. If you disagree with your primary care provider, you can:

- *Call* your insurance company or, in a managed-care plan, the medical director or the member-services department. Explain your concern. Explain that you requested a referral but your doctor has refused to make one. You'll have to present a strong case.
- *Persist* with your primary care provider. Evidence from

Checking Up on a Specialist

Most physicians display their certifications and diplomas on their office walls. If you don't see them, you can ask:

- What specialty training have you completed?
- Are you board certified? If so, by what boards?
- With what hospitals are you affiliated?

Second Opinions

If you disagree with a specialist on what constitutes good care for you, getting a second opinion from another specialist may be a good idea.

Second opinions are especially important for maladies for which there are no definitive solutions, or those which call for surgery and other "invasive" procedures. In fact, many insurers *require* second opinions before certain types of surgery.

To find an appropriate person to give you a second opinion, ask your primary care provider or contact the Massachusetts Medical Society, 1440 Main St., Waltham 02254 (617)893-4610 or (800)322-2303.

your own library research might convince him or her that a specialist's care is warranted.

- *Find* a specialist on your own and foot the bill yourself, at least until the specialist provides the evidence you need to convince your primary care provider or insurer of your need for such care.

In choosing a specialist, look for many of the same qualities you seek in anyone from whom you receive health care. First, the specialist must be *competent* to treat your illness. Second, the specialist should inspire *trust* and *respect.* Look for a specialist who treats you as an individual, *listens* to you, and *explains* your problems and options in language you can understand, without condescension.

You can assess personal characteristics by interviewing a specialist. However, judging competency is a challenge. As a start, the Massachusetts Board of Registration in Medicine can provide some information about licensing and credentials. It keeps public records on all physicians in the state, including:

- Medical school and date of graduation;
- Board certification; *and*
- Hospital privileges.

Bad Docs?

Nationwide, physician disciplinary actions hit an all-time high in 1993, with 3,078 doctors disciplined by state medical boards. In 1,176 cases, boards revoked or suspended doctor's licenses, while imposing milder sanctions on the others. In Massachusetts, find out whether anyone has made a formal complaint about a physician by calling the Board of Registration in Medicine at (617)727-1788. Information on complaints that the board is still investigating is not available. The board will also provide the court docket numbers of medical malpractice suits against physicians, and you can look up the case at the relevant courthouse. Unfortunately, the courts don't notify the board of all the cases they are required to report, so this information may be incomplete. For more information or assistance with the search process, contact the Massachusetts chapter of the National Center for Patient Rights at (508)543-6379.

You can also consult *Questionable Doctors,* available from Public Citizen's Health Research Group. It names 10,289 doctors disciplined by the states and the federal government since 1986. About 70 percent of these doctors were allowed to keep practicing. Nationally, the cases include 1,346 criminal convictions, 1,130 instances of over-prescribing drugs or prescribing the wrong ones, 817 instances of alcohol or drug abuse, and 173 instances of sexual misconduct with a patient. Massachusetts ranked very low on the number of doctors disciplined, according to the last survey.

Disciplinary Record

To order a copy of *Questionable Doctors,* contact the Public Citizen Health Research Group, 2000 P St., NW, Washington, DC 20036 (202)833-3000. $15 for the Massachusetts listing; also available at many libraries.

Resources

American Board of Medical Specialties
1007 Church St.
Evanston, IL 60201
(708)491-9091
Certification Line: (800)776-2378
Call or write to check if a specialist is certified.

Ask-A-Nurse
(800)544-2424
Registered nurses staff this 24-hour hotline. Call for health information on any illness or injury, advice in a medical emergency, and referrals to local physicians. All calls are confidential. The service is sponsored by 15 Boston-area hospitals.

Massachusetts Board of Registration in Medicine
10 West St.
Boston 02111
(617)727-1788
Call or write to register a complaint or to obtain complaint information about a physician. The board licenses physicians to practice in Massachusetts and can provide credential information as well.

Massachusetts League of Community Health Centers
100 Boylston St.
Boston 02116
(617)426-2225
Call or write for information on community health centers.

Massachusetts Medical Society
1440 Main St.
Waltham 02254
(617)893-4610
(800)322-2303
Call or write for a list of primary care physicians and specialists in your community and for certain information, such as certification and hospital privileges, on particular physicians.

Massachusetts Coalition of Nurse Practitioners
2464 Massachusetts Ave.
Cambridge 02140
(617)575-1565
Call or write for information on nurse practitioners.

Chapter 3 Hospitals

By Joseph Restuccia, Alan Labonte, and Jeffrey Gelb

Western hospitals date from medieval times when monks provided hospitality and care for weary and sick travelers. In fact, the word hospital derives from the Latin word for guest. How different those welcoming images are from the high-tech, fast-paced, and seemingly impersonal institutions of today.

Fortunately, much of the mystery and anxiety fades for health care consumers who understand how hospitals are organized. With careful planning and knowledge, you can be a valuable—and valued—partner with your hospital and the team of caregivers you encounter there.

The Types of Hospital

The many varieties of hospitals generally fall into four main categories: general medical and surgical, specialty, rehabilita-

---

Joseph Restuccia, DrPH, is Associate Professor of Health Care and Operations Management at Boston University School of Management. He also holds faculty appointments at the university's medicine and public health schools. Alan Labonte has 20 years of experience in hospital management. Jeffrey Gelb, MD, is a physician with clinical training in general and orthopedic surgery.

tion and chronic disease, and psychiatric. Within those categories, hospitals can be teaching or non-teaching, for-profit or nonprofit, or small community-based facilities or large tertiary care centers serving whole metropolitan areas.

A *teaching hospital* is affiliated with a medical school and has a teaching program for medical students, interns, and residents. A *community hospital* primarily serves the needs of its local area with general medical and surgical services. Many community hospitals are also teaching hospitals.

Future Sense

The time to learn about hospitals is when you are well and in a position to make a careful, informed, and objective decision. Try to get a sense now of your family's potential need for hospital care, taking into account any current illnesses or conditions, your family's medical history, your insurance coverage—and your personal preferences.

Tertiary care hospitals (usually teaching hospitals) provide highly specialized care for severe health problems, such as that given in intensive-care, coronary-care, and trauma units. Community hospitals not equipped to handle such cases often refer acute care patients to tertiary hospitals.

From the consumer's point of view, the principle strength of teaching hospitals lies in their ability to provide round-the-clock physician services and highly sophisticated technology and medical techniques. Interns and residents—the "house staff"—manage day-to-day care under the guidance and supervision of fully trained, attending in-house physicians who are members of the hospital and medical-school faculty.

Nevertheless, resist the temptation automatically to select a prestigious teaching hospital as your family's primary source of hospital care. You and your physician may well prefer a smaller hospital that is closer to your home and perhaps less expensive. The quality at smaller community hospitals often compares to that found at large teaching institutions, particularly for routine illnesses or surgeries. And the accessibility of a local hospital for family and friends is also important. Remember, the support of loved ones is integral to the healing process.

Nationally, about 1,000 hospitals *specialize.* That is, they treat a specific category of patient, or patients with a specific type of disease or condition. Hospitals can be dedicated to a number of special purposes or constituencies, such as cancer, psychiatry, rehabilitation, orthopedics, elders, and children. If someone in your family has a chronic condition that warrants ongoing, specialized medical support and access to the latest treatment methods, talk to your current providers about establishing a relationship with a hospital specializing in that condition.

However, specialty hospitals may be far from your home and lack the facilities and staff necessary to treat an unrelated medical complication. And even if you use a specialty hospital for

Nonprofit and For-Profit Hospitals

A hospital can be owned by a city, a county, a state, the federal government, a church, a university, investors, or a nonprofit corporation. Or the owner can be any combination of these types.

For-profit hospitals are owned by corporations or, less often, by individuals, such as doctors who practice at the hospital. In the Boston area, no general medical and surgical hospitals are for-profit.

Nonprofit hospitals are owned by private nonprofit corporations, as well as by cities, states, the federal government, and church groups. Sometimes, the nonprofit "owners" hire for-profit companies to manage the hospital.

Most studies have found for-profit and nonprofit hospitals to be almost indistinguishable. No overwhelming evidence indicates major differences in either efficiency or quality, especially when comparing nonprofit hospitals to investor-owned for-profit hospitals. Both types of hospitals receive most of their revenue from insurance companies. And except for public hospitals owned by local governments, neither nonprofits nor for-profits provide much "free care." In the absence of more definitive evidence, it's up to you to weigh the facts about *each* hospital individually; seek the best providers and the best care, whether it's at a nonprofit or a for-profit institution.

> **Required Reading**
>
> A hospital's patient handbook can answer many of your questions about a facility. If the hospital doesn't give you a copy when you come in, ask to see it. At the same time, ask for a copy of the Patient Bill of Rights and get full information on your rights and responsibilities.
>
> *For more information on your rights as a hospital patient, turn to Chapter 12.*

one problem, you still need to think about your family's general medical care. Select a primary care physician and a hospital that will work together to address your family's needs.

Making a Choice

Although in many cases your choices are limited by the type of care you need, where your doctor has admitting privileges, where you live, and your health plan, you often have some options. The decisions you make affect the experiences you'll have at the hospital. Put another way, the more you know about *any* hospital, the better off you'll be and the more likely you are to be a competent partner in your care.

You want to find two aspects of good hospital care: the right *medical care* and a *caring atmosphere.* Both are critical to the outcome of your hospital visit. Quality is the most important component in your choice of a hospital; it's a universal concern. Other factors depend on your personal preferences and needs. Do you prefer a less expensive hospital? One closer to home? A smaller one? One with a national reputation?

Ask your current primary care provider or any health care professionals you know personally what hospitals they use and why. For example, hospital nurses have direct experience with such critical factors as the coordination of each patient's care, the caring atmosphere, and staff satisfaction. One telling question to ask a nurse—or any other health care provider—is whether she or he would send a family member to a particular hospital.

You can also ask your employer's or union's benefits department to recommend good hospitals and to provide information about their experiences with them. And talk to friends, family, and colleagues about their experiences.

Check the Services: High-Quality Care

Inquire about a hospital's ability to meet your particular needs, such as care for cancer, heart disease, or kidney disease. Does it have the services and specialties you need? Does it have experience with any conditions you or your family have now or anticipate in the future? Think about both your family's medical history and its current health status.

In addition, ask whether a hospital has:

- Staff trained and designated to prepare and manage your plan of care;
- Staff trained and designated to prepare and manage your discharge plan;
- Pre-admission services, so you can obtain as much outpatient care as possible;
- Education programs for patients, families, and members of the community, which you might want to attend to see how the programs describe the hospital;
- Referral networks in case you need to transfer to a more specialized facility;
- Social workers to help you access social, clinical, physical, and financial services; *and*
- Hospice services.

If you can, learn about the nursing staff. Nurses are the only medical personnel immediately available to you around the clock. And they're the ones most likely to be familiar with all aspects of your care. Generally, one nurse can care for three to six patients. If a hospital has a higher average ratio of patients

Practice Makes Perfect?

An effective means of comparing the ability of two or more hospitals to treat you is to determine how often each one encounters cases like yours. In general, hospitals—and specialists—that perform a certain procedure often tend to be safer. How many patients with your condition has the hospital treated? What is its success rate with specific medical procedures?

Ask your doctor or the hospital for data on the relevant experience of both the facility and the people who would handle your surgery or other hospital care. Your doctor will help you interpret the information.

per nurse, seek an explanation. If the ratio is lower, the hospital's overall philosophy may be based on a commitment to patient-centered care.

▼ FOR MORE INFORMATION

on the nursing staff levels at Boston area hospitals, turn to the listings that begin on Page 98.

Accreditation

Accreditation indicates that a hospital meets at least minimum standards of quality—perhaps much more. The *Joint Commission on Accreditation of Healthcare Organizations (JCAHO)*, an independent, nonprofit organization, conducts a quality assessment of most hospitals every three years. This process is voluntary, and about 80 percent of U.S. hospitals participate.

A few hospitals receive accreditation with commendation, conditional accreditation, or no accreditation. Conditionally accredited facilities have six months to correct deficiencies cited by the JCAHO.

In late 1994, the JCAHO began to make detailed data on hospitals available to the public. Reports cover a wide variety

Death Rates and Quality

The federal government compiles mortality data—death rates—for U.S. hospitals. Unfortunately, these statistics are hard to interpret. For example, a high number could indicate a problem, but it's just as likely to indicate an excellent hospital that accepts the most complex cases. Although adjusted rates can correct somewhat for such factors, death-rate statistics best serve to help hospitals monitor and improve themselves.

You can get the rates for 5,500 hospitals from the *Consumer's Guide to Hospitals*, which advises readers to use them as a starting point, not as a definitive mark of quality. *To order the guide, contact the Center for the Study of Services, 733 15th St., NW, Washington, DC 20005 (800)475-7283. The cost is $12.*

of areas, including nursing care, infection control, patient rights, and safety. The charge to receive this record is $30 per facility. Only reports compiled after January 1, 1994 are available. For more information, contact the JCAHO at (708)916-5800.

Make sure the hospital you use is accredited. All hospitals listed in *Health Care Choices* are accredited by the JCAHO. Among other things, that means they have programs, staff, or procedures related to:

• *Handling patient complaints.* You want a hospital to have a patient advocate or representative on staff or at least a clearly stated process for handling complaints.

• *Infection control.* Is there an infection-control practitioner on staff or a clear system for coordinating such activities?

• *End-of-life decisions.* An ethics committee or consultant should be available to help patients, providers, and their families deal with these difficult questions.

Emergency Departments

If several hospitals near your home have emergency departments, you may want to compare their capabilities before a crisis arises.

A strong indicator of capability is volume. The more visits a department handles, the more capable it's likely to be.

Another important factor is the qualifications of the physicians staffing the department. Some hospitals use only doctors who are board-certified in emergency medicine, surgery, or other specialties geared to the types of emergency commonly seen—for example, pediatricians in a children's hospital. Others rely on residents or other physicians with little training in the treatment of major traumas and other emergency conditions.

Check the Services: The Caring Hospital

Your recovery in a hospital depends on environmental factors as well as medical ones. Is your hospital a *caring* institution?

A caring atmosphere is often as difficult to identify as high-quality care. Among others factors to consider, a hospital should offer emotional support to your friends and family if you are seriously ill. Obviously, the staff is key. Are nurses, doctors, and other hospital employees courteous, polite, and friendly toward patients and visitors? Do they answer questions, or are they rushed and distracted when you try to talk with them? It's hard to know about these matters before you enter the hospital, but if you experience problems while using a hospital, talk to your admitting physician.

You might be able to determine ahead of time whether a hospital:

- Accommodates your special diet requests;
- Allows visitors to bring you food if your doctor approves;
- Sets liberal hours for receiving visitors and making phone calls;
- Provides accommodations for parents to spend the night with their children and helps make arrangements for other out-of-town visitors;
- Allows patients to sit outside of their rooms; *and*
- Keeps waiting rooms and patients' rooms clean.

Hospitality Houses

Friends and family are integral to health care. However, many patients must use hospitals far from home. For example, a person in need of major surgery or complicated radiation treatments may travel to a tertiary care center or specialty hospital far away for several weeks or more.

To meet the need for affordable lodging of patients' families and friends, *hospital hospitality houses* are located near many hospitals. For the most part, these are nonprofit organizations that offer a variety of services—overnight lodging, kitchen and laundry facilities, transportation, and children's playrooms. They offer a warm and supportive alternative to the isolation and expense of hotel rooms. The minimal charge for an overnight stay varies, and in many cases services are free. Talk to someone in the hospital social services department for assistance with locating or paying for such lodging.

These are some of the hospital hospitality houses in the Boston area:

The Family Inn serves families of organ transplant patients at any Boston hospital. 70 Seawall Ave., Brookline 02146 (617)566-3430.

Halcyon Place serves family members of patients at Massachusetts General Hospital, Massachusetts Eye and Ear Infirmary, Shriners Burns Institute, New England Medical Center, Children's Hospital, and others. 27 Commonwealth Ave., Boston 02116 (617)267-4242.

The Hospitality Program arranges lodging in the homes of local hosts for families of patients at any local hospital. 138 Tremont St., Boston 02111 (617)482-4338.

John Jeffries House, owned by Massachusetts Eye and Ear Infirmary, is open to the general public as well as families of patients at the Infirmary and Massachusetts General Hospital. 14 Embankment Rd., Boston 02115 (617)367-1866.

Ronald McDonald House primarily serves families of children with cancer who are 18 years or under and at Children's Hospital and Dana Farber Cancer Institute. 229 Kent St., Brookline 02146 (617)734-3333.

Hospitals and Foreign Languages

If you or someone in your family doesn't speak English fluently, you will need a competent language translator from the moment you enter a hospital.

In the past, hospitals and patients used anyone available as a translator: a family member, a friend, another patient, a person employed in another capacity at the hospital. All of these choices are inadequate.

For one thing, rarely will any of these people understand medical terminology in one, let alone two, languages. Also, translators must be available 24 hours a day. After all, a patient who wakes up in pain at 3 a.m. may need a translator immediately.

Most importantly, few relatives, friends, or even hospital employees have training in a critical part of health care: respecting each patient's rights to privacy and information. For example, a parent may hesitate to speak frankly if his or her child is the translator. Or an adult translator may censor the conversation between a child and a physician. The patient needs to know the doctor heard everything she or he says, and vice versa.

More and more often, hospitals train and enlist translators for the languages they encounter regularly. For emergencies, many hospitals subscribe to the AT&T Language Line; it provides translators for 140 languages, 24 hours a day.

Registering a Complaint

If you feel you've received poor care or unfair treatment in a hospital, bring your problem to the attention of hospital authorities. If you aren't satisfied with the institution's response or if it responds slowly, you can register a complaint either during your hospital stay or afterwards. State your case in writing as clearly as possible. Document it with information from your own record and the hospital's official record, if you have a copy.

To lodge a complaint about hospital care, you can contact:

• The Massachusetts Department of Public Health, Division of Health Care Quality, 10 West St., Boston 02111 (617)727-5860; *or*

• The Joint Commission on Accreditation of Healthcare Organizations, 1 Renaissance Blvd., Oakbrook, IL 60181 (708)916-5800.

Resource for Medicare Patients

If you receive hospital care through the Medicare program, register complaints about quality by contacting the Massachusetts Peer Review Organization, 235 Wyman St., Waltham 02154-1231 (617)890-0011. *For more information, turn to Chapter 6.*

Resources

Health Care for All
30 Winter St.
Boston 02108
(617)350-6207
(800)272-4232
Call with problems receiving access to Massachusetts hospitals—for instance, if you were denied care at a hospital or you think you qualify for free or reduced-cost care and need assistance with applying.

Massachusetts Department of Medical Security
One Ashburton Pl.
Boston 02108
(617)727-8300
(800)238-0990
This office is responsible for ensuring that hospitals follow the eligibility criteria for providing free care. Call if you think you have been wrongfully denied such care.

Massachusetts Peer Review Organization
235 Wyman St.
Waltham 02154-1231
(617)890-0011
(800)252-5533
MassPRO is responsible for ensuring that Medicare patients receive complete, high quality care. Call if you receive Medicare and think a hospital has mistreated you or discharged you too quickly.

What Nurses Say About Metropolitan Boston's Hospitals

By the Staff of *Health Care Choices*

Health Care Choices surveyed nurses about their experiences with the hospitals where they work. We received survey information and comments from about 500 nurses who reported on 40 hospitals.

A strong word of caution: the *Health Care Choices* survey was a first step in a long process. Rather than giving you guidance on specific hospitals, it points to broad areas that may be cause for consumer concern. We strongly invite academic researchers, government agencies, coalitions, and the hospitals themselves to follow up the results of this preliminary survey with scientific studies on both individual hospitals and hospitals as a whole. Based on such studies, hospitals could improve the quality of their services, and consumers could make more informed decisions about their hospital care.

The *Health Care Choices* survey offers two types of information for you to consider as you choose and use a hospital:

• Potential areas to watch for—and watch out for. These conclusions are based on answers to 12 questions the survey asked about nurses' perceptions of the hospitals' teamwork and overall quality. We also asked nurses if they would recommend their hospital to family and friends.

- Written comments by the nurses.

The Survey Responses

Survey responses strongly reflect the turmoil in the health care industry as a whole and suggest that it affects nurses' opinions of how well they and the hospitals they work for deliver patient care.

The best news: nurses overwhelmingly recommend the hospitals where they work as a place where families and friends could receive care. Nurses are also generally positive about how well their hospital adheres to quality-assurance procedures, responds to patient concerns, and works with patients to ensure comprehensive discharge planning.

Not surprisingly given national changes in hospital staffing, the greatest dissatisfaction concerns nurse-to-patient ratios in a respondent's hospital and in the specific unit in which she or he works. However, the variation from hospital to hospital—and from unit to unit in one hospital—may be great.

Perhaps most troubling, if borne out by further studies, is the low opinion nurses hold about the quality of teamwork—coordination and communication among administrators, physicians, nurses, and support staff. Despite the overall low opinion, there may be a great variation in this from hospital to hospital, so further studies of such differences would greatly help you decide which hospitals you'd prefer to use.

The Nurses' Comments

Following are a few of the hundreds of comments nurses made about hospitals in the Boston area. The comments are edited slightly for clarity, punctuation, and spelling, and the names of hospitals have been removed.

Clearly, nurses have a lot to say that could benefit consumers: in terms of hospital care as a whole, care at particular institutions, and, what nurses know about best, care in their own units. The nurses' comments strongly reveal their concern for patients and their love of and commitment to their work.

Nurses expressed strong views—both good and bad—on the impact of hospital mergers. And the views on staffing levels at hospitals were an especially common cause for complaint, both due to declining nurse-to-patient ratios and, even more, because of the replacement of nurses, especially registered nurses, with patient-care technicians.

• When are consumers going to demand better nurse-to-patient ratios? The staffing on our own unit is dangerous, at times, to providing safe patient care.

• Patients deserve all the time and care they can get, and it doesn't happen, because there is not enough staff anymore. It also is a potential injury hazard for nursing staff.

• My recommendation to readers—don't get sick.

• I have seen Hospital A grow and change with the continually changing health system. However, the patient always comes first.

• I have been a patient at Hospital A myself twice and received excellent care. For a community hospital, I feel that the level of medical and nursing care provided here is good to excellent.

• Patients at Hospital A receive excellent medical care, but physician availability, unfortunately, is on a 9-5, Monday-Friday basis. If an urgent need develops, there is a 90 percent chance the physician won't come in until his rounds!

• I have worked at three other hospitals as a student and feel Hospital B is a model in holistic, patient-centered care. There is a strong collaborative effort between nursing and medicine. Discharge planning is addressed as soon as a patient is admitted.

• There are too many patient-care technicians at Hospital C. A member of my family is presently in the hospital. When I asked a staff member for Tylenol, I was told his nurse is at supper and he must wait until she returns.

• Hospital D is very caring to the poor, sensitive to different cultures, and family-oriented.

• I believe most of the problems at Hospital D relate to the lack of input from nursing. This bureaucratic institution does not respect nurses' input.

• By decreasing the number of professional RNs who provide direct patient care, Hospital E has stated that lower quality care is okay.

• Hospital E is losing its ability to deliver quality care. The nursing division has been raped along with any ancillary services. Patients go home sicker, faster, and we are unable to teach them very much! And the administration *does not care!*

• Parents are definitely considered part of the team caring for the child at Hospital F. Their questions and concerns are addressed, and they are encouraged to participate in the care of their child.

• I have worked in other hospitals in the area and have come back to Hospital G for less pay because of the quality of care we are able to give our patients.

• In fulfilling my role as client advocate, I have consistently had the support of the administration to best meet client needs. I have always felt Hospital H is client- and quality-oriented.

• My reason not to recommend Hospital I is because the physicians who would provide the care are not of the highest standards.

• No raise for three years. Hospital J is continually buying new clinics throughout Massachusetts. When it buys a new one, it fires any union employee and will re-hire at a lower non-union rate.

• It is unfortunate that because of cutbacks, the patients at Hospital J have to suffer with fewer nurses on staff. The patients do know and often comment that they've noticed a difference in care.

• Hospital K considers secretaries and aides as part of the patient ratio. It is not unusual on a weekend to have the care of 15 patients with an aide. I've talked with other nurses in other facilities, and the staffing is similar.

• Hospital L, like so many others, is going through a lot of changes. The facility spends a lot of money for PR to say how much they care about quality. It is my opinion that they only care about the budget and the cost-effectiveness of the staffing numbers.

• I think Hospital M is an excellent hospital. Because it is a teaching hospital, the nurses are an integral part of the health care team. I do think discharge planning could be improved.

• Even though Hospital N has interpreters for all languages, non-English-speaking clients are not given options and are not aware that they can refuse prescriptions if they wish. This also happens to English-speaking clients.

• Hospital O is a private hospital newly affiliated with another hospital. It now offers an even wider range of services.

• Hospital P is like an army rather than a corporation—its structure, mentality, and demands. I do feel it is a good hospital and will survive the '90s.

• Patients at Hospital Q are provided with videos, pamphlets, and other handouts regarding their illnesses and medicines, but due to poor staffing, nurses find out about discharges only hours beforehand, leaving little time to educate patients or their families.

• Hospital R is replacing RNs with patient-care technicians. Some have little or no experience. New generic name tags do not reflect status, so patients do not know who really is caring for them. Staff are happy when everyone makes it through the day okay, not necessarily when care is given.

The Listings

I. Health Plans

The staff of *Health Care Choices* assembled the following information on 21 Boston-area health plans from a variety of sources. Unless otherwise noted, the information comes from questionnaires *Health Care Choices* sent to the plans. Included in the list are all area HMOs, the four PPOs with the most local members, and the six largest traditional indemnity insurers, according to the 1992 premiums they collected. Most plans responded to the questionnaire; the few that didn't are noted in the listings. When possible, *Health Care Choices* compared data reported by plans to data collected by independent researchers, consumer organizations, and government agencies.

HMOs and PPOs receive many requests for information from employers and other organizations, and are usually responsive. Traditional indemnity insurers are less equipped to handle such requests because the insurance products they sell are customized for each employer and employee group. Also, indemnity insurers are not required to submit plan information to the Division of Insurance, so less public data is available; *Health Care Choices* lists only the names, addresses, and phone numbers of these companies.

Consider the information presented in *Health Care Choices* together with the promotional materials, member handbook, and other data you find when you are choosing a health plan.

Get details about the benefits package, community-hospital affiliations, facility sites, and other topics from the handbook or by asking a plan representative specific questions.

An important consideration when choosing a health plan is its hospital affiliations. In response to our questionnaire, health plans listed anywhere from 25 to 70 affiliated hospitals, although in reality a plan may cover only select services at any one hospital. Find out ahead of time which of your local hospitals are in the plan's referral circle and for what types of services.

As reported by the plans to *Health Care Choices*, the standard benefits packages offered to employee groups by each plan are very similar. All are subject to state and federal mandates that require insurers to offer certain benefits. Most offer extra benefits, such as coverage for prescriptions, dental care, and vision care as "riders" that employers can purchase. Because the plans' standard benefits packages are so similar and vary according to what your employer chooses, that information does not appear here. All of the benefits offered in a plan should be in the benefits handbook or member contract.

Health Care Choices does not list premiums or other out-of-pocket expenses. Details about costs for group plans are negotiated between the insurance company and your employer. When estimating your out-of-pocket costs, also consider what you will pay for services not covered by your plan.

Key to the Data on Health Plans

Plan Type: *HMO/Staff Model:* Individual physicians are on staff and work directly at a health center. *HMO/Group Model:* Doctors are in established group practices that contract with the HMO. *HMO/IPA Model:* The HMO contracts directly with independent physicians or a formal association of physicians for health services delivered at the doctors' offices or health care facilities. *PPO:* Preferred Provider Organizations. *Indemnity:* Traditional indemnity insurer.

Enrollment: Subscribers (members) and dependents as of December 31, 1993, unless otherwise noted. For HMOs, as reported to the Division of Insurance. For PPOs, as reported by the plan to *Health Care Choices*.

Established: For HMOs, reported to the Division of

Insurance as "date commenced business." For PPOs, as reported by the plan to *Health Care Choices.* Older companies tend to be larger and more stable financially. They also have a track record with providers and consumers, so it's easier to get information about them.

Accreditation: The National Committee on Quality Assurance (NCQA), a nonprofit organization, reviews the quality of HMOs. These reviews are new, so award "bonus points" to an HMO that is accredited but don't penalize one that isn't. Scheduled reviews mean that the HMO has applied for accreditation and will undergo review on the date listed. One-year accreditation means that the plan will be reviewed in a year to determine if it can move up to full accreditation. Accreditation applies only to HMOs.

Languages: Many health plans have health care providers and member-service representatives who speak more than one language fluently. Some also subscribe to the AT&T Language Line, which offers 24-hour translation services in 140 languages.

Typical Copayments: In HMOs and PPOs, copayments are a fixed dollar amount you pay for health care services. Listed here are the copayments for each plan's standard package for an office visit, emergency-room visit, and prescription. These amounts are reported by the plan for the standard package offered to most of its members; however, the amount can vary for each plan depending on the benefits package.

Quality Improvement Initiatives: As reported by the insurer to *Health Care Choices.* Reports are edited for clarity and consistency but not content. Many quality-improvement activities focus on saving money; others note improvements in member services. Use this information to gain some insight into the efforts a plan makes to respond to members' concerns. Voicing concerns *can* result in changes and better service.

Points to Consider: This section includes miscellaneous information specific to each plan such as:

• Options for enrolling as an individual, not as part of a group. In general, most PPOs and HMOs enroll non-group individuals on a conversion basis only—that is, a member who leaves a group policy can "convert" to non-group coverage, but usually with fewer benefits and at a higher cost. HMO policies usually provide better conversion benefits than policies offered by indemnity insurers.

• Recent mergers and other developments that may affect consumers in the future.

• Specialized firms with which a plan contracts to provide certain services, most commonly mental health care, dental care, and prescription drugs. The specialty firm, rather than the health plan, could determine what care you receive and who provides it. You may need to contact it to obtain detailed information on the provider network and how to obtain care.

• Names of point-of-service (POS) plans—an option to see providers outside of an HMO network for some services at a higher expense.

• Significant results on Boston-area health plans from a national survey of federal employees conducted by the Center for the Study of Services (publisher of *Checkbook* magazine in Washington, DC, and San Francisco).

Physician Information:

• **Accepting New Patients:** Percentage of primary care providers who are accepting new patients. This is the number that counts for members, rather than a health plan's promotional materials about its total number of affiliated physicians. The average among reporting plans is 86 percent.

• **Certification:** Percentage of all affiliated physicians who are certified by one of the member organizations of the American Board of Medical Specialties. Higher levels of certification could signify higher standards of care, although many excellent doctors aren't certified. Not included is the percentage of board-eligible physicians—usually another 5 to 10 percent of physicians—who have trained for certification but not yet taken the exams. Nationally, about 85 percent of HMO physicians and 60 percent of all physicians are certified. The average among reporting plans is 83 percent.

• **Physician Turnover:** The percentage of primary care providers who left or whose contracts were terminated compared to the total number affiliated with the plan in 1993. A high turnover could indicate problems with the plan administration and continuity-of-care problems for members. Nationally, turnover averages 5 to 12 percent annually for large group practices. The average among reporting plans is 2.8 percent.

Quality Information (for HMOs only):

In 1994, the New England HEDIS Coalition, a collaborative effort of health plans, employers, and health care purchaser associations, collected and analyzed data from HMOs. The National Committee for Quality Assurance developed the Health Plan Employer Data and Information Set (HEDIS), a core set of measures on health plan performance.

Nine health plans in *Health Care Choices* provided information to the coalition. Plans that didn't participate in 1994 are noted.

The listings provide the reported rate for each measure, based on the records of non-Medicaid health plan members in 1993.

Although the coalition made efforts to standardize data across plans, it did not audit the reports of the plans. Also, in some cases, differences between plans in data-collection and measurement techniques hinder the comparability of reports. Please read the descriptions of each measure carefully. This is the first year the coalition has collected this information, so the data is best considered as a baseline for evaluating plan improvements in following years.

Keep in mind the limitations of this data. For example, the indicators don't inform you about other aspects of quality pertaining to the particular condition or concern, such as the process for receiving care. Nor do they tell you about the enormous number of health concerns not addressed by the measures.

The indicators from the New England HEDIS Coalition are:

• **Childhood Immunization:** Percentage of enrolled children who received all recommended immunizations by age 2. Immunization is one of the best ways to prevent a variety of serious illnesses that can affect children. The U.S. Public Health Service's national goal is to have at least 90 percent of

▶ CIGNA HEALTHCARE OF MASSACHUSETTS

101 Federal St., Boston, MA 02110
Member Service: (617)737-3800 or (800)345-9458

Type: HMO/IPA
Enrollment: 32,706
Established: 1986
Accreditation: Scheduled 6/26/95
Languages: N/A

Typical Copayments
Office Visit: N/A
Emergency Room Visit: N/A
Prescriptions: N/A

Quality Improvement Initiatives: N/A

Points to Consider

- CIGNA did not respond to the *Health Care Choices* questionnaire.
- CIGNA did not participate in the New England HEDIS Coalition Survey in 1994.

▶ FALLON COMMUNITY HEALTH PLAN

10 Chestnut St., Worcester 01608
Patient Relations: (800)283-2556 or (508)799-2100

Type: HMO/Group model
Enrollment: 165,259
Established: 1977
Accreditation: Full
Languages: The Fallon Interpreter Services offers translators in more than 18 languages; Language Link, a local service, can send interpreters to sites within 30 minutes; and Fallon subscribes to the AT&T Language Line. Interpreter Services: (508)852-3522.

Typical Copayments
Office Visit: $2-$10
Emergency Room Visit: $0-$25
Prescriptions: $5

Quality Improvement Initiatives

Fallon reports that it has undertaken a number of quality-improvement projects, including distributing preventive-care guidelines to providers resulting in improved rates of screening for high cholesterol and breast cancer and increased child immunization rates; decreasing cesarean-section rates; increasing the numbers of flu vaccines given to elderly patients; expanding interpreter services; and establishing a women's wellness center. In response to member concerns about access to routine appointments and telephone waiting times, Fallon added physicians to the plan, designed "Quik Phys" shorter physical exams, improved scheduling practices in some offices, increased urgent care availability, and installed a new phone system.

Points to Consider

- Non-group individuals may enroll by converting from a group policy or on their own. For individual enrollment, benefits are the same as for the standard Fallon HMO plan, without prescription drug coverage, and a health screen is required. The monthly premium rate for the individual plan is $153.42.
- Fallon Flex is the POS option.
- Serves primarily central Massachusetts
- Part of the Fallon Healthcare System, which includes Fallon Clinic, Saint Vincent Hospital, and other facilities. The provider network includes 26 Fallon Clinics, four UMass Group Practice sites, and about 60 individual Fallon Affiliate physicians. Copayments are higher when members see Fallon Affiliates.
- In the survey by the Center for the Study of Services, 87% of respondents were satisfied with their plan, about average for all plans surveyed. A significantly higher-than-average percentage of respondents rated CMHC highly on coverage.

PHYSICIAN INFORMATION	
Accepting New Patients:	78%
Board Certification:	87.5%
Turnover: 4%	

QUALITY INFORMATION	
Childhood Immunization:	90.0%
Cholesterol Screening:	91.8%
Mammography Screening:	80.4%
Prenatal Care:	100%
Mental Health Follow-up:	95.5%

▌ = average for physician information, median for quality information; data on all reporting plans.

▶ GUARDIAN LIFE INSURANCE CO.

201 Park Avenue South, New York, NY 10003

Member Services: (212)598-8000

Type: Indemnity

▶ HARVARD COMMUNITY HEALTH PLAN

10 Brookline Pl. West, Brookline 02146
Member Services: (617)739-6161 or (800)338-4247

Type: Both HMO/staff and HMO/group models
Enrollment: 458,284
Established: 1969
Accreditation: Full
Languages: Spanish, Russian, and others; translation services vary among sites; many clinicians are bilingual.

Typical Copayments
Office Visit: $5
Emergency Room Visit: $25
Prescriptions: $5

Quality Improvement Initiatives

HCHP reports that it made five improvements in 1993 based on HCHP data: implementing practice guidelines for the prevention and detection of urinary tract infections, resulting in a decrease of cultures taken and cost savings; implementing an education program for parents and clinicians about children's asthma, resulting in a reduction of hospital admissions for asthmatic children in the program; improving cholesterol screening and patient-notification system; increasing child immunization rates; and improving patient satisfaction with access to mammography facilities.

Points to Consider

- Non-group individuals can enroll by converting from a group policy or on their own through the Personal Plan; a prescription drug benefit is not available and a health screen is required. The monthly premium rate for the individual plan is $159.57, $319.14 for the two-person plan, and $430.84 for the family plan.
- Added Choice is the POS option.
- In the survey by the Center for the Study of Services, 87% of respondents were satisfied with their plan, about average for all plans surveyed. A significantly higher-than-average percentage of respondents rated HCHP highly on quality of care, ability to find a satisfactory doctor, coverage, and customer services in general.
- HCHP is a group/staff model HMO, with a network of 19 health centers that it owns and operates, plus over 70 contracted medical groups providing care at over 100 locations in Massachusetts, Rhode Island, and New Hampshire.
- In 1994, HCHP signed letters of intent to merge with both Matthew Thornton Health Plan and Pilgrim Health Plan. These mergers have not been completed and are awaiting approval from the divisions of insurance in Massachusetts and New Hampshire. The impact of these mergers is not known in part because the final terms have not yet been decided.

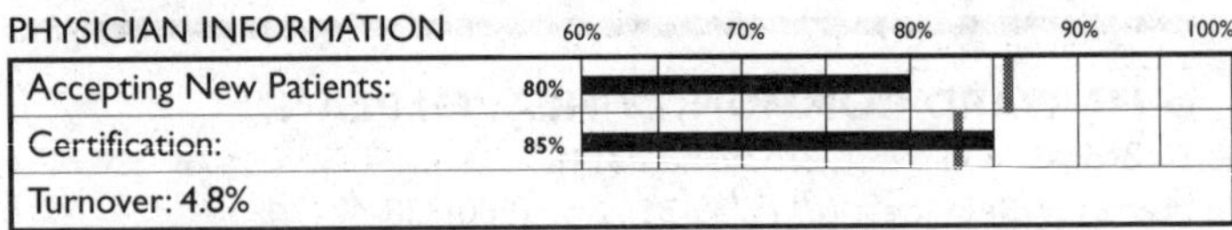

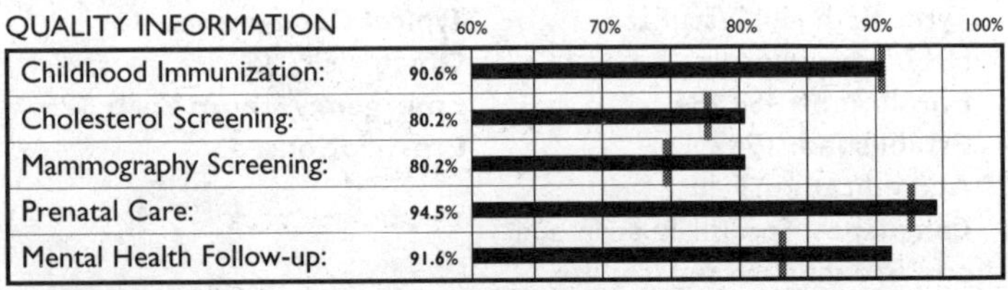

▌= average for physician information, median for quality information; data on all reporting plans.

▶ HMO BLUE

100 Summer St., Boston 02110

Member Services: (617)956-2000 or (800)368-6392

Type: HMO/IPA
Enrollment: 439,729
Established: 1992
Accreditation: Scheduled 12/4/95
Languages: Many of the network providers and employees are fluent in numerous foreign languages.

Typical Copayments
Office Visit: $5
Emergency Room Visit: $25
Prescriptions: $10 brand-name drugs; $5 generic drugs

Quality Improvement Initiatives: N/A

Points to Consider

- Non-group individuals may enroll only by converting from a group policy.
- HealthFlex Blue is the POS option.
- HMO Blue and Bay State, the other Blue Cross/Blue Shield HMO, operate separately.
- Biodyne, Inc. administers mental health benefits.
- In the survey by the Center for the Study of Services, 82% of respondents were satisfied with their plan, about average for all plans surveyed; 14% were extremely satisfied, significantly below the average for all plans surveyed. A significantly lower-than-average percentage of respondents rated HMO Blue highly on customer services in general. The survey covered former members.

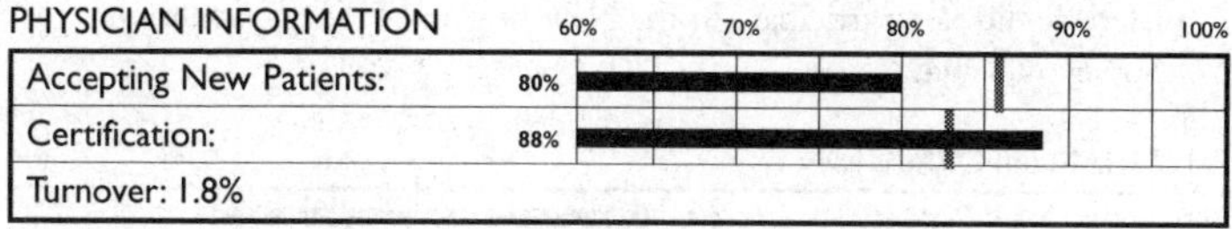

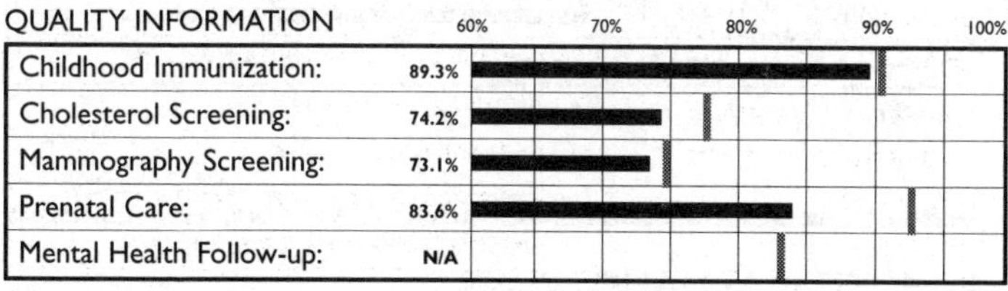

| = average for physician information, median for quality information; data on all reporting plans.

▶ JOHN HANCOCK MUTUAL LIFE INSURANCE CO.

P.O. Box 111, Boston 02117
Member Services: (617)572-6000
Type: Indemnity

▶ METLIFE HEALTHCARE NETWORK OF MASSACHUSETTS

99 High St., Boston 02110
Member Services: (800)444-7855

Type: HMO/IPA
Enrollment: 1,896
Established: 1987
Accreditation: None
Languages: None

Typical Copayments
Office Visit: $10
Emergency Room Visit: $50
Prescriptions: $5-$10

Quality Improvement Initiatives

In 1993, MetLife reports, it streamlined its medical-management and physician-referral processes. MetLife conducts member-satisfaction surveys four times a year. Identifying and addressing problems are handled on a department-by-department basis.

Points to Consider

- Non-group individual enrollment is not available.
- POS Network is the POS option.
- In June 1994, Metropolitan Life Insurance Company and Travelers Inc. announced that they were combining health care insurance operations nationally. The joint venture is expected to have no impact on Massachusetts MetLife HMO members.

- MetLife did not participate in the New England HEDIS Coalition Survey in 1994.

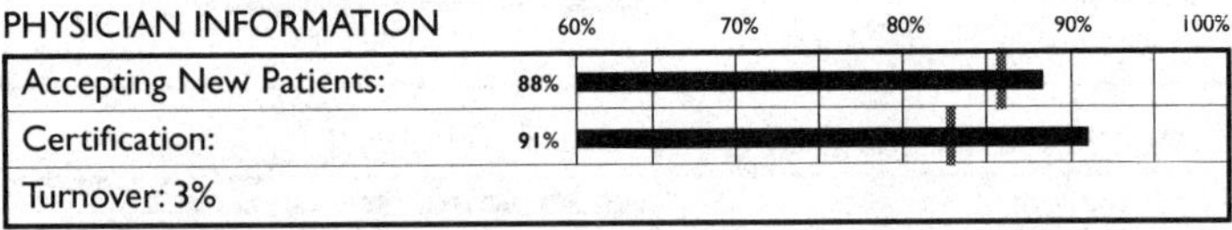

▌= average for all reporting plans.

▶ MUTUAL ALLIANCE PLAN

440 Lincoln St., Worcester 01653
Member Services: (508)855-4033

Type: PPO
Enrollment: 11,000
Established: 1988
Languages: Spanish

Typical Copayments
Office Visit: $5-$15 for network providers
Emergency Room Visit: $25 or $50
Prescriptions: Vary

Quality Improvement Initiatives

Mutual Alliance Plan reports that it added physicians and hospital facilities to the network, particularly in eastern Massachusetts.

Points to Consider

- Non-group individual enrollment in the PPO is not available.
- State Mutual Life Assurance Co. of America, a division of Allmerica Financial, owns Mutual Alliance Plan.
- The primary criteria for network physician selection is admitting privileges to a network hospital; other credentialing aspects are confidential.

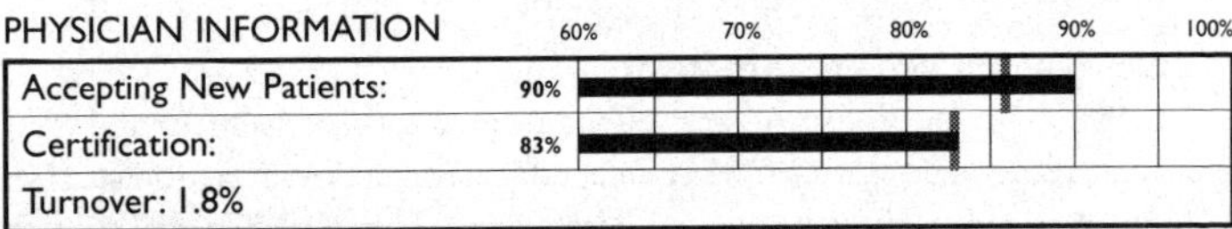

▌= average for all reporting plans.

▶ NEIGHBORHOOD HEALTH PLAN

253 Summer St., Boston 02210-1120
Member Services: (617)772-5500 or (800)433-5556
Type: HMO/IPA
Enrollment: 41,261
Established: 1988
Accreditation: None

Languages: A wide variety. Every new member receives a "Welcome Call" in her or his native language from a bilingual NHP member-service representative who explains how to obtain benefits and referrals.

Typical Copayments
Office Visit: $0
Emergency Room Visit: $0
Prescriptions: $3

Quality Improvement Initiatives

NHP reports it made the following improvements in quality and efficiency: assessing waiting times for routine and urgent appointments and working with the primary care sites to improve access; improving newborns' health outcomes through identifying and monitoring pregnant women at risk for delivering premature infants; developing a school-based system of care to enhance access to health care by children and adolescents; developing a system-wide asthma management program; conducting provider educational programs through the "NHP University;" increasing the control over cost and quality of the home care delivery system; and improving the timeliness of hospital discharge planning.

Points to Consider

- Non-group individuals may enroll only by converting from a group policy.
- NHP does not have a POS option.
- NHP is unique in that it serves as a managed-care system for many patients of over 60 Massachusetts community health centers. Recently, NHP has expanded to include 20 private group practices in its network as well.
- Unlike other HMOs, the majority of NHP members are enrolled through Medicaid or small employer groups and live in urban areas. As a result, NHP members tend to have lower incomes and higher health care needs and NHP was unable to submit as much non-Medicaid data as other HMOs. These factors can contribute to lower-than-normal rates on HEDIS quality measures.
- Board-certification rate applies to primary care physicians only.
- Data on physician turnover is not available because NHP contracts with health centers and group practices rather than individual physicians.

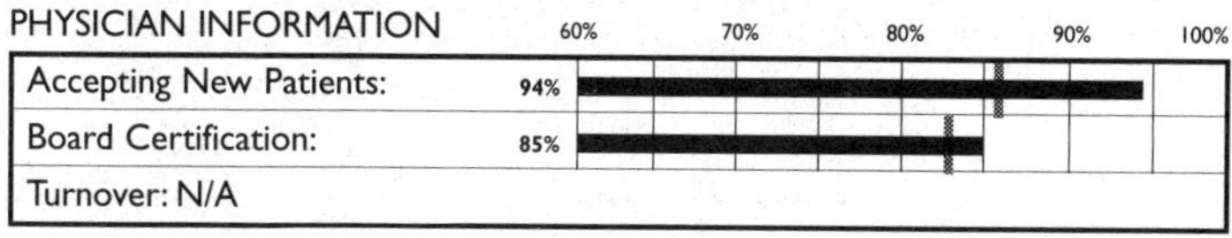

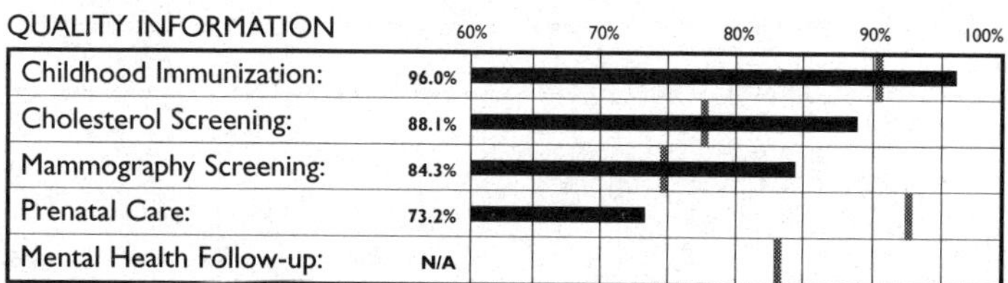

▌ = average for physician information, median for quality information; data on all reporting plans.

▶ PILGRIM HEALTH CARE

P.O. Box 9102, Norwell 02061
Member Services: (617)871-3950 or (800)742-8326

Type: HMO/IPA
Enrollment: 281,099
Established: 1981
Accreditation: None
Languages: Subscribes to the AT&T Language Line; has written translations of benefits summaries in languages predominant in the service area.

Typical Copayments
Office Visit: $5
Emergency Room Visit: $30
Prescriptions: $9 brand-name drugs; $3 generic drugs

Quality Improvement Initiatives

In 1993, Pilgrim reports, it instituted a computer program to link medical-outcome data and patient complaints with provider evaluations and developed a database that documents provider patterns of care. This assists in performance reviews. Two areas that members identified as needing improvement were premium rates and selecting primary care physicians. In response, Pilgrim's cost-control team implemented programs to reduce the growth rate of medical costs, members are educated about the plan's gatekeeper function, and a provider database was created to enhance provider selection.

Points to Consider

- Non-group individuals may enroll only by converting from a group policy. An indemnity option through the Allianz Life Insurance Company of North America is available to members who become ineligible for membership and who do not live in the service area.
- Pilgrim's Point of Service is the POS option.
- In 1994 Pilgrim signed a letter of intent to merge with Harvard Community Health Plan. The merger has not been completed and is awaiting approval from the Division of Insurance. The impact of the merger is not known in part because the final terms are not yet decided.
- NORCAP provides substance-abuse benefits.

PHYSICIAN INFORMATION		60%	70%	80%	90%	100%
Accepting New Patients:	82%					
Board Certification:	N/A					
Turnover: 1.5%						

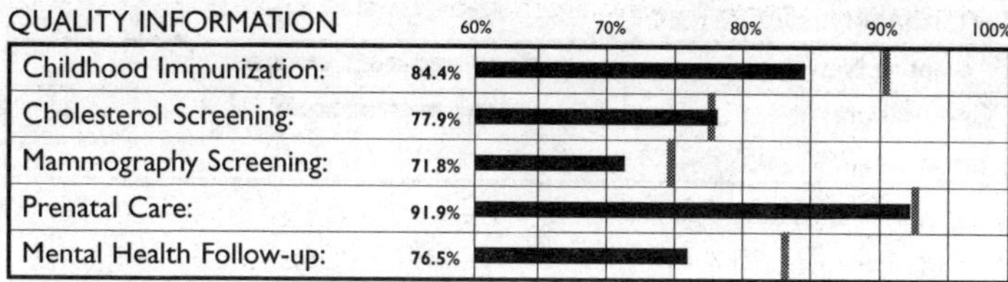

= average for physician information, median for quality information; data on all reporting plans.

▶ PRUCARE PLUS

10 New England Business Center, Andover 01810
Customer Services: (800)422-7399

Type: POS
Enrollment: 76,801
Established: 1986
Accreditation: One-year
Languages: Subscribes to the AT&T Language Line

Typical Copayments
Office Visit: $10
Emergency Room Visit: $50
Prescriptions: $10 brand-name drugs; $5 generic drugs

Quality Improvement Initiatives

In response to a member-satisfaction survey conducted in 1993, PruCare Plus reports, it demanded and received more compliance from network physicians with referral and billing procedures; increased the size of the physician network; educated provider offices about PruCare Plus procedures; and conducted more training in the Customer Service unit.

Points to Consider

- PruCare Plus is a point-of-service plan that is much like a PPO except that members must choose a primary care physician.
- Non-group individual enrollment in the POS is not available. Individuals can convert to the Prudential indemnity plan.
- Prudential Insurance Co. owns PruCare Plus.
- Enrollees are subject to preexisting-condition exclusions for one year if they enroll at any time other than their employer's open-enrollment period.
- Behavioral Health Management Solutions, Inc., administers mental health benefits.
- In 1993, Prudential Insurance Co. established PruCare HMO, which has about 445 members. All of the HMO physicians are in the POS network.

PHYSICIAN INFORMATION

		60%	70%	80%	90%	100%
Accepting New Patients:	83%					
Certification:	80%					
Turnover: 1.0%						

▌ = average for all reporting plans.

▶ PRUDENTIAL INSURANCE CO.

751 Broad St., Newark, NJ 07102
Member Services: (201)802-6000
Type: Indemnity

▶ TRAVELERS INSURANCE CO.

125 High St., Boston 02110
Member Services: (617)772-2670
Type: Indemnity

▶ TRAVELERS MANAGED CARE SYSTEM

125 High St., Boston 02110
Member Services: (800)842-3014

Type: PPO
Enrollment: N/A
Established: 1987
Languages: N/A

Typical Copayments
Office Visit: N/A
Emergency Room Visit: N/A
Prescriptions: N/A

Quality Improvement Initiatives: N/A

Points to Consider

- Travelers Managed Care did not respond to the *Health Care Choices* questionnaire.
- In June 1994, Metropolitan Life Insurance Company and Travelers Inc. announced that they were combining their health care insurance operations nationally. The joint venture is expected to have little impact on Travelers Managed Care members.

▶ TUFTS ASSOCIATED HEALTH MAINTENANCE ORGANIZATION, INC.

333 Wyman St., Waltham 02254
Customer Relations: (800)462-0224

Type: HMO/IPA
Enrollment: 234,818
Established: 1981
Accreditation: One-year
Languages: Subscribes to the AT&T Language Line; the Customer Relations Department is equipped with a Telecommunications Device for the Deaf.

Typical Copayments
Office Visit: Vary
Emergency Room Visit: Vary
Prescriptions: Vary

Quality Improvement Initiatives

As part of ongoing quality improvement initiatives, Tufts Health Plans reports, new programs in three areas brought together existing initiatives. The Healthy Birthday Program offers services to pregnant members at risk for preterm delivery and to obstetrical caregivers to help manage prenatal care through to a successful delivery. The Cesarean Section Awareness Program aims to reduce c-section rates without compromising care for mothers or babies. Preventive Health Services Guidelines encourage members and providers to engage in preventive health measures; among the areas of concentration are childhood immunizations, cervical and breast cancer prevention and early detection, and asthma management; in addition, physicians are encouraged to remind members about when and how often to receive routine tests. Each year, Tufts Health Plans conducts customer-satisfaction and physician-satisfaction surveys to help it determine areas of strength and target areas for improvement.

Points to Consider:

- Non-group individuals may enroll only by converting from a group policy.
- Tufts Total Health Plan is the POS option.

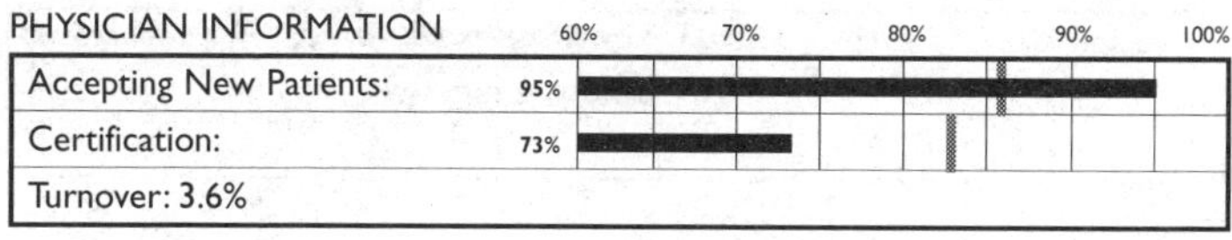

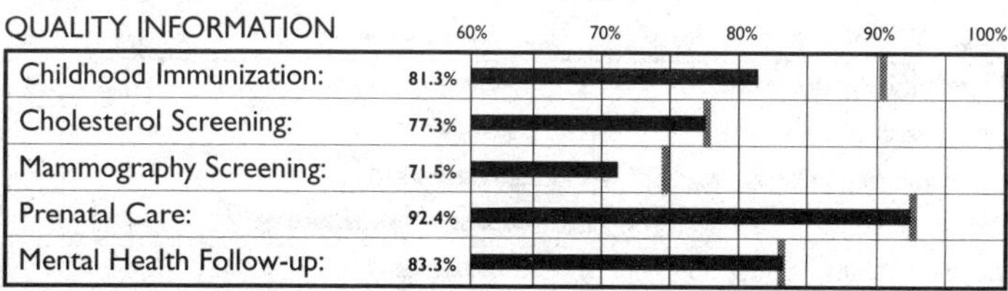

▌ = average for physician information, median for quality information; data on all reporting plans.

▶ U.S. HEALTHCARE

3 Burlington Woods Dr., Burlington 01803
Member Solutions: (800)323-9930

Type: HMO/IPA
Enrollment: 44,457
Established: 1988
Accreditation: Full
Languages: Subscribes to the AT&T Language Line; Spanish-speaking customer representatives; prints bilingual member handbooks.

Typical Copayments
Office Visit: $5
Emergency Room Visit: $35
Prescriptions: $5

Quality Improvement Initiatives

As a result of quality-assessment efforts in 1993, U.S. Healthcare reports, it took action in five areas: it revamped the provider-compensation system to place more emphasis on quality of care rather than utilization statistics; engaged in the NCQA accreditation process and received full accreditation; initiated a specialist recertification program; tracked adverse events with hospitalizations and delivered feedback to network hospitals; and addressed deficiencies with primary care physicians by "freezing" or terminating offices that do not meet U.S. Healthcare standards.

Points to Consider

- Non-group individuals may enroll only by converting from a group policy.
- Versatile, Choice of Excellence, and Quality Point Programs are the POS options.
- U.S. Healthcare owns and operates HMOs in eight northeastern states.
- Board-certification rate applies to primary care physicians only.
- U.S. Healthcare also has 28,900 members enrolled through employer self-insured plans.

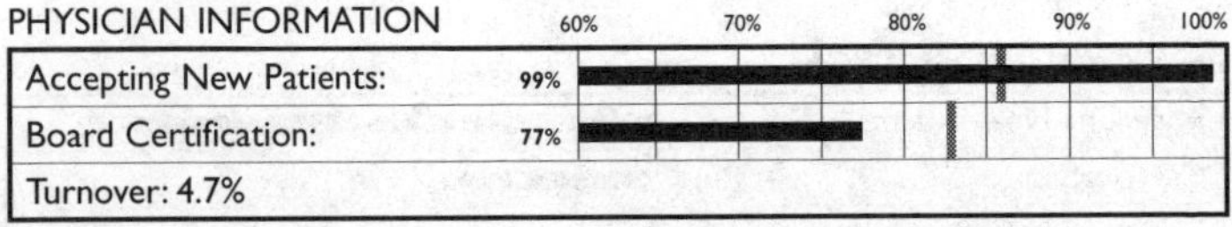

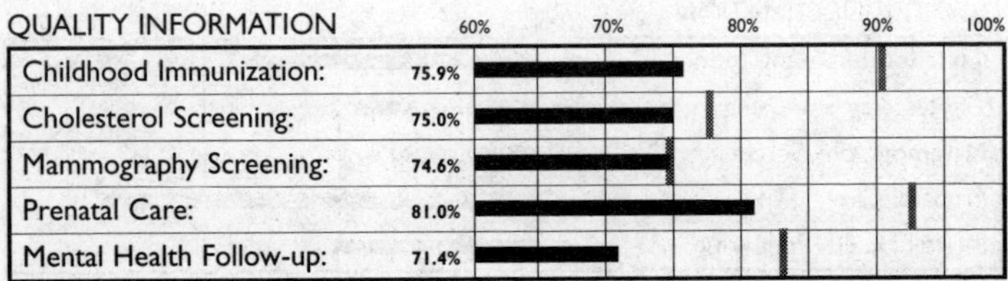

▌= average for physician information, median for quality information; data on all reporting plans.

II. Primary Care Providers

These listings can help you locate a primary care provider. Inclusion here does not constitute an endorsement. Not listed here are nurse practitioners and physician assistants and, for the most part, obstetricians, gynecologists, and pediatricians. Nurse practitioners and physician assistants most often deliver primary care in collaborative settings, such as group practices, HMOs, and community health centers.

▼ FOR MORE INFORMATION

on obstetricians and gynecologists, turn to Chapter 5; on pediatricians, turn to Chapter 4.

Primary Care Physicians

These doctors responded to a *Health Care Choices* questionnaire distributed to all internists, family physicians, and general-practice physicians in the Boston metropolitan area, according to the records of the Massachusetts Board of Registration in Medicine in March 1994. The physicians supplied the data and stated that they accept new patients.

Type: An *individual* physician practices alone or in conjunction with a nurse or physician assistant. *Group* practices have several physicians and other health professionals on staff. *HMOs* are health maintenance organizations.

Certifications: Professional medical societies set requirements for training and offer specialty examinations and certification. While certification is not required and measures knowledge more than skill, it offers some confirmation of competence in a particular field. Conversely, physicians practicing outside their specialty may be less experienced. There is no certification in primary care, per se, or general practice, but related certifications include credentials in family practice, internal medicine, pediatrics, preventive medicine, gynecology, and obstetrics. About two-thirds of U.S. physicians are certified. *Board eligible* signifies that a physician has completed the requirements to take the certification exam but has not yet been certified through the examination process.

Plans: Major health plans with which the physician is affiliated. This does not necessarily mean that *anyone* can use this physician through a listed plan. Ask the physician and the plan. Note also that some health plans allow you to use any licensed primary care physician. Check with your insurer.

Hospitals: The hospitals to which the physician can admit a patient.

N/A signifies no answer, an illegible entry on the questionnaire, or not applicable.

Arlington

Carole E. Allen
Carole Allen Pediatric Associates
22 Mill St.
Arlington 02174
Type: group
Certification: pediatrics
Plans: Tufts, HMO Blue, Blue Care Elect, HCVM, Pilgrim, Cost Care, Medicare, Travelers
Hospitals: Children's, Mt. Auburn, Beth Israel, Brigham and Women's, Cambridge

Patricia Guastella
Carole Allen Pediatric Associates
22 Mill St.
Arlington 02174
Type: group
Certification: pediatrics
Plans: Tufts, HMO Blue, Blue Care Elect, HCVM, Pilgrim, Cost Care, Medicare, Travelers
Hospitals: Children's, Mt. Auburn, Beth Israel, Brigham and Women's, Cambridge

Bedford

David S. Newcombe
Bedford VA Hospital
200 Springs Rd.
Bedford 01730
Type: hospital-based
Certification: internal medicine, rheumatology
Plans: none
Hospitals: Bedford VA

James J. Steinberg
Bedford VA Hospital
200 Springs Rd.
Bedford 01730
Type: hospital-based
Certification: internal medicine, subspecialty in endocrinology
Plans: N/A
Hospitals: Bedford VA

Ruth M. Liberfarb
Brighton Marine Health Center Pediatric Clinic
Hanscom AFB
Bedford 02135
Type: group
Certification: pediatrics, medical genetics
Plans: US Federal Health Plan
Hospitals: Massachusetts General, Children's

Beverly

Frank S. Carbone, Jr.
550 Cabot St.
Beverly 01915
Type: group—Lahey Community
Certification: internal medicine
Plans: HCHP, plus others
Hospitals: Beverly, Lahey

William R. Dorsey
Beverly Pediatric Associates
Parkhurst Professional Building
Herrick St.
Beverly 01915
Type: group
Certification: pediatrics
Plans: many
Hospitals: Beverly, Salem, Children's, Brigham and Women's

Gordon P. Elmeer
112 Sohier Rd.
Beverly 01915
Type: individual
Certification: internal medicine, gastroenterology
Plans: Bay State, HMO Blue, PruCare, CIGNA
Hospitals: Beverly

Carol S. Kessler
Beverly Pediatrics
Parkhurst Building
Beverly 01915
Type: two-person practice
Certification: N/A
Plans: BC/BS, Tufts, U.S. Healthcare, MetLife, PruCare, Bay State, Travelers, Aetna, CIGNA, John Hancock, Medicaid, Pilgrim
Hospitals: Beverly, North Shore Medical Center

Boston

J. Barclay Adams
110 Francis St.
Boston 02215
Type: individual
Certification: internal medicine
Plans: All BC/BS products
Hospitals: Deaconess, Brigham and Women's, New England Baptist

J. Andrew Billings
Chelsea Health Associates/Internal Medicine Associates

Massachusetts General Hospital
Fruit St.
Boston 02114
Type: group
Certification: internal medicine
Plans: Tufts, Bay State, HMO Blue, MGH Plus, Pilgrim, John Hancock
Hospitals: Massachusetts General

Thomas L. Delbanco
Health Care Associates
Beth Israel Hospital
330 Brookline Ave.
Boston 02215
Type: group
Certification: internal medicine
Plans: multiple
Hospitals: Beth Israel

Peter H. Dragonas
333 Longwood Ave.
Boston 02115
Type: individual
Certification: ob/gyn
Plans: many
Hospitals: Brigham and Women's, New England Baptist, Deaconess

Kenneth C. Edelin
720 Harrison Ave.
Boston 02118
Type: individual
Certification: ob/gyn
Plans: most major health plans
Hospitals: Boston University Medical Center

Susan E. Frankl
Evans Medical Group
University Hospital
720 Harrison Ave.
Boston 02118
Type: group
Certification: internal medicine
Plans: HMO Blue, Pilgrim, U.S. Healthcare, HCHP (for BU employees)
Hospitals: Boston University Medical Center

Laura N. Goldman
New England Health Associates
77 Summer St.
Boston 02110
Type: group
Certification: family practice
Plans: Tufts, Bay State, HMO Blue, CIGNA, Aetna, and others
Hospitals: New England Medical Center

Robert A. Goodell
Downtown Medical Associates
294 Washington St.
Boston 02108
Type: group (four physicians)
Certification: pediatrics, family practice
Plans: Tufts, HMO Blue, Bay State, U.S. Healthcare
Hospitals: New England Medical Center

Pamela Hartzband
Deaconess Medicine
110 Francis St.
Boston 02215
Type: group
Certification: internal medicine, endocrinology and metabolism
Plans: HMO Blue, BC/BS, Bay State, Commonwealth PPO, Master Health Plus
Hospitals: New England Deaconess

Barbara C. Holbert
Downtown Medical Associates
294 Washington St.
Boston 02108
Type: group
Certification: internal medicine
Plans: Tufts, U.S. Healthcare, CIGNA, Aetna, Travelers, John Hancock, Bay State, Pilgrim
Hospitals: Boston University Medical Center, New England Medical Center

Gail H. Kaufman
Blackwell Medical
125 Parker Hill Ave.
Boston 02120
Type: individual
Certification: internal medicine, gastrointestinal medicine
Plans: Tufts, Pilgrim, U.S. Healthcare, Bay State
Hospitals: New England Baptist, New England Deaconess

K.J. Kelly
Massachusetts General Hospital
Renal Unit
Boston 02114
Type: group
Certification: nephrology
Plans: to be established
Hospitals: Massachusetts General

Stephen J. Lerman
Harvard Community Health Plan
2 Fenway Plaza
Boston 02215
Type: HMO
Certification: pediatrics
Plans: HCHP
Hospitals: Children's, Brigham and Women's

Alexandra M. Matzner
270 Clarendon St.
Boston 02116
Type: individual
Certification: N/A
Plans: N/A
Hospitals: N/A

Alan F. Meyers
Child Health Foundation
Department of Pediatrics
Boston City Hospital
Boston 02118
Type: hospital-based clinic
Certification: pediatrics
Plans: HCHP, Tufts, NHP, Pilgrim
Hospitals: Boston City

Joanne Mitchell
Birth Defects Service
Children's Hospital
300 Longwood Ave.
Boston 02115
Type: group
Certification: pediatrics
Plans: all
Hospitals: Children's

Sara J. Nuciforo
Boston City Hospital Primary Care
ACC-3, PCC
818 Harrison Ave.
Boston 02118
Type: public-hospital group, also takes HMO patients
Certification: internal medicine
Plans: HCHP, Tufts, NHP, (HMO Blue soon)
Hospitals: Boston City

Cindy Osman
Codman Square Health Center
Boston City Hospital
818 Harrison Ave.
Boston 02130
Type: community health center
Certification: pediatrics
Plans: Tufts, BC/BS, NHP
Hospitals: Boston City, (Carney soon)

Jan Paradise
Boston City Hospital
818 Harrison Ave.
Boston 02118
Certification: pediatrics
Plans: Pilgrim, NHP, Medicaid
Hospitals: Boston City

David E. Rosengard
Rosengard Clinic Medical Center
West Broadway
Boston 02127
Type: three-doctor group
Certification: family practice, psychiatry, neurology, quality assurance, forensic examiners
Plans: Tufts
Hospitals: New England Medical Center, Boston University Medical Center, Boston City

Roy M. Rubin
Harvard Community Health Plan
2 Fenway Plaza
Boston 02215
Type: HMO
Certification: internal medicine
Plans: HCHP
Hospitals: Brigham and Women's, Beth Israel

Suzanne E. Salamon
Shattuck Hospital
170 Morton St.
Boston 02130
Type: hospital-based, inpatient and outpatient
Certification: internal medicine, geriatrics
Plans: Medicaid, Medicare
Hospitals: Shattuck Hospital

Susan C. Thomas
Medical Care Associates
One Boylston Plaza
Boston 02118
Type: group
Certification: internal medicine
Plans: all major health plans except HCHP
Hospitals: Boston University Medical Center, St. Elizabeth's

Karen E. Victor
Deaconess Medical Associates
1 Autumn St.
Boston 02146
Type: academic group
Certification: internal medicine
Plans: HMO Blue, Bay State
Hospitals: N/A

Susan Wainger
Savitz & Wainger Medical Associates
294 Washington St.
Boston 02108
Type: group
Certification: internal medicine
Plans: most
Hospitals: Beth Israel, New England Medical Center

Robert M. Weiss
Boston University Gynecology Associates
88 E. Newton St.
Boston 02118
Type: group
Certification: ob/gyn, reproductive endocrinology
Plans: HMO Blue, Pilgrim, U.S. Healthcare, CostCare, BC/BS
Hospitals: Boston University Medical Center

Boston/Allston

Benjamin Brown
Joseph M. Smith Community Health Center
51 Stadium Way
Allston 02134
Type: group
Certifications: family practice
Plans: Medicaid; in progress: NHP, PruCare, Aetna Health Plans, Tufts, Pilgrim, HMO Blue, Bay State, PHCS, Health Care Value
Hospitals: St. Elizabeth's

H. Carroll Eastman
Joseph M. Smith Community Health Center
51 Stadium Way
Allston 02134
Type: group
Certification: none—general practitioner
Plans: Medicaid, NHP
Hospitals: N/A

Leora Fishman
Joseph M. Smith Community Health Center
51 Stadium Way
Allston 02134

Type: group
Certification: family practice
Plans: Medicaid, NHP, PruCare, Aetna, Tufts, Pilgrim, HMO Blue; in progress: Bay State, PHCS, Health Care Value
Hospitals: St. Elizabeth's

Janet O. Yardley
Joseph M. Smith Community Health Center
51 Stadium Way
Allston 02134
Type: group
Certification: family practice
Plans: Medicaid, NHP, PruCare, Aetna, Tufts, Pilgrim, HMO Blue, Bay State, Affordable Health; in progress: PHCS, Health Care Value
Hospitals: St. Elizabeth's

Boston/Brighton

Robert A. Bonanno
Stanton Medical Associates
697 Cambridge St.
Brighton 02135
Type: group
Certification: internal medicine
Plans: Pilgrim, PruCare, Tufts, Bay State, HMO Blue
Hospitals: St. Elizabeth's, Newton-Wellesley

Richard C. Galgano
Stanton Medical Associates
697 Cambridge St.
Brighton 02135
Type: group
Certification: internal medicine
Plans: Pilgrim, PruCare, Tufts, Bay State, HMO Blue
Hospitals: St. Elizabeth's, Newton-Wellesley

Martin L. Gelman
Greater Boston Medical Associates
280 Washington St.
Brighton 02135
Type: group
Certification: internal medicine, nephrology
Plans: Bay State, Tufts, U.S. Healthcare, PruCare, HMO Blue, Health Source, Travelers, Affordable Health
Hospitals: St. Elizabeth's, Whidden, Malden, Milford

Emilie S. Hitron
Stanton Medical Associates
697 Cambridge St.
Brighton 02135
Type: group
Certification: internal medicine
Plans: Pilgrim, PruCare, Tufts, Bay State, HMO Blue
Hospitals: St. Elizabeth's, Newton-Wellesley

Walter J. Lee
280 Washington St.
Brighton 02135
Type: individual
Certification: internal medicine
Plans: Tufts, Bay State, Pilgrim, HMO Blue, U.S. Healthcare, Aetna
Hospitals: St. Elizabeth's

Ralph M. Porter
Stanton Medical Associates
697 Cambridge St.
Brighton 02135
Type: group
Certification: internal medicine
Plans: Pilgrim, PruCare, Tufts, Bay State, HMO Blue
Hospitals: St. Elizabeth's, Newton-Wellesley

Janice T. Powell
Stanton Medical Associates
697 Cambridge St.
Brighton 02135
Type: group
Certification: internal medicine
Plans: Pilgrim, PruCare, Tufts, Bay State, HMO Blue
Hospitals: St. Elizabeth's, Newton-Wellesley

Rohrer Associates
11 Nevine St.
Brighton 02135
Type: group
Certification: internal medicine, geriatrics
Plans: multiple
Hospitals: St. Elizabeth's, WalthamWeston, Beth Israel

Ashraf S. Selim
Greater Boston Medical Associates
280 Washington St.
Brighton 02135
Type: group
Certification: internal medicine, nephrology
Plans: Tufts, Bay State, Medicaid, HMO Blue, Health Source, Affordable Health
Hospitals: St. Elizabeth's, Malden, Whidden, Milford

Alec J. Style
Brighton Marine Health Center
77 Warren St.
Brighton 02135
Type: group
Certification: family practice
Plans: Tufts, HMO Blue, PruCare, Aetna, Bay State
Hospitals: St. Elizabeth's

Elizabeth B. Wood
Brookline Associates in Internal Medicine
11 Nevins St.
Brighton 02135
Type: group
Certification: internal medicine
Plans: Tufts, Pilgrim, BC/BS, Bay State, Aetna, Medicare
Hospitals: St. Elizabeth's

Boston/Dorchester

Barbara L. Anderson
Bowdoin St. Health Center
200 Bowdoin St.
Dorchester 02122
Type: health center
Certification: family practice
Plans: NHP, Tufts
Hospitals: Carney

Mary Lou C. Ashur
Carney Hospital
2100 Dorchester Ave.
Boston 02124
Type: group
Certification: internal medicine, preventive medicine
Plans: N/A
Hospitals: Carney, Boston City

Boston Medical Group
2100 Dorchester Ave.
Dorchester 02124
Type: group (25 primary care physicians)
Certifications: various, including internal medicine, family practice, and pediatrics
Plans: many
Hospitals: most for Carney, others include Quincy, Milton, and others

Shreekant Chopra
Renal Medical Care, PC
2110 Dorchester Ave.
Dorchester 02124
Type: group
Certification: internal medicine, nephrology
Plans: BC/BS, HMO Blue, Pilgrim, Tufts, Bay State, Medicare, Medicaid
Hospitals: Carney, Goddard Memorial, New England Baptist

Tai J. Chung
Renal Medical Care, PC
2110 Dorchester Ave.
Dorchester 02124
Type: two-physician group
Certification: internal medicine
Plans: BC/BS, HMO Blue, Pilgrim, Tufts, Bay State, Medicare, Medicaid
Hospitals: Carney, New England Baptist

Byron R. Diggs
Harvard Street Health Center
632 Blue Hill Ave.
Dorchester 02121
Type: group
Certification: internal medicine
Plans: NHP
Hospitals: N/A

Jayne M. Doherty
Harvard Street Health Center
632 Blue Hill Ave.
Dorchester 02121
Type: health center
Certification: internal medicine
Plans: NHP
Hospitals: N/A

Mary Elizabeth Dore
Neponset Health Center
398 Neponset Ave.
Dorchester 02122
Type: group
Certification: internal medicine
Plans: almost all, including HCHP
Hospitals: Carney

Mina A. Gillers
Upham's Corner Health Center
500 Columbia Road
Dorchester 02125
Type: group
Certification: pediatrics
Plans: NHP, Tufts, HCHP
Hospitals: Boston City

Holly H. Goodale
Dorchester House Multi-Service Center
1353 Dorchester Ave.
Dorchester 02122
Type: group
Certification: pediatrics
Plans: Tufts, NHP, HMO Blue
Hospitals: Boston City, New England Medical Center (newborns)

Karen O. Kennedy
Codman Square Health Center
637 Washington St.
Dorchester 02124
Type: health center
Certification: pediatrics
Plans: NHP, Tufts, Pilgrim
Hospitals: Carney, Boston City, New England Medical Center

Janet L. Levatin
1993 Dorchester Ave.
Boston 02124
Type: individual
Certification: pediatrics, homeopathy
Plans: Medicaid, BC/BS indemnity
Hospitals: Carney

Mark S. Ostrem
2100 Dorchester Ave.
Boston 02124
Type: group
Certification: internal medicine, geriatrics
Plans: Tufts, Bay State, PruCare, Pilgrim, John Hancock, BC/BS
Hospitals: Carney

Susan Racine
2110 Dorchester Ave.
Dorchester 02124
Type: individual
Certification: internal medicine
Plans: Tufts, HCHP, Hancock, Prudential, Aetna, CIGNA, Cost Care
Hospitals: Carney

Gary L. Taylor
Boston Medical Group
2110 Dorchester Ave.
Dorchester 02124
Type: group
Certification: internal medicine, geriatrics
Plans: HMO Blue, BC/BS, Pilgrim, Tufts, MetLife, U.S. Healthcare, PruCare, NHP, Medicaid, Medicare, Health Choice
Hospitals: Carney

J. Tuakli-Williams
Blue Hill Avenue Medical Associates
512 Blue Hill Ave.

Dorchester 02121
Type: individual
Certification: pediatrics
Plans: BC/BS, Tufts, U.S. Healthcare, Pilgrim
Hospitals: Children's, Brigham and Women's, Beth Israel

Juan C. Vera
212 Ashmont St.
Dorchester 02124
Type: individual
Certification: internal medicine
Plans: Tufts, Aetna, Pilgrim, Bay State, PruCare, HMO Blue, Cost Care, MetLife, Medicaid
Hospitals: Milton, Carney

Boston/East Boston

Peter G. Stringham
East Boston Neighborhood Health Center
10 Gove St.
East Boston 02128
Type: group
Certification: family practice
Plans: HCHP, Tufts, Bay State
Hospitals: Children's, Boston City

Bertstrand W. Williams
East Boston Neighborhood Health Center
10 Gove St.
East Boston 02128
Type: HMO
Certification: adult medicine, pediatrics
Plans: HCHP, Tufts
Hospitals: Boston City, Children's

Boston/Hyde Park

Charles W. Lowney
Lowney Medical Associates
1234 Hyde Park Ave.
Hyde Park 02136
Type: individual
Certification: family medicine
Plans: Tufts, Pilgrim, U.S. Healthcare, PruCare, CIGNA, HMO Blue, MetLife, BC/BS
Hospitals: New England Baptist, Newton-Wellesley

Carolyn F. Sax
Hyde Park Pediatrics, PC
695 Truman Pkwy.
Hyde Park 02136
Type: group
Certification: pediatrics
Plans: all except U.S. Healthcare
Hospitals: Children's

Robert Schwartz
1017 River St.
Hyde Park 02136
Type: individual
Certification: family practice
Plans: HMO Blue, Medicaid
Hospitals: Boston University Medical Center

Boston/Jamaica Plain

Farshid Fararooy
Lemuel Shattuck Hospital
170 Morton St.
Jamaica Plain 02130
Type: hospital-based
Certification: internal medicine
Plans: many
Hospitals: Lemuel Shattuck

Barbara R. Gottlieb
Brookside Community Health Center
3297 Washington St.
Jamaica Plain 02130
Type: health center/group
Certification: internal medicine
Plans: NHP, HMO Blue, Medicaid, Bay State, PCC
Hospitals: Brigham and Women's

Steven W. Greer
Martha Eliot Health Center
33 Bickford St.
Jamaica Plain 02130
Type: health center/group
Certification: pediatrics
Plans: NHP
Hospitals: Children's

Li-Wen Jen
Southern Jamaica Plain Health Center
687 Centre St.
Jamaica Plain 02146
Type: health center
Certification: pediatrics
Plans: NHP, PCC, BC/BS, John Hancock
Hospitals: Children's, Brigham and Women's

Nancy H. Kahn
Brookside Community Health Center
3297 Washington St.
Jamaica Plain 02130
Type: group
Certification: pediatrics
Plans: HMO Blue, Bay State, NHP
Hospitals: Brigham and Women's, Children's

Eng-Hwi Kwa
1155 Centre St.
Jamaica Plain 02130
Type: individual
Certification: internal medicine, addiction medicine
Plans: Pilgrim, Tufts, Bay State, BC/BS, John Hancock
Hospitals: Faulkner, Mt. Auburn

Katherine McGowan
Faulkner Hospital
1153 Centre St.
Jamaica Plain, MA 02130
Type: individual
Certification: internal medicine, infectious disease
Plans: Tufts, HMO Blue, Medicaid, John Hancock, Bay State
Hospitals: Faulkner

Cathryn L. Samples
Martha Eliot Health Center
33 Bickford St.
Jamaica Plain, MA 02130

Type: health center
Certification: pediatrics
Plans: NHP, Bay State
Hospital: Children's

Boston/Mattapan

Jerline S. Dixon
Boston Medical Group
438 River St.
Mattapan 02126
Type: group
Certification: internal medicine
Plans: Pilgrim, Tufts, Bay State, U.S. Healthcare, Aetna, MetLife, NHP
Hospitals: Carney, Beth Israel, Boston University Medical Center, Boston City

Carl Singletary
Mattapan Community Health Center
1425 Blue Hill Ave.
Mattapan 02126
Type: health center
Certification: internal medicine
Plans: Tufts, Bay State, BC/BS, U.S. Healthcare
Hospitals: Faulkner, Boston City

Boston/Roslindale

David W. Chen
942 South St.
Roslindale 02131
Type: individual
Certification: internal medicine
Plans: Tufts, Bay State, HMO Blue, Pilgrim, John Hancock
Hospitals: Faulkner

Carol A. O'Neil
Greater Roslindale Medical and Dental Center
6 Cummins Hwy.
Roslindale 02131
Type: health center
Certification: family practice
Plans: Tufts, Bay State, HMO Blue, Pilgrim, NHP
Hospitals: Faulkner

Mitchell O. Tunick
Roslindale Pediatric Associates
950 South St.
Roslindale 02131
Type: group
Certification: pediatrics
Plans: most except HCHP
Hospitals: Children's

Boston/Roxbury

Mark R. Drews
Whittier Street Neighborhood Health Center
20 Whittier St.
Roxbury 02120
Type: health center
Certification: internal medicine
Plans: NHP, Tufts
Hospitals: Boston City

Boston/South Boston

Selim R. Chakar
580 East Broadway
South Boston 02127
Type: individual
Certification: surgery
Plans: PruCare, Aetna, Tufts, Pilgrim
Hospitals: St. Elizabeth's

Yung Y. Teng
Rosengard Clinic
380 W. Broadway
South Boston 02127
Type: group
Certification: none
Plans: BC/BS
Hospitals: New England Medical Center

Boston/West Roxbury

Robert W. Mullins
77 Corey St.
West Roxbury 02132
Type: individual
Certification: general medicine
Plans: Tufts, Bay State
Hospitals: Faulkner

Brookline

David G. Blom
209 Harvard St.
Brookline 02146
Type: group
Certification: internal medicine
Plans: N/A
Hospitals: St. Elizabeth's

Bruce W. Bunnell
Centre Pediatric Associates
One Brookline Pl.
Brookline 02146
Type: group
Certification: pediatrics
Plans: Tufts, HCHP, HMO Blue, PruCare
Hospitals: Beth Israel, Children's, Massachusetts General, Brigham and Women's

Daniel G. Heller
Centre Pediatric Associates
One Brookline Pl.
Brookline 02146
Type: group
Certification: pediatrics
Plans: Tufts, HCHP, HMO Blue, PruCare
Hospitals: Beth Israel, Children's, Massachusetts General, Brigham and Women's

Parnag H. Kasarjian
1199 Beacon St.
Brookline 02146
Type: individual
Certification: internal medicine
Plans: Tufts, Pilgrim, BC/BS, Bay State, CIGNA
Hospitals: Beth Israel

James A. Marquardt

33 Pond Ave.
Brookline 02146
Type: group
Certification: ob/gyn
Plans: HMO Blue, HCHP, Pilgrim, Bay State, Travelers PPO
Hospitals: Brigham and Women's

Izabella A. Mazhbits
209 Harvard St.
Brookline 02146
Type: individual
Certification: N/A
Plans: Medicaid, Medicare, BC/BS, HMO Blue, Bay State
Hospitals: St. Elizabeth's

Michael K. Rees
Rees Medical Associates
1195 Beacon St.
Brookline 02146
Type: group
Certification: internal medicine
Plans: many
Hospitals: Beth Israel, Brigham and Women's, St. Elizabeth's

Susan D. Reuter
Centre Pediatric Associates
One Brookline Pl.
Brookline 02146
Type: group
Certification: pediatrics
Plans: Tufts, HCHP, HMO Blue, PruCare
Hospitals: Beth Israel, Children's, Massachusetts General, Brigham and Women's

Sandhya T. Shah
1180 Beacon St.
Brookline 02146
Type: individual
Certification: ob/gyn
Plans: many
Hospitals: Beth Israel, St. Elizabeth's

Debbie Tesler
Centre Pediatric Associates
One Brookline Pl.
Brookline 02146
Type: group
Certifications: pediatrics
Plans: Tufts, HCHP, HMO Blue, PruCare
Hospitals: Beth Israel, Children's, Massachusetts General, Brigham and Women's

Amnon Wachman
1101 Beacon St.
Brookline 02146
Type: individual
Certification: internal medicine
Plans: HMO Blue, Pilgrim, Travelers, Bay State, BC/BS
Hospitals: Brigham and Women's

Richard Wolff
1180 Beacon St.
Brookline 02146
Type: individual
Certification: internal medicine, cardiovascular disease
Plans: many
Hospitals: Beth Israel

Pamela M. Zuckerman
Centre Pediatric Associates
One Brookline Pl.
Brookline 02146
Type: group
Certification: pediatrics
Plans: Tufts, HCHP, HMO Blue, PruCare
Hospitals: Beth Israel, Children's, Massachusetts General, Brigham and Women's

Burlington

Richard G. Ruben
Burlington Pediatric Associates
281 Cambridge St.
Burlington 01803
Type: group
Certification: pediatrics
Plans: most
Hospitals: Children's, Winchester

Benjamin Scheindlen
Burlington Pediatric Associates
281 Cambridge St.
Burlington 01803
Type: group
Certification: pediatrics
Plans: most
Hospitals: Children's, Winchester

Cambridge

Steele Beloi
300 Mt. Auburn St.
Cambridge 02238
Type: group
Certification: internal medicine
Plans: Tufts, Bay State, Pilgrim, HMO Blue, Aetna, Travelers
Hospitals: Mt. Auburn

Mary L. Brown
MIT Medical Department
77 Massachusetts Ave.
Cambridge 02139
Type: HMO
Certification: internal medicine
Plans: MIT Health Plan
Hospitals: Mt. Auburn

Cambridge Hospital
Primary Care Center
1493 Cambridge St.
Cambridge 02139
Type: group
Certification: internal medicine
Plans: Bay State, HMO Blue, U.S. Healthcare, NHP
Hospitals: Cambridge

Lisa Dobberteen
North Cambridge Health Center
266B Rindge Ave.
Cambridge 02140
Type: health center

Certification: pediatrics
Plans: Tufts, HMO Blue, U.S. Healthcare, BC/BS, Medicaid
Hospitals: Cambridge, Mt. Auburn, Massachusetts General

Alan Drabkin
Riverside Health Center
205 Western Ave.
Cambridge 02139
Type: health center
Certification: family practice
Plans: Bay State, BC/BS, HMO Blue, U.S. Healthcare
Hospitals: Cambridge

Dianne E. Drake
Harvard University Health Services
75 Mt. Auburn St.
Cambridge 02138
Type: HMO—students
Certification: internal medicine
Plans: Harvard University Community Health Plan, Health Flex
Hospitals: N/A

Eric M. Flint
Pediatric Associates
330 Mt. Auburn St.
Cambridge 02238
Type: group
Certification: internal medicine
Plans: Tufts, BC/BS, CIGNA, Bay State
Hospitals: Mt. Auburn, Cambridge

Alan C. Garber
Mt. Auburn Primary Care Center
330 Mt. Auburn St.
Wyman-3
Cambridge 02238
Type: group
Certification: internal medicine
Plans: Tufts, HMO Blue, Pilgrim
Hospitals: Mt. Auburn

Morris Gorfine
897 Massachusetts Ave.
Cambridge 02139
Type: individual
Certification: family practice
Plans: BC/BS, HMO, HealthFlex, Bay State, Pilgrim, Tufts
Hospitals: St. Elizabeth's, Cambridge, Somerville

Susan W. Hardt
Cambridge Hospital Primary Care
1493 Cambridge St.
Cambridge 02139
Type: group/hospital-based
Certification: internal medicine, geriatrics
Plans: U.S. Healthcare, Bay State, BC/BS
Hospitals: Cambridge

Karen T. Isselbacher
Physician Associates
Mt. Auburn Hospital
330 Mt. Auburn St., Suite 410
Cambridge 02159
Type: group
Certification: internal medicine
Plans: Tufts, Bay State, HMO Blue, Pilgrim, CIGNA, John Hancock
Hospitals: Mt. Auburn

Edward O. Leitao
East Cambridge Health Center/Cambridge Hospital
650 Cambridge St.
Cambridge 02141
Type: N/A
Certification: N/A
Plans: Bay State, HMO Blue, Medicare, Medicaid
Hospitals: Cambridge

Joan H. Mathews
777 Concord Ave
Cambridge 02138
Type: individual
Certification: pediatrics
Plans: Tufts, Bay State, HMO Blue, Aetna, John Hancock, Travelers, Pilgrim
Hospitals: Massachusetts General, Children's

Philip P. McGovern
1458 Cambridge St.
Cambridge 02139
Type: individual
Certification: ob/gyn
Plans: Cost Care, PruCare, Tufts, HMO Blue, Bay State, Travelers, Pilgrim, CIGNA, U.S. Healthcare
Hospitals: Cambridge, Mt. Auburn, Winchester

Barbara R. Ogur
Cambridge Hospital Neighborhood Health Centers
1493 Cambridge St.
Cambridge 02139
Type: community health center
Certification: internal medicine
Plans: NHP, HMO Blue, U.S. Healthcare
Hospitals: Cambridge

Gregorio E. Pedroza
1611 Cambridge St.
Cambridge 02138
Type: HMO
Certification: internal medicine
Plans: HCHP
Hospitals: Mt. Auburn, Cambridge

Bernard Shepen
300 Mt. Auburn St.
Cambridge 02138
Type: individual
Certification: internal medicine, nephrology
Plans: Bay State, HMO Blue, John Hancock, MetLife
Hospitals: Mt. Auburn

Ellen Spar
Physician Associates
300 Mt. Auburn St.
Cambridge 02238

Type: group
Certification: internal medicine
Plans: HMO Blue, Tufts, CIGNA, Bay State, Pilgrim, Aetna, Medicaid, MetLife
Hospitals: Mt. Auburn

Triphon P. Vlagopoulos
575 Mt. Auburn St.
Cambridge 02138
Type: individual
Certification: internal medicine, allergy
Plans: Tufts, HMO Blue, Bay State, Pilgrim, John Hancock, Travelers
Hospitals: Mt. Auburn, Waltham Weston

Lori A. Wroble
MIT Health Service
77 Massachusetts Ave.
Cambridge 02139
Type: HMO
Certification: ob/gyn
Plans: MIT Health Service
Hospitals: Brigham and Women's

Michael W. Yogman
135 Huron Ave.
Cambridge 02138
Type: individual
Certification: pediatrics
Plans: Tufts, Pilgrim, HMO Blue, Travelers, John Hancock
Hospitals: Children's, Massachusetts General, New England Medical Center, Beth Israel, Mt. Auburn, Brigham and Women's

William M. Zinn
Cambridge Hospital Primary Care Unit
1493 Cambridge St.
Cambridge 02139
Type: group
Certification: internal medicine, geriatrics
Plans: HMO Blue, Bay State, Pilgrim, U.S. Healthcare
Hospitals: Cambridge

Canton

C.S. Chong
442 Washington St.
Canton 02021
Type: individual
Certification: N/A
Plans: N/A
Hospitals: N/A

Robert L. D'Agostino
40 Revere St.
Canton 02021
Type: individual
Certification: family practice
Plans: BC/BS, Medicare, Pilgrim, Travelers
Hospitals: Norwood

Theodore J. Goodman
800 Washington St.
Canton 02021
Type: individual
Certification: pediatrics
Plans: Pilgrim, HMO Blue, Tufts, Bay State
Hospitals: Norwood

Chelsea

Sefik Abdulhayoglu
383A Washington Ave.
Chelsea 02150
Type: individual
Certification: internal medicine
Plans: Bay State, BC/BS, U.S. Healthcare, Medicare, Medicaid
Hospitals: Whidden Memorial, Everett

Nancy S. Adams
111 Everett Ave.
Chelsea 02150
Type: individual
Certification: internal medicine
Plans: HMO Blue, Tufts, PruCare, U.S. Healthcare
Hospitals: Beth Israel

Colleen M. Collins
MGH/Chelsea Health Center
100 Bellingham St.
Chelsea 02150
Type: health center
Certification: internal medicine
Plans: many
Hospitals: Massachusetts General

M. Sheila Desmond
MGH/Chelsea Health Center
100 Bellingham St.
Chelsea 02150
Type: group
Certification: pediatrics
Plans: Bay State, BC/BS, Tufts, Pilgrim
Hospitals: Massachusetts General

Judith S. Fisch
MGH/Chelsea Health Center
100 Bellingham St.
Chelsea 02150
Type: group
Certification: internal medicine, geriatrics
Plans: BC/BS, Bay State, Tufts, and others
Hospitals: Massachusetts General

Thomas C. Sterne
Adult Medicine Unit
Chelsea Health Center
100 Bellingham St.
Chelsea 02150
Type: group
Certification: internal medicine
Plans: most except for HCHP
Hospitals: Massachusetts General

Andrew Billings
Chelsea Health Associates
Internal Medicine Associates
100 Bellingham St.
Chelsea 02150
Type: group
Certification: internal medicine
Plans: Tufts, Bay State, HMO Blue, MGH Plus, Pilgrim, John Hancock
Hospitals: Massachusetts General

Chestnut Hill

Patti J. Colevas
Brigham and Women's Physician's Group
850 Boylston St.
Chestnut Hill 02167
Type: group
Certification: internal medicine
Plans: HMO Blue, HCHP, Travelers, Bay State
Hospitals: Brigham and Women's

M. David Kelleher
Boylston Medical Group
830 Boylston St.
Chestnut Hill 02061
Type: group
Certification: internal medicine
Plans: HMO Blue, Bay State, Pilgrim, U.S. Healthcare, NHP, John Hancock
Hospitals: Boston University Medical Center

Harold J. Kosasky
Chestnut Hill Medical Center
25 Boylston St.
Chestnut Hill 02167
Type: individual
Certification: ob/gyn
Plans: N/A
Hospitals: Brigham and Women's, Newton-Wellesley

Evelyn S. Picker
Brigham Physician's Group
850 Boylston St.
Chestnut Hill 02167
Type: group
Certification: internal medicine
Plans: BC/BS, HMO Blue, Travelers, HCHP, Bay State, Medicare, Medicaid
Hospitals: Brigham and Women's, New England Baptist, New England Deaconess, Newton-Wellesley

Jerome D. Siegel
CRA/Occupational Health & Rehabilitation
69 Thornton Rd.
Chestnut Hill 02167
Type: hospital-based
Certification: internal medicine, occupational medicine, public health
Plans: N/A
Hospitals: New England Baptist, Newton-Wellesley

Lester A. Steinberg
25 Boylston St.
Chestnut Hill 02167
Type: N/A
Certification: N/A
Plans: N/A
Hospitals: Beth Israel

Cohasset

Daniel R. Bonetzky
Cohasset Medical
152 King St.
Cohasset 02025
Type: group
Certification: N/A
Plans: most
Hospitals: N/A

Concord

Concord Hillside Medical Associates
242 Baker Ave.
Concord 01742
Type: group
Certification: various
Plans: Aetna, BC/BS, HCHP, PruCare, and many more
Hospitals: Emerson

Danvers

James J. Hagerty
6 Graystone Dr.
Danvers 01923
Type: individual
Certification: internal medicine
Plans: BC/BS, Tufts, Bay State, CIGNA, Travelers, PruCare, U.S. Healthcare, Medicare
Hospitals: Beverly

Steven L. Keenholtz
140 Commonwealth Ave.
Danvers 01923
Type: individual
Certification: internal medicine, infectious diseases
Plans: N/A
Hospitals: Beverly

Mark B. Mengel
Family Practice Center/Residency Program
75 Lindall St.
Danvers 01923
Type: group
Certification: family practice, preventive medicine
Plans: BC/BS, Pilgrim, Tufts, Bay State, and many more
Hospitals: Beverly

Dedham

David G. Bekker
Dedham Medical Associates
One Lyons St.
Dedham 02026
Type: multispecialty group
Certification: pediatrics
Plans: HCHP and many others
Hospitals: Children's, Newton-Wellesley

Everett

Jonathan D. Strongin
Pulmonary Associates of Greater Boston
103 Garland St.
Everett 02149
Type: group
Certification: internal medicine, pulmonary disease, critical care
Plans: HMO Blue, Pilgrim, PruCare, Tufts
Hospitals: Whidden Memorial, Malden, Melrose-Wakefield, Beth Israel

Framingham

Joel L. Bass
Metrowest Medical Center

115 Lincoln St.
Framingham 02192
Type: hospital-based
Certification: pediatrics
Plans: Medicaid
Hospitals: Metrowest Medical Center

Stephen B. Berkowitz
Ob/Gyn Associates
95 Lincoln St.
Framingham 01701
Type: group
Certification: ob/gyn
Plans: HMO Blue, Pilgrim, Tufts, Bay State
Hospitals: Metrowest Medical Center

Leon Herman
Ob/Gyn Associates
95 Lincoln St.
Framingham 01701
Type: group
Certification: ob/gyn
Plans: Medicaid, Medicare, Tufts, Pilgrim, and others
Hospitals: Metrowest Medical Center

Shun-How Lee
600 Worcester Rd.
Framingham 01701
Type: individual
Certification: internal medicine, endocrinology
Plans: HMO Blue, Bay State, Tufts, Pilgrim, Aetna, PruCare
Hospitals: Metrowest Medical Center

Carol Moore
Metrowest Medical Center
115 Lincoln St.
Framingham 02192
Type: hospital-based
Certification: pediatrics
Plans: Medicaid
Hospitals: Metrowest Medical Center

Daniel J. Roth
Framingham Pediatrics
161 Worcester Rd.
Framingham 01701
Type: group
Certification: pediatrics
Plans: Pilgrim, Tufts, HMO Blue, U.S. Healthcare, Bay State, PruCare, MetLife
Hospitals: Metrowest Medical Center

Lexington

Cynthia A. Carpenter
Lexington Pediatric Associates
19 Muzzey St.
Lexington 02173
Type: group
Certification: pediatrics
Plans: Tufts, CIGNA, MetLife, BC/BS, HCHP, PruCare, John Hancock, Travelers
Hospitals: Children's

Mitchell J. Feldman
Lexington Pediatric Associates
19 Muzzey St.
Lexington 02173
Type: group
Certification: pediatrics
Plans: Tufts, CIGNA, MetLife, BC/BS, HCHP, PruCare, John Hancock, Travelers
Hospitals: Children's

Nancy G. Geis
Lexington Pediatric Associates
19 Muzzey St.
Lexington 02173
Type: group
Certification: pediatrics
Plans: Tufts, CIGNA, MetLife, BC/BS, HCHP, PruCare, John Hancock, Travelers
Hospitals: Children's

Edward M. Gerber
Lexington Pediatric Associates
394 Lowell St.
Lexington 02173
Type: group
Certification: none
Plans: Tufts, HMO Blue, Pilgrim, BC/BS, Bay State, Aetna, Medicare, Health Source
Hospitals: Symmes, Winchester, Mt. Auburn

Francine M. Henessey
Lexington Pediatric Associates
19 Muzzey St.
Lexington 02173
Type: group
Certification: N/A
Plans: Tufts, CIGNA, MetLife, BC/BS, HCHP, PruCare, John Hancock, Travelers
Hospitals: Children's

Risa J. Korn
Beth Israel Hospital Medical Group Foundation
482 Bedford St.
Lexington 02173
Type: group
Certification: internal medicine
Plans: most
Hospitals: Beth Israel

Chawki E. Nahabet
19 Muzzey St.
Lexington 02173
Type: individual
Certification: ob/gyn
Plans: all except HCHP
Hospitals: Mt. Auburn, Winchester

Daniel I. Palant
Lexington Pediatric Associates
19 Muzzey St.
Lexington 02173
Type: group
Certification: pediatrics
Plans: HCHP, Tufts, BC/BS, Bay State, Aetna, John Hancock, MetLife, Travelers
Hospitals: Children's, Beth Israel, Brigham and Women's, Mt. Auburn

Julian L. Pearlman
Lexington Pediatric Associates
19 Muzzey St.

Lexington 02173
Type: group
Certification: N/A
Plans: Tufts, CIGNA, MetLife, BC/BS, HCHP, PruCare, John Hancock, Travelers
Hospitals: Children's

Douglas C. Pollard
16 Clarke St.
Lexington 02173
Type: individual
Certification: internal medicine
Plans: N/A
Hospitals: Lawrence Memorial, Symmes, Mt. Auburn, Winchester

Martin K. White
Lexington Pediatric Associates
19 Muzzey St.
Lexington 02173
Type: group
Certification: N/A
Plans: Tufts, CIGNA, MetLife, BC/BS, HCHP, PruCare, John Hancock, Travelers
Hospitals: Children's

Wendy L. Wornham
Lexington Pediatric Associates
19 Muzzey St.
Lexington 02173
Type: group
Certification: N/A
Plans: Tufts, CIGNA, MetLife, BC/BS, HCHP, PruCare, John Hancock, Travelers
Hospitals: Children's

Lynn

Christopher Chen
Pediatric Health Care Associates
225 Boston St.
Lynn 01904
Type: group
Certification: pediatrics
Plans: all major plans
Hospitals: North Shore Children's

Habibullah Habibi
225 Boston St.
Lynn 01904
Type: individual
Certification: internal medicine
Plans: N/A
Hospitals: Atlanticare Medical Center

Walter L. Harrison
34 Lynnfield St.
Lynn 01902
Type: individual
Certification: pediatrics
Plans: many
Hospitals: N/A

Jacob R. Karas
Respiratory Care Physicians
583 Chestnut St.
Lynn 01904
Type: group
Certification: internal medicine, pulmonary disease
Plans: Aetna, Bay State, HCHP, HMO Blue, Pilgrim, Tufts, PruCare
Hospitals: Union, Salem, Beverly

Mary M. Parr
Pediatric Health Care Associates
225 Boston St.
Lynn 01904
Type: group
Certification: pediatrics
Plans: all except U.S. Healthcare
Hospitals: Salem/North Shore, Melrose-Wakefield

Peter R. Sheckman
North Shore Medical Group
496 Lynnfield St.
Lynn 01904
Type: group
Certification: internal medicine, infectious diseases
Plans: N/A
Hospitals: Union, Salem, Beverly

Lynnfield

Ruth A. Hazen
Post Office Square
Lynnfield 01940
Type: individual/partnership
Certification: pediatrics
Plans: Bay State, HMO Blue, Tufts
Hospitals: North Shore Medical Center

John A. Schey
Post Office Square
Lynnfield 01940
Type: individual/partnership
Certification: pediatrics
Plans: Bay State, HMO Blue, Tufts, PruCare
Hospitals: North Shore Medical Center

Malden

John G. Goulding
440 Pleasant St.
Malden 02148
Type: partnership
Certification: family practice
Plans: Pilgrim, Healthsource, PruCare, CIGNA, HMO Blue
Hospitals: New England Memorial, Malden, Melrose-Wakefield

Peter F. Jeffries
Malden Family Health Center
100 Hospital Rd.
Malden 02148
Type: group
Certification: family practice
Plans: Pilgrim, U.S. Healthcare, Medicaid
Hospitals: Malden

Chander M. Nagpaul
380 Pleasant St.
Malden 02148
Type: group
Certification: internal medicine
Plans: Pilgrim, BC/BS, Bay State, U.S. Healthcare
Hospitals: Malden, New England Memorial, Melrose-Wakefield, Lawrence

Carl J. Turissini
Middlesex Cardiology Associates
Malden Hospital
100 Hospital Rd.
Malden 02148
Type: group
Certification: internal medicine, cardiology
Plans: most
Hospitals: Boston University Medical Center, Malden, Melrose-Wakefield, Whidden

Medfield

Mark H. Abensohn
266 Main St.
Medfield 02052
Type: individual
Certification: internal medicine
Plans: John Hancock, MetLife, BC/BS, Travelers, Aetna
Hospitals: Leonard Morse, Newton-Wellesley

Medford

Bruce F. Goodman
101 Main St.
Medford 02155
Type: individual
Certification: internal medicine
Plans: Tufts, Bay State, HMO Blue, BC/BS, BC Elect, Aetna, Pilgrim, MetLife, PruCare, U.S. Healthcare
Hospitals: Lawrence Memorial, Malden, Winchester

Poul M. LaPlante
Medford Family Practice
92 High St.
Medford 02155
Type: individual
Certification: family practice
Plans: Tufts, Bay State, Pilgrim, U.S. Healthcare, PruCare, Travelers, many others
Hospitals: Malden, Lawrence Memorial, Melrose-Wakefield, Winchester

Melvyn B. Levine
Pediatric Associates of Medford
101 Main St.
Medford 02155
Type: group
Certification: pediatrics
Plans: Bay State, Tufts, HMO Blue, PruCare, MetLife, Aetna, Pilgrim, Travelers
Hospitals: Malden, Winchester, Lawrence Memorial

Doina F. Marina
Medford Ob/Gyn Associates
46 Salem St.
Medford 02155
Type: N/A
Certification: N/A
Plans: BC/BS, HMO Blue, Tufts, U.S. Healthcare, Bay State, Pilgrim
Hospitals: Winchester, Malden, Lawrence Memorial

Rosario A. Scandura
Medford Ob/Gyn Associates
46 Salem St.
Medford 02155
Type: N/A
Certification: N/A
Plans: BC/BS, HMO Blue, Tufts
Hospitals: Winchester, Malden, Lawrence Memorial

Robert P. Williamson
43 Forest St.
Medford 02155
Type: individual
Certification: internal medicine
Plans: Tufts, Bay State, BC/BS
Hospitals: Lawrence Memorial

Melrose

John D. Mudrock
536 Franklin St.
Melrose 02176
Type: individual
Certification: internal medicine
Plans: Tufts, Travelers, MetLife, U.S. Healthcare
Hospitals: Melrose-Wakefield, Malden, New England Memorial

Natick

Kais R. Alhadi
Natick Medical Associates
6 Dewey St.
Natick 01760
Type: individual
Certification: pediatrics
Plans: Tufts, Pilgrim, HMO Blue, Medicaid, many others
Hospitals: Metrowest Medical Center

Robert Gottlieb
Metrowest Ob/Gyn Associates
67 Union St.
Natick 01760
Type: group
Certification: ob/gyn
Plans: most
Hospitals: Metrowest Medical Center

Sofia B. Melenevskaya
67 Union St.
Natick 01760
Type: individual
Certification: ob/gyn
Plans: all but HCHP
Hospitals: Metrowest Medical Center

Wanda D. Ryan
Endocrine & Diabetes Associates
67 Union St.
Natick 01760
Type: group
Certification: internal medicine, endocrinology
Plans: CostCare, Pilgrim, John Hancock, Tufts, Pilgrim, MetLife, HMO Blue
Hospitals: Metrowest Medical Center

Jennifer R. Thulin
67 Union St.
Natick 01760
Type: individual
Certification: ob/gyn
Plans: HMO Blue, Bay State, Pilgrim, Tufts, and many others
Hospitals: Metrowest Medical Center

Frank E. Wilson
Metrowest Ob/Gyn Associates
67 Union Street
Natick 01760
Type: group
Certification: ob/gyn
Plans: most
Hospitals: Metrowest Medical Center

Needham

Perminder Dhillon
111 Lincoln St.
Needham 02192
Type: individual
Certification: internal medicine, cardiology
Plans: most except U.S. Healthcare
Hospitals: Gloucester, Newton-Wellesley

Peter A. Ostrow
17 Oak St.
Needham 02192
Type: individual
Certification: internal medicine, pulmonary medicine
Plans: Aetna, Bay State, HMO Blue, Pilgrim, Tufts
Hospitals: Newton-Wellesley, Deaconess-Glover

Yatish Patel
Internist Associates
105 Chestnut St.
Needham 02192
Type: group
Certification: internal medicine, pulmonary
Plans: BC/BS, HMO Blue, PruCare, Medicare, Medicaid, Tufts, Pilgrim
Hospitals: Deaconess-Glover, Newton-Wellesley, WalthamWeston

Nicholas J. Rencricca
Oak Street Medical Associates
17 Oak St.
Needham 02192
Type: group
Certification: internal medicine
Plans: most
Hospitals: New England Deaconess, Deaconess-Glover, Newton-Wellesley

Earle G. Woodman
91 Dedham Ave.
Needham 02192
Type: individual
Certification: internal medicine
Plans: Tufts, HMO Blue, Pilgrim, Bay State, MetLife, Travelers, and others
Hospitals: Deaconess-Glover, Newton-Wellesley

Newton

Eugene Aron
Newton-Wellesley Ob/Gyn
2000 Washington St.
Newton 02162
Type: group
Certification: ob/gyn
Plans: all except HCHP and U.S. Healthcare
Hospitals: Newton-Wellesley

Carol S. Englender
1126 Beacon St.
Newton 02161
Type: individual
Certification: N/A
Plans: BC/BS
Hospitals: N/A

Jeanne T. Hubbuch
1126 Beacon St.
Newton 02161
Type: individual
Certification: environmental medicine
Plans: N/A
Hospitals: N/A

Martin E. Leber
588 Walnut St.
Newton 02160
Type: individual
Certification: pediatrics
Plans: Tufts, HMO Blue, PruCare, Aetna, Traveler, MetLife, Pilgrim, CostCare, HCVM
Hospitals: Newton-Wellesley, Children's, Brigham and Women's

Newton Lower Falls

R. James Klingenstein
2000 Washington St.
Newton Lower Falls 02162
Type: individual
Certification: internal medicine, gastroenterology
Plans: Tufts, HMO Blue, Pilgrim, CIGNA, Aetna
Hospitals: Newton-Wellesley

Elisabeth B. Pedersen
2000 Washington St.
Newton Lower Falls 02162
Type: group
Certification: internal medicine
Plans: many
Hospitals: Newton-Wellesley

Norwood

Abraham A. Litt
825 Washington St.
Norwood 02062
Type: individual
Certification: ob/gyn
Plans: Tufts, Bay State, Pilgrim, HMO Blue, PruCare, MetLife
Hospitals: Norwood, Newton-Wellesley, Brigham and Women's

Steven R. Maynard
Dedham Medical Associates
325 River Ridge Dr.

Norwood 02062
Type: multispecialty group
Certification: ob/gyn
Plans: HCHP, Aetna, BC/BS, Cost Care, Pilgrim, Healthcare Value, Travelers, Tufts
Hospitals: Newton-Wellesley

North Weymouth

Martin Iser
Hingham Weymouth Family Medical
795 Bridge St.
North Weymouth 02191
Type: group
Certification: family practice
Plans: many
Hospital: South Shore

Grace Niklas
Hingham-Weymouth Family Medical Associates
795 Bridge St.
North Weymouth 02191
Type: group
Certification: internal medicine
Plans: many
hospitals: Quincy, (South Shore soon)

Peabody

Charlotte Dick
Peabody Medical Associates
North Shore Mall
Peabody 01960
Type: HMO
Certification: pediatrics
Plans: HMO Blue, BC/BS, Bay State, and others
Hospitals: North Shore Children's

Miriam C. Dunau
North Shore Community Health Center
150 Main St.
Peabody 01960
Type: health center
Certification: pediatrics
Plans: BC/BS, HMO Blue, Bay State, Tufts, NHP, Medicaid, and others
Hospitals: North Shore Medical Center, Salem

Elysia C. Griswold
Peabody Medical Associates
North Shore Mall
Peabody 01960
Type: group
Certification: internal medicine
Plans: HMO Blue, BC/BS
Hospitals: Salem

Murray A. Leavitt
North Shore Medical and Dental Center
Essex Center Dr.
Peabody 01960
Type: individual
Certification: internal medicine
Plans: BC/BS, Blue Care Elect, HMO Blue, Tufts, Bay State, Pilgrim,
Hospitals: Salem, Union

Richard P. Lipman
Pediatric Health Care Associates
One Roosevelt Ave.
Peabody 01960
Type: group
Certification: pediatrics
Plans: Tufts, Bay State, HMO Blue, HCHP, Pilgrim
Hospitals: North Shore Medical Center

Carolyn S. Moneymaker
North Shore Community Health Center
150 Main St.
Peabody 01960
Type: community health center
Certification: pediatrics
Plans: BC/BS, HMO Blue, Bay State, Tufts, NHP, Medicaid, and others
Hospitals: North Shore Medical Center

Thomas S. Natale
Pediatric Health Care Associates
One Roosevelt Ave.
Peabody 01960
Type: group
Certification: pediatrics
Plans: Bay State, BC/BS, HCHP, Tufts, PruCare
Hospitals: North Shore Medical Center, Melrose-Wakefield

William C. Wiswall
One Roosevelt Ave.
Peabody 01960
Type: individual
Certification: pediatrics
Plans: most
Hospitals: North Shore Children's

Quincy

Frank J. Archbald
Harvard Community Health Plan
1250 Hancock St.
Quincy 02169
Type: HMO
Certification: ob/gyn
Plans: HCHP
Hospitals: Brigham and Women's

Richard W. Ashburn
Medical Associates of Quincy, Inc.
Crown Colony
500 Congress St.
Quincy 02169
Type: group
Certification: internal medicine, pulmonary medicine, critical care medicine
Plans: Health Care Value, CIGNA, Medicare, HMO Blue, Blue Care Elect, Private Healthcare Systems, Tufts, U.S. Healthcare, Pilgrim, PruCare, John Hancock
Hospitals: Quincy, South Shore

Leslie R. Blachman
Crown Colony Pediatrics
500 Congress St.
Quincy 02169
Type: group

Certification: N/A
Plans: Medicaid, Aetna, PruCare, BC/BS, Bay State, Tufts, Total Health
Hospitals: Carney, South Shore

Charlotte S. Brody
South Shore Gynecology
21 School St.
Quincy 02169
Type: group
Certification: ob/gyn
Plans: Tufts, Bay State, Pilgrim, PruCare
Hospitals: South Shore, Quincy

Kenneth J. Einstein
Medical Associates of Quincy
500 Congress St.
Quincy 02169
Type: group
Certification: internal medicine
Plans: HMO Blue, Tufts, Bay State, Pilgrim, U.S. Healthcare
Hospitals: Quincy, South Shore

Moses J. Entin
37 Woodward Ave.
Quincy 0216
Type: individual
Certification: family practice
Plans: BC/BS, CIGNA, Pilgrim, John Hancock, Medicare, Medicaid
Hospitals: Quincy

Margot C. Pariser
Crown Colony Pediatrics
500 Congress St.
Quincy 02169
Type: group
Certification: N/A
Plans: Medicaid, Aetna, PruCare, BC/BS, Bay State, Tufts, Total Health
Hospitals: Carney, South Shore

Gerald Rosenblatt
Medical Associates of Quincy
500 Congress St.
Quincy 02169
Type: group
Certification: internal medicine
Plans: Aetna, Bay State, Pilgrim, CIGNA, Guardian, Healthcare Value, John Hancock, Private Health Care
Hospitals: Quincy

Daniel M. Sheff
Medical Associates of Quincy
500 Congress St.
Quincy 02169
Type: group
Certification: internal medicine, rheumatology
Plans: Bay State, Tufts, Travelers, PruCare, HMO Blue, Pilgrim, Cost Care, Pilgrim, CIGNA, MetLife, U.S. Healthcare
Hospitals: Quincy, South Shore

Bernard Spiegel
South Shore Gynecology Associates
21 School St.
Quincy 02169
Type: group
Certification: ob/gyn
Plans: Pilgrim, HMO Blue, Tufts, Bay State, BC/BS, Aetna, PruCare
Hospitals: Quincy, South Shore

Robert M. Weinberg
Wollaston Medical Associates
7 Elm Ave.
Quincy 02170
Type: group
Certification: internal medicine
Plans: most
Hospitals: Carney, Quincy, South Shore

Paula S. Wright
Crown Colony Pediatrics
500 Congress St.
Quincy 02169
Type: group
Certification: N/A
Plans: Medicaid, Aetna, PruCare, BC/BS, Bay State, Tufts, Total Health
Hospitals: Carney, South Shore

Randolph

Vitaly A. Bernstein
100 Lafayette St.
Randolph 02368
Type: individual
Certification: N/A
Plans: BC/BS, Medicare, Tufts, Pilgrim
Hospitals: Good Samaritan

Revere

Randall S. Bock
Medical Treatment Center of Revere
372 Broadway
Revere 02151
Type: individual
Certification: N/A
Plans: Bay State, Medicaid
Hospitals: Malden

Sharda Jain
570 Broadway
Revere 02151
Type: individual
Certification: none
Plans: BC/BS, Medicare, Medicaid, U.S. Healthcare
Hospitals: St. Elizabeth's, Newton-Wellesley

Michael T. Nathan
MGH/Revere Health Associates
300 Broadway
Revere 01890
Type: hospital-based outpatient
Certification: internal medicine
Plans: Bay State, Tufts, John Hancock, Cost Care, Pilgrim, NHP, HMO Blue, Blue Choice, Blue Care Elect
Hospitals: Massachusetts General

Laura J. Olson
MGH/Revere Health Associates
300 Broadway
Revere 02151

Type: group, affiliated with Massachusetts General Hospital
Certification: internal medicine
Plans: Tufts, Bay State, NHP, HMO Blue, John Hancock
Hospitals: Massachusetts General

Salem

Betsy S. August
Salem Women's Health Associates
331 Highland Ave.
Salem 01970
Type: group
Certification: ob/gyn
Plans: Tufts
Hospitals: Salem

Arthur J. Kavanagh
26 Chestnut St.
Salem 01970
Type: group
Certification: N/A
Plans: BC/BS, Tufts, John Hancock, U.S. Healthcare, CIGNA, Pilgrim
Hospitals: Salem

Mark H. Mandell
Pediatric Associates of Greater Salem
72 Highland Ave.
Salem 01970
Type: group
Certification: pediatrics
Plans: Pilgrim, HCHP, Bay State, Tufts, Travelers, MetLife, CIGNA
Hospitals: North Shore Medical Center, New England Medical Center

Thomas A. Raskauskas
Women's Health
55 Highland Ave.
Salem 01970
Type: group
Certification: ob/gyn
Plans: Medicare, Bay State, BC/BS, HMO Blue, Tufts, Medicaid
Hospitals: Salem

Richard B. Rudolph
Salem Ob/Gyn Associates
86 Highland Ave.
Salem 01970
Type: group
Certification: ob/gyn
Plans: Tufts, Pilgrim, HMO Blue, Medicaid, Bay State
Hospitals: North Shore Medical Center

John T. Szymanski
Puritan Medical Center
331 Highland Ave.
Salem 01970
Type: group
Certification: internal medicine
Plans: HCHP, Tufts, Bay State, HMO Blue, Travelers, Medicaid
Hospitals: Salem, Union

Saugus

Michael P. Harrigan
269 Central St.
Saugus 01906
Type: individual
Certification: internal medicine
Plans: Bay State, Pilgrim, U.S. Healthcare, Tufts, HMO Blue
Hospitals: New England Medical Center, Atlanticare Medical Center

James B. Hickey
320 Central St.
Saugus 01906
Type: individual
Certification: internal medicine
Plans: HMO Blue, Bay State, Tufts, Pilgrim, Medicaid, Aetna
Hospitals: Atlanticare Medical Center

Gregory C. Meyer
Medical Treatment Center of Saugus
320 Central St.
Saugus 01906
Type: group
Certification: pediatrics, emergency
Plans: Medicaid, BC/BS, Medicare
Hospitals: Atlanticare (emergency room)

Sharon

Steven E. Ross
Sharon Medical Associates
23 Pond St.
Sharon 02067
Type: individual
Certification: internal medicine, family medicine, school physician
Plans: Pilgrim, Tufts, HMO Blue, Aetna, PruCare, Medicare
Hospitals: Norwood, Southwood, Goddard, Cushing

Somerville

Mary Ann Cromer
Somerville Pediatric Associates
East Somerville Health Center
42 Cross St.
Somerville 02145
Type: group
Certification: N/A
Plans: many
Hospitals: many

Frederick W. Dekow
Harvard Community Health Plan
40 Holland St.
Somerville 02144
Type: HMO
Certification: internal medicine
Plans: HCHP
Hospitals: Mt. Auburn, Brigham and Women's

David C. Osler
Somerville Pediatric Associates
230 Highland Ave.
Somerville 02143
Type: hospital-based group

Certification: pediatrics
Plans: Bay State, HMO Blue, U.S. Healthcare, NHP
Hospitals: Somerville, Massachusetts General, Children's, Cambridge, St. Elizabeth's

Floyd B. Russak
Somerville Family health
35 Bow St./Union Square
Somerville 02143
Type: group
Certification: internal medicine
Plans: HMO Blue, Tufts, Pilgrim, CIGNA, PruCare, Aetna, HCVM, Bay State, U.S. Healthcare
Hospitals: Mt. Auburn

Stoneham

Bruce H. Churchill
Family Care Center
5 Woodland Rd.
Stoneham 02180
Type: group
Certification: family practice
Plans: HCHP
Hospitals: New England Memorial

Daniel M. Feinn
Women's Medical Arts
3 Woodland Rd.
Stoneham 02180
Type: group
Certification: ob/gyn
Plans: HMO Blue, Pilgrim, Tufts
Hospitals: New England Memorial, Malden, Lawrence Memorial, Melrose-Wakefield

Jeffrey Gorvine
3 Woodland Rd.
Stoneham 02180
Type: individual
Certification: internal medicine
Plans: N/A
Hospitals: New England Memorial, Melrose-Wakefield

Gordon M. Magonet
Family Care Center
5 Woodland Rd.
Stoneham 02180
Type: group
Certification: family practice
Plans: HCHP
Hospitals: New England Memorial

Suzanne B. Rothchild
Women's Medical Arts
3 Woodland Rd.
Stoneham 02180
Type: group
Certification: ob/gyn
Plans: HMO Blue, Pilgrim, Tufts
Hospitals: New England Memorial, Malden, Lawrence, Melrose-Wakefield

Leo Sorger
Women's Medical Arts
3 Woodland Rd.
Stoneham 02180
Type: group
Certification: ob/gyn
Plans: HMO Blue, Pilgrim, Tufts
Hospitals: New England Memorial, Malden, Lawrence, Melrose-Wakefield

Timothy D. Stryker
106 Main St.
Stoneham 02180
Type: individual
Certification: internal medicine, endocrinology
Plans: HMO Blue, Tufts, Pilgrim, PruCare
Hospitals: Melrose-Wakefield, New England Memorial

Stoughton

Kilinc A. Erkan
Park Pediatric Associates, Inc.
966B Park St.
Stoughton 02072
Type: group
Certification: pediatrics allergist
Plans: Pilgrim, Tufts, CIGNA, Bay State, PruCare, BC/BS, MetLife
Hospitals: Goddard Memorial, Cardinal Cushing

James H Tyer
Park Ob/Gyn Associates
966B Park St.
Stoughton 02072
Type: individual
Certification: ob/gyn
Plans: Medicare, Medicaid, Blue Choice, Blue Care Elect, Pilgrim, Tufts, Bay State, HMO Blue, Pilgrim, MetLife, MedView
Hospitals: Good Samaritan

Joseph M. Weinstein
Park Medical Associates
966C Park St.
Stoughton 02072
Type: group
Certification: internal medicine, cardiology
Plans: Pilgrim, Tufts, PruCare, U.S. Healthcare, HMO Blue
Hospitals: Good Samaritan

Swampscott

Donald B. Barkan
990 Paradise Rd.
Swampscott 01907
Type: individual
Certification: internal medicine
Plans: Tufts, HMO Blue, BC/BS
Hospitals: Union, Salem

Wakefield

Saul H. Cohen
15 Richardson Ave.
Wakefield 01880
Type: individual
Certification: pediatrics
Plans: Tufts, BC/BS, U.S. Healthcare, Pilgrim, Travelers, Bay State
Hospitals: Melrose-Wakefield

Thomas R. Jevon
300 Quannapowitt Pkwy.
Wakefield 01880
Type: individual
Certification: family medicine
Plans: Tufts, HMO Blue, Pilgrim, Bay State
Hospitals: Melrose-Wakefield

Walpole

Charles S. Chen
1426 Main St.
Walpole 02081
Type: individual
Certification: internal medicine, hematology, medical oncology
Plans: Tufts, HMO Blue, Bay State, Pilgrim, CIGNA, and others
Hospitals: Norwood, Southwood Community

Laura C. Knobel
130 West St.
Walpole 02081
Type: individual
Certification: family practice
Plans: Pilgrim, Bay State, Tufts, HMO Blue, Aetna, Cost Care, Health Care Value Management
Hospitals: Newton-Wellesley, Norwood

Waltham

Radha Agarwal
Eastern Mass. Health Assoc.
WalthamWeston Hospital
Waltham 02254
Type: individual
Certification: none
Plans: Medicare, Medicaid, BC/BS, Bay State, Tufts, Pilgrim
Hospitals: WalthamWeston

William M. Soybel
20 Hope Ave.
Waltham 02154
Type: individual
Certification: internal medicine
Plans: Tufts, BC/BS, Pilgrim, and others
Hospitals: WalthamWeston, Newton

Watertown

Trevor H. Kaye
Mt. Auburn Medical Associates
521 Mt. Auburn St.
Watertown 02172
Type: group
Certification: internal medicine
Plans: HMO Blue, Tufts, Pilgrim, Bay State, John Hancock
Hospitals: Mt. Auburn, Cambridge

Henry Rikkers
Harvard Community Health Plan
485 Arsenal St.
Watertown 02172
Type: HMO, staff model
Certification: pediatrics
Plans: HCHP
Hospitals: Massachusetts General, Children's, Mt. Auburn

Linda C. Loney
Watertown Health Center
85 Main St.
Watertown 02172
Type: group
Certification: pediatrics
Plans: Pilgrim, HMO Blue, PruCare, and others
Hospitals: St. Elizabeth's

Wellesley

Stephen B. Smith
8 Grove St.
Wellesley 02181
Type: individual
Certification: ob/gyn
Plans: BC/BS, Medicare, Cost Care, John Hancock, Tufts, HMO Blue, Blue Care Elect, Bay State, Health Flex Blue
Hospitals: Newton-Wellesley

Weston

Shelley C. Bernstein
Weston Pediatric Physicians
486 Boston Post Rd.
Weston 02193
Type: group
Certification: pediatrics
Plans: HMO Blue, HCHP, Bay State, Pilgrim
Hospitals: Children's, Newton-Wellesley

Ralph Earle
Weston Pediatric Physicians
486 Boston Post Rd.
Weston 02193
Type: group
Certification: pediatrics
Plans: HMO Blue, HCHP, Bay State, Pilgrim
Hospitals: Children's, Newton-Wellesley

Corinne S. Ertel
Weston Pediatric Physicians
486 Boston Post Rd.
Weston 02193
Type: group
Certification: pediatrics
Plans: HMO Blue, HCHP, Bay State, Pilgrim
Hospitals: Children's, Newton-Wellesley

Margaret W. Manion
Weston Pediatric Physicians
486 Boston Post Rd.
Weston 02193
Type: group
Certification: pediatrics
Plans: HMO Blue, HCHP, Bay State, Pilgrim
Hospitals: Children's, Newton-Wellesley

Karen McCarte
Weston Pediatric Physicians
486 Boston Post Rd.
Weston 02193
Type: group
Certification: pediatrics
Plans: HMO Blue, HCHP, Bay State, Pilgrim
Hospitals: Children's, Newton-Wellesley
Donna Staton
Weston Pediatric Physicians
486 Boston Post Rd.

Weston 02193
Type: group
Certification: pediatrics
Plans: HMO Blue, HCHP, Bay State, Pilgrim
Hospitals: Children's, Newton-Wellesley

Weymouth
Mary Delaney
851 Main St.
Weymouth 02190
Type: individual
Certification: internal medicine and metabolism, endocrinology, diabetes
Plans: Pilgrim, MetLife, Tufts, Travelers, BC/BS
Hospitals: South Shore

Wilmington
Josephine A. Albano
25 Lowell St.
Wilmington 01887
Type: individual
Certification: internal medicine, endocrinology
Plans: Tufts, Bay State, Pilgrim, CIGNA, PruCare
Hospitals: Lawrence Memorial, Winchester

Sarah Andrew
Wilmington Pediatrics
500 Salem St.
Wilmington 01887
Type: group
Certification: pediatrics
Plans: most
Hospitals: Winchester

Winchester
Susan Auerbach
955 Main St.
Winchester 01890
Type: individual
Certification: internal medicine
Plans: Tufts, Pilgrim, Travelers, Cost Care, Aetna, HCVM, and others
Hospitals: Winchester

Ronald F. Backer
11 Elmwood Ave.
Winchester 01890
Type: group
Certification: family practice
Plans: Tufts, Pilgrim, MetLife, HMO Blue, Travelers, Pilgrim, CIGNA, HCVM, BC/BS, Bay State, Blue Choice, PruCare
Hospitals: Winchester

Franklin B. Waddell
Russell Hill Ob/Gyn
955 Main St.
Winchester 01890
Type: group
Certification: ob/gyn
Plans: most
Hospitals: Winchester

Winthrop
Haren P. Desai
249 Washington Ave.
Winthrop 02152
Type: group
Certification: internal medicine, geriatrics
Plans: HMO Blue, Bay State, Tufts, Pilgrim, CIGNA
Hospitals: Whidden Memorial, Melrose-Wakefield, Malden

Victor F. Saldanha
54 Lincoln St.
Winthrop 02152
Type: individual
Certification: N/A
Plans: HMO Blue, Tufts, Pilgrim, U.S. Healthcare, Bay State
Hospitals: Whidden Memorial, Melrose-Wakefield, Malden

Woburn
Michele A. Crage
Woburn Medical Associates
23 Warren Ave.
Woburn 01801
Type: group
Certifications: internal medicine, nephrology
Plans: Tufts, HMO Blue, Bay State, John Hancock, Pilgrim, Medicare, Medicaid
Hospitals: Lawrence Memorial, Winchester, New England Memorial

Roy A. Epstein
400 W. Cummings Park
Woburn 01801
Type: group
Certification: ob/gyn
Plans: most
Hospitals: New England Memorial, Winchester, Lawrence Memorial

Richard L. McDowell
400 W. Cummings Pk.
Woburn 01801
Type: group
Certification: ob/gyn
Plans: N/A
Hospitals: New England Memorial

David Tager
Woburn Medical Associates
23 Warren Ave.
Woburn 01801
Type: group
Certifications: internal medicine, gastroenterology
Plans: Bay State, HMO Blue, John Hancock, CIGNA, Pilgrim, Tufts, Aetna, Travelers
Hospitals: Winchester

Community Health Centers

This list includes all Boston-area members of the Massachusetts League of Community Health Centers, plus selected other centers that offer primary care. All charge based on ability to pay, accept most types of insurance, and offer some free care to low-income clients. Most have translators available for the major languages spoken in the neighborhood and have some evening and weekend hours. Check with the center and your health plan about coverage by your insurance. Most community health centers participate in Neighborhood Health Plan for Medicaid enrollees. Listed here are the hospitals to which physicians at the center have authorization to admit a patient.

Boston

Boston Evening Medical Center
388 Commonwealth Ave.
Boston 02215
(617)267-7171
Hospitals: New England Medical Center, New England Deaconess

Fenway Community Health Center
7 Haviland St.
Boston 02115
(617)267-0900
Hospitals: Beth Israel

North End Community Health Center
332 Hanover St.
Boston 02113
(617)742-9570
Hospitals: Massachusetts General

South Cove Community Health Center
885 Washington St.
Boston 02111
(617)482-7555
Hospitals: Beth Israel

South End Community Health Center
400 Shawmut Ave.
Boston 02118
(617) 425-2000
Hospitals: Boston City, Brigham and Women's, Children's

Boston/Allston

Joseph M. Smith Community Health Center
51 Stadium Way
Allston 02134
(617)783-0500
Hospitals: St. Elizabeth's, Franciscan Children's

Boston/Charlestown

Bunker Hill Health Center
73 High St.
Charlestown 02129
(617)724-8160
Hospitals: Massachusetts General, Brigham and Women's

Boston/Dorchester

Bowdoin Street Health Center
200 Bowdoin St.
Dorchester 02122
(617)825-9800
Hospitals: Carney, St. Elizabeth's, Beth Israel (maternity)

Codman Square Health Center
637 Washington St.
Dorchester 02124
(617)825-9660
Hospitals: Boston City, New England Medical Center, Boston University Medical Center, Carney, and others

Dorchester House Multi-Service Center
1353 Dorchester Ave.
Dorchester 02122
(617)288-3230
Hospitals: Boston City, Carney, New England Medical Center

Geiger-Gibson Community Health Center
250 Mt. Vernon St.
Dorchester 02125
(617)288-1140
Hospitals: Boston City, Carney, Brigham and Women's

Harvard Street Neighborhood Health Center
895 Blue Hill Ave.
Dorchester 02121
(617)825-3400
Hospitals: Boston City

Little House Health Center
990 Dorchester Ave.
Dorchester 02125
(617)282-3700
Hospitals: Carney, Beth Israel (ob/gyn), St. Elizabeth's

Neponset Health Center
398 Neponset Ave.
Dorchester 02122
(617)282-3200
Hospitals: Boston City, Carney, New England Medical Center

Upham's Corner Health Center
500 Columbia Rd.
Dorchester 02125
(617)287-8000
Hospitals: Boston City, New England Medical Center

Boston/East Boston

East Boston Neighborhood Health Center
10 Gove St.
East Boston 02128
(617)569-5800
Hospitals: Boston City

Boston/Jamaica Plain

Brookside Community Health Center
3297 Washington St.
Jamaica Plain 02130
(617)522-4700
Hospitals: Brigham and Women's

Martha Eliot Health Center
33 Bickford St.
Jamaica Plain 02130
(617)522-5300
Hospitals: Children's, Brigham and Women's

Southern Jamaica Plain Health Center
687 Center St.
Jamaica Plain 02130
(617)278-0710
Hospitals: Brigham and Women's

Boston/Mattapan

Mattapan Community Health Center
1425 Blue Hill Ave.
Mattapan 02126
(617)296-0061
Hospitals: Beth Israel, Boston City, Carney, Lemuel Shattuck

Boston/Roslindale

Greater Roslindale Medical and Dental Center
6 Cummings Hwy.
Roslindale 02131
(617)323-4440
Hospitals: Faulkner

Boston/Roxbury

Dimock Community Health Center
55 Dimock St.
Roxbury 02119
(617)442-8800
Hospitals: Boston City, Children's, Beth Israel

Roxbury Comprehensive Community Health Center
435 Warren St.
Roxbury 02119
(617)442-7400
Hospitals: Deaconess, Beth Israel, Boston City, Lemuel Shattuck

Whittier Street Neighborhood Health Center
20 Whittier St.
Roxbury 02120
(617)427-1000
Hospitals: Boston City, Boston University Medical Center

Boston/South Boston

Laboure Center, Inc.
371 W. Fourth St.
South Boston 02127
(617)268-9670
Hospitals: N/A

Mary Ellen McCormack Health Center
10 Logan Way
South Boston 02127
(617)288-3119
Hospitals: Boston City, Carney, Brigham and Women's

South Boston Community Health Center
133 Dorchester St.
South Boston 02127
(617)269-7500
Hospitals: New England Medical Center, Carney

Cambridge

Cambridgeport Neighborhood Health Center
150 Erie St.
Cambridge 02139
(617)498-1105
Hospitals: Cambridge

East Cambridge Neighborhood Health Center
650 Cambridge St.
Cambridge 02141
(617)498-1131
Hospitals: Cambridge

North Cambridge Health Center
266 Rindge Ave.
Cambridge 02140
(617)498-1119
Hospitals: Cambridge

Riverside Neighborhood Health Center
205 Western Ave.
Cambridge 02139
(617)498-1109
Hospitals: Cambridge

Teen Health Center
459 Broadway
Cambridge 02139
(617)498-1548
Hospitals: Cambridge

Windsor Street Neighborhood Health Center
105 Windsor St.
Cambridge 02139
(617)498-1098
Hospitals: Cambridge

Chelsea
Chelsea Health Center
100 Bellingham St.
Chelsea 02150
(617)884-8300
Hospitals: Massachusetts General

Hull
Hull Medical Center
180 George Washington Blvd.
Hull 02045
(617)925-4550
Hospitals: Quincy

Lynn
Lynn Community Health Center
269 Union St.
Lynn 01901
(617)581-3900
Hospitals: Atlanticare, Beverly, Salem, North Shore Children's

Peabody
North Shore Community Health Center
150 Main St.
Peabody 01960
(508)532-4903
Hospitals: Salem

Quincy
Manet Community Health Center
1193 Sea St.
Quincy 02169
(617)471-8683
Hospitals: Quincy

Manet Community Health Center at Snug Harbor
9 Bicknell St.
Quincy 02169
(617)471-4715
Hospitals: Quincy

Revere
MGH/Revere Health Associates
300 Broadway
Revere 02151
(617)284-0064
Hospitals: Massachusetts General

Somerville
East Somerville Health Center
42 Cross St.
Somerville 02145
(617)776-6120
Hospitals: Somerville, Cambridge, St. Elizabeth's, Mt. Auburn

Mystic Health Center
510 Mystic Ave.
Somerville 02145
(617)623-8686
Hospitals: Somerville, St. Elizabeth's

Somerville Primary Care
230 Highland Ave.
Somerville 02143
(617)666-4400
Hospitals: Somerville

60+ Health Center
167 Holland St.
Somerville 02144
(617)628-4972
Hospitals: Somerville

Watertown
Watertown Health Center
85 Main St.
Watertown 02172
(617)923-0001
Hospitals: St. Elizabeth's

Winchester
Winchester Hospital Family Medical Center
500 Salem St.
Wilmington 01887
(508)657-3910
Hospitals: Winchester

III. Hospitals

The hospital listing that follow focus on general medical and surgical hospitals, with limited data on hospitals that specialize in fields like rehabilitation and chronic disease care.

▼ **FOR A LIST**
of psychiatric hospitals, turn to Chapter 7.

Health Care Choices gathered this information from a number of sources. One of the main sources was a questionnaire sent to the hospitals. Almost all hospitals responded; facilities that declined are noted in their entry. Other sources of information include the Massachusetts Rate Setting Commission and *The AHA Guide to the Healthcare Field* (published by the American Hospital Association).

Much of the publicly available data on hospitals comes from the facilities themselves, and unbiased agencies or organizations rarely audit it. When possible, we present data that is at least collected in a consistent manner from every hospital. If such data is not available, *Health Care Choices* uses the answers the hospitals gave on the questionnaires.

That said, *Health Care Choices* collected an immense amount of information; it is boiled down here to a few meaningful items in a format useful to you as a consumer. Consider the information *as a starting point* for a discussion between you and your physician when you are deciding which hospital to go to or which health plan to join.

Almost every hospital accepts credit cards, Medicaid, Medicare, and Blue Cross/Blue Shield for payment. On the other hand, the insurance companies and health plans that hospitals contract with vary greatly and change frequently: get that information directly from your insurance company.

Keep in mind that different people with varying needs look for different things in a hospital. A great hospital for one person may fall short in some areas for another person. You need to decide what's important to you and to gather as much information as you can now, when you have the time.

Key to the Data on Hospitals

Patient Advocate: Large hospitals often have patient advocates on staff to help you navigate the bureaucracy. They can sometimes handle complaints. At the very least, they can help you understand how the hospital works. In the absence of a "patient advocate" per se, some hospitals provide the phone number of the public-affairs department, administrative office, or volunteer office.

Type: For-profit or nonprofit; city, state or church-owned; general medical and surgical or specialty; teaching.

Languages: Translators available, but not necessarily 24 hours a day.

Outpatient Visits: The number of 1993 outpatient visits as reported to the Massachusetts Rate Setting Commission (unless otherwise noted). This number offers a very rough indicator of the scope of outpatient services.

Emergency Visits: The number of 1993 emergency visits as reported to the Massachusetts Rate Setting Commission (unless otherwise noted). This number offers an indication of the experience of the emergency department; that, in turn, is a very rough indicator of the quality of emergency care; more experience means higher quality.

Maternity Service: The number of births in 1993.

Points to Consider: This section contains a variety of information, depending on the hospital's special circumstances. Among the items noted are:

- The hospital reports that it excels in particular fields;
- The hospital reports that it is the sole Boston-area provider of a particular service;
- JCAHO has awarded accreditation with commendation, the highest level a hospital can receive. Nationally, only about 5 percent of all hospitals have achieved this. All other hospitals listed in *Health Care Choices* have standard accreditation;
- If the hospital performs coronary artery bypass graft procedures, the number of 1993 surgeries performed, as reported to *Health Care Choices* by the hospital. The American Heart Association and American College of Cardiology advise pick-

ing a hospital that does at least 200 to 300 open-heart operations per year and a surgeon who performs at least 100 to 150 a year;

• Recent mergers between two or more hospitals. Often, mergers don't affect the quality of patient services, but in some cases they can lead to disruption and layoffs. Unhappy nurses and other staff can have a direct effect on patient care;

• The affiliated medical school for teaching hospitals.

Board Certification: Percentage of active medical staff at the hospital who have board certification. Specialty societies certify physicians to practice particular specialties if they receive extra training and pass advanced tests in the field. Although certification measures knowledge more than skill, a high proportion of board-certified physicians on a hospital's medical staff suggests a higher level of expertise on hand. About two-thirds of U.S. physicians are certified. The average for all hospitals reporting to *Health Care Choices* is 87 percent.

ICU Staffing: The number of intensive care nurse hours divided by the number of patient days in intensive care units in 1993, as reported to the Massachusetts Rate Setting Commission. In general, a higher number is better, but keep in mind that many factors contribute to legitimate variations among hospitals on nurse staffing levels. Consider the data as one among many pieces of data on any hospital. This scale ranges from 14 to 25 for Boston-area hospitals, with an average of 20 for all reporting hospitals.

Inpatient Staffing: The number of inpatient nurse hours divided by the number of inpatient days in 1993, as reported to the Massachusetts Rate Setting Commission. In general, a higher number is better, but keep in mind that many factors contribute to legitimate variations among hospitals on nurse staffing levels. Consider the data as one among many pieces of data on any hospital. This scale ranges from 4 to 10 for Boston-area hospitals, with an average of 8 for all reporting hospitals.

N/A in an entry signifies no answer, not applicable, or unusable data.

General Medical and Surgical Hospitals

▶ ATLANTICARE MEDICAL CENTER

500 Lynnfield St., Lynn 01904 (617)581-9200
Patient Relations Coordinator: (617)477-3011
Type: Nonprofit general medical and surgical hospital
Languages: Khmer, Russian, Spanish
Outpatient Visits: 96,757 (hospital-provided data)
Emergency Visits: 44,241 (hospital-provided data)
Maternity Service: None
Points to Consider:

- Sole provider of alternative healing programs to complement traditional treatments (hospital-provided data).
- Excelling fields are oncology, cardiology, and diabetes management services (hospital-provided data).
- The center is comprised of the Union Hospital Division and the Atlanticare Hospital Division for psychiatric and substance-abuse treatment.

		60%	70%	80%	90%	100%
Board Certification:	86.5%					
		0	5	10	15	20	25
ICU Staffing:	N/A					
Inpatient Staffing:	N/A					

▮ = average for all reporting hospitals

▶ BETH ISRAEL HOSPITAL

330 Brookline Ave., Boston 02215 (617)735-2000
Public Affairs: (617)735-4431
Type: Nonprofit general medical and surgical teaching hospital
Languages: Russian, Spanish; arrangements can be made for translating any language
Outpatient Visits: 199,302
Emergency Visits: 52,491
Maternity Service: 5,393 births in 1993
Points to Consider:

- Excelling fields are cardiology, oncology, and ob/gyn services (hospital-provided data).
- Affiliated with Harvard Medical School.
- Known for its nursing care (hospital-provided data).

		60%	70%	80%	90%	100%
Board Certification:	86%					
		0 5 10 15 20 25				
ICU Staffing:	N/A					
Inpatient Staffing:	N/A					

▌ = average for all reporting hospitals

▶ BEVERLY HOSPITAL

Herrick St., Beverly 01915 (508)922-3000

Admission Office: (508)922-3000, ext. 2900

Type: Nonprofit general medical and surgical hospital

Languages: 20 languages, including American Sign, Cambodian, French, Italian, Spanish, and Vietnamese

Outpatient Visits: 31,726

Emergency Visits: 42,275

Maternity Service: 2,598 births in 1993

Points to Consider:

- Accreditation with commendation from JCAHO.
- Excelling fields are the midwife-managed birth center, elder-care, and kidney dialysis (hospital-provided data).

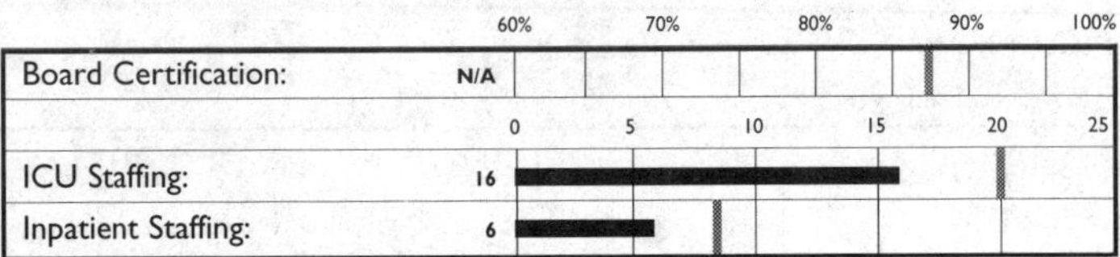

▶ BOSTON CITY HOSPITAL

818 Harrison Ave., Boston 02118 (617)534-5000

Patient Representative: (617)534-4970

Type: City-owned general medical and surgical teaching hospital

Languages: 26 languages

Outpatient Visits: 225,000 (hospital-provided data)

Emergency Visits: 62,000 (hospital-provided data)

Maternity Service: 1,300 births in 1993

Points to Consider:

- Excelling fields are primary care, maternity services, and pediatrics (hospital-provided data).
- Recently expanded into a new facility, placing all inpatient services under one roof.
- Level I accreditation for the trauma center (jointly operated with Boston

University Medical Center) from the American College of Surgeons (the only Boston trauma center to go through this voluntary accreditation process).

- Affiliated with Boston University School of Medicine.

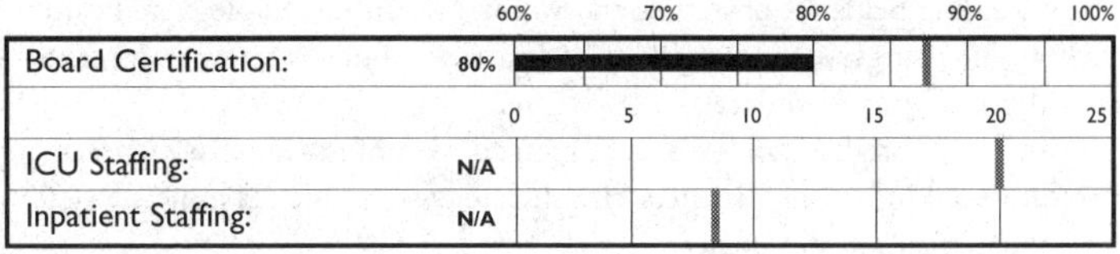

		60%	70%	80%	90%	100%
Board Certification:	80%					
		0	5	10	15	20 / 25
ICU Staffing:	N/A					
Inpatient Staffing:	N/A					

▌ = average for all reporting hospitals

▶ BOSTON UNIVERSITY MEDICAL CENTER

88 E. Newton St., Boston 02118-2393 (617)638-8000
Patient Advocate: (617)638-6856
Type: Nonprofit general medical and surgical teaching hospital
Languages: American Sign, Cantonese, Cape Verdean, Czechoslovakian, German, French, Greek, Haitian, Italian Japanese, Korean, Polish, Portuguese, Russian, Spanish, Vietnamese, and Yiddish
Outpatient Visits: 86,550
Emergency Visits: 15,777
Maternity Service: None
Points to Consider:

- Excelling fields are cardiac services, cancer, and neurosciences (hospital-provided data).
- Sole provider for spinal cord injury treatment (hospital-provided data).
- Affiliated with Boston University School of Medicine.
- Operates a Level I trauma center with Boston City Hospital.
- Performed 380 coronary artery bypass graft procedures in 1993.

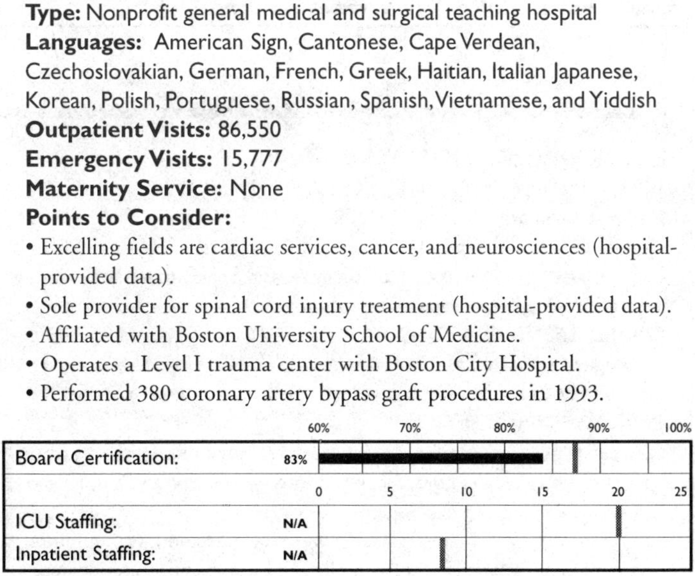

		60%	70%	80%	90%	100%
Board Certification:	83%					
		0	5	10	15	20 / 25
ICU Staffing:	N/A					
Inpatient Staffing:	N/A					

▌ = average for all reporting hospitals

▶ BRIGHAM AND WOMEN'S HOSPITAL

75 Francis St., Boston 02115 (617)732-5500
Patient Relations: (617)732-6636
Type: Nonprofit general medical and surgical teaching hospital
Languages: All of the major foreign languages and dialects found within the Boston area.

Outpatient Visits: 393,912
Emergency Visits: 49,011
Maternity Service: 8,693 births in 1993
Points to Consider:

- Excelling fields are obstetrics and women's health, cardiology and cardiovascular surgery, and lung, kidney, heart, and bone marrow transplants (hospital-provided data).
- In 1993, Brigham and Women's merged with Massachusetts General Hospital to become Partners HealthCare System, Inc. The specifics of the merger are still unclear.
- Affiliated with Harvard Medical School.
- Performed 1,408 coronary artery bypass graft procedures in 1993.

		60% – 100%
Board Certification:	N/A	
		0 – 25
ICU Staffing:	N/A	
Inpatient Staffing:	10	

I = average for all reporting hospitals

▶ CAMBRIDGE HOSPITAL

1493 Cambridge St., Cambridge 02139 (617)498-1000
Patient Relations: (617)498-1278
Type: City-owned general medical and surgical teaching hospital
Languages: Haitian Creole, Portuguese, and Spanish, full-time; translators for 14 other languages on call
Outpatient Visits: 150,442
Emergency Visits: 28,071
Maternity Service: 889 births in 1993
Points to Consider:

- Excelling fields are care for disadvantaged populations, primary care medical training, and comprehensive ambulatory services (hospital-provided data).
- Received the 1993 Foster-McGaw Award for outstanding community services. Such services include Cambridge Hospital's nurse-midwifery program, multidisciplinary AIDS program, and elders home-care program.
- Affiliated with Harvard Medical School and Tufts Medical School.

		60% – 100%
Board Certification:	79%	
		0 – 25
ICU Staffing:	21	
Inpatient Staffing:	10	

I = average for all reporting hospitals

▶ CARNEY HOSPITAL

2100 Dorchester Ave., Boston 02124 (617)296-4000
Patient Liaison: (617)296-4000, ext. 2025
Type: Nonprofit general medical and surgical teaching hospital
Languages: American Sign, Arabic, Chinese, Cape Verdean, Dutch, French, German, Greek, Haitian Creole, Hebrew, Indian, Italian, Korean, Latvian, Lithuanian, Persian, Polish, Portuguese, Pakistani, Russian, Spanish, Tagalog, Turkish, Vietnamese, and Yiddish.
Outpatient Visits: 75,907 (hospital-provided data)
Emergency Visits: 37,301 (hospital-provided data)
Maternity Service: Prenatal care only
Points to Consider:

- Excelling fields are primary care, cardiology, and psychiatry services (hospital-provided data).
- Member of the Daughters of Charity National Health System.

		60%	70%	80%	90%	100%
Board Certification:	83%					
		0 5	10	15	20	25
ICU Staffing:	N/A					
Inpatient Staffing:	N/A					

| = average for all reporting hospitals

▶ DEACONESS-GLOVER MEMORIAL HOSPITAL

148 Chestnut St., Needham 02192 (617)444-5600
Vice President: (617)444-5600, ext. 1050
Type: Non-profit general medical and surgical hospital
Languages: Spanish
Outpatient Visits: 35,892 (hospital-provided data)
Emergency Visits: 11,637 (hospital-provided data)
Maternity Service: None
Points to Consider:

- Excelling fields are oncology, diabetes, and eldercare (hospital-provided data).
- Sole community provider of a urinary incontinence program (hospital-provided data).
- The former Glover Memorial Hospital, this recently came under the ownership of New England Deaconess Hospital Corp.

		60%	70%	80%	90%	100%
Board Certification:	88%					
		0 5	10	15	20	25
ICU Staffing:	N/A					
Inpatient Staffing:	N/A					

| = average for all reporting hospitals

▶ EMERSON HOSPITAL

Old Road to Nine Acre Corner, Concord 01760 (508)369-1400

Patient Care Assessment: (508)287-3095

Type: Nonprofit general medical and surgical hospital

Languages: Arabic, Albanian, American Sign, Cambodian, Chinese, Czech, Danish, Finish, French, German, Greek, Gujerati, Hindi, Italian, Latin, Lithuanian, Pampanago, Tagalog, Russian, Spanish, Swahili, Swedish, Tagalog, Ukrainian, Vietnamese.

Outpatient Visits: 50,534

Emergency Visits: 21,110

Maternity Service: 1,589 births in 1993

Points to Consider:

- Excelling fields are preventive care, outpatient rehabilitative services (hospital-provided data).
- Home care program is one of the first hospital-based programs of its kind in Massachusetts (hospital-provided data).

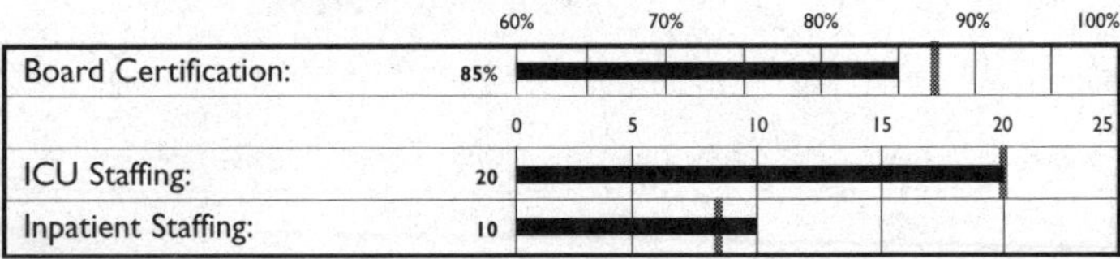

▮ = average for all reporting hospitals

▶ FAULKNER HOSPITAL

1153 Centre St., Jamaica Plain 02130 (617)983-7000

Patient Advocate Office: (617)983-7425

Type: Nonprofit general medical and surgical hospital

Languages: N/A

Outpatient Visits: 124,162

Emergency Visits: 36,829

Maternity Service: N/A

Points to Consider:

- Faulkner Hospital did not respond to the *Health Care Choices* questionnaire.

		60% 70% 80% 90% 100%
Board Certification:	N/A	
		0 5 10 15 20 25
ICU Staffing:	20	
Inpatient Staffing:	9	

▮ = average for all reporting hospitals

▶ GOOD SAMARITAN MEDICAL CENTER, GODDARD CAMPUS

909 Sumner St., Stoughton 02072 (617)344-5100
Patient Advocate Office: (617)344-5100, ext. 2030
Type: Nonprofit general medical and surgical teaching hospital
Languages: Haitian Creole, Portuguese, Spanish
Outpatient Visits: 42,826
Emergency Visits: 28,519
Maternity Service: 1,438 births in 1993
Points to Consider:

- Excelling fields are oncology, gerontology, and cardiology services (hospital-provided data).
- Part of the Caritas Christi Catholic Healthcare System.
- Affiliated with Tufts University School of Medicine.
- Center includes the former Goddard Memorial and Cardinal Cushing hospitals; the Cushing Campus is in Brockton (508)427-3000.

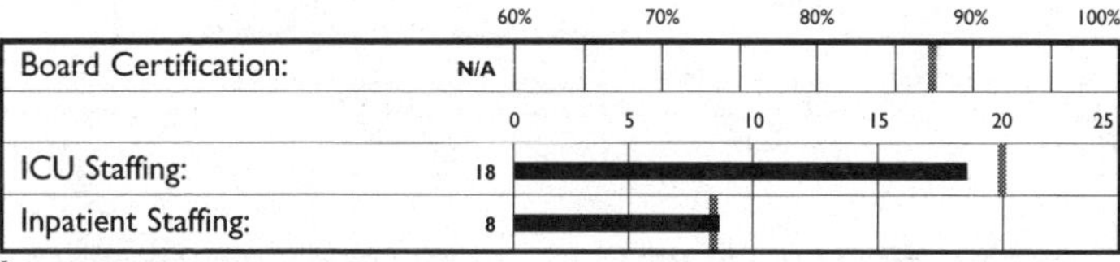

= average for all reporting hospitals

▶ LAHEY CLINIC

41 Mall Rd., Burlington 01805 (617)273-5100
Patient Representative: (617)273-5100, ext. 8837
Type: Nonprofit general medical and surgical hospital
Languages: Portuguese, Spanish
Outpatient Visits: 604,679
Emergency Visits: 66,456
Maternity Service: None
Points to Consider:

- Accreditation with commendation from JCAHO.
- Excelling fields are gastroenterology, cardiology/cardiac surgery, and urology (hospital-provided data).
- Recently acquired Symmes Hospital.

		60% – 100%
Board Certification:	95%	
		0 – 25
ICU Staffing:	22	
Inpatient Staffing:	8	

= average for all reporting hospitals

▶ LAWRENCE MEMORIAL HOSPITAL

170 Governors Ave., Medford 02155 (617)396-9250
Administration Office: (617)396-9250, ext. 419
Type: Nonprofit general medical and surgical teaching hospital
Languages: American Sign, Arabic, Armenian, Chinese, French, Greek, Hebrew, Italian, Japanese, Romanian, Turkish
Outpatient Visits: 39,908
Emergency Visits: 13,894
Maternity Service: None
Points to Consider:

- Excelling fields are geriatrics, cardiac care, and oncology services (hospital-provided data).
- Affiliated with Tufts University Medical School.

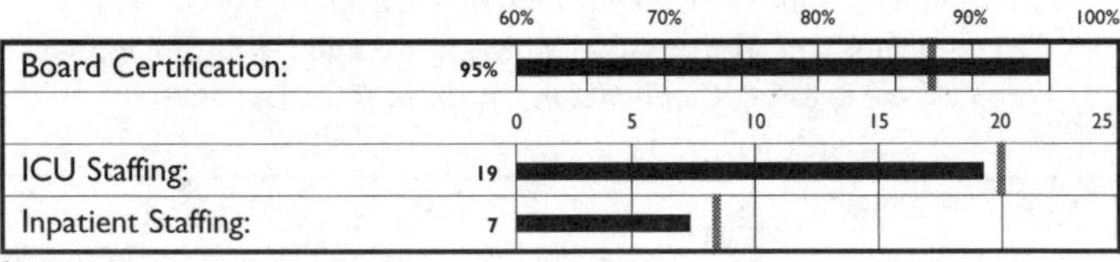

▮ = average for all reporting hospitals

▶ MALDEN HOSPITAL

100 Hospital Rd., Malden 02148 (617)322-7560
Administration Office: (617)322-2221, ext. 5554
Type: Nonprofit general medical and surgical hospital
Languages: Subscribes to AT&T Language Line
Outpatient Visits: 19,567
Emergency Visits: 24,392
Maternity Service: 1,427 births in 1993
Points to Consider:

- Excelling fields are primary care and family medicine, obstetrics and maternity services, and geriatric services (hospital-provided data).

		60%	70%	80%	90%	100%
Board Certification:	74%					
		0 5	10	15	20	25
ICU Staffing:	20					
Inpatient Staffing:	7					

▮ = average for all reporting hospitals

▶ MASSACHUSETTS GENERAL HOSPITAL

32 Fruit St., Boston 02114 (617)726-2000
Patient Care Representative: (617)726-3370
Type: Nonprofit general medical and surgical teaching hospital
Languages: All major foreign languages
Outpatient Visits: 558,446 (hospital-provided data)
Emergency Visits: 67,357 (hospital-provided data)
Maternity Service: Started November 1, 1994
Points to Consider:

- Sole provider of proton beam therapy and intraoperative radiation services (hospital-provided data).
- Merged with Brigham and Women's in 1993 to become Partners HealthCare System, Inc. The specifics of the merger are still unclear.
- Affiliated with Harvard Medical School.
- Performed 936 coronary artery bypass graft procedures in 1993.

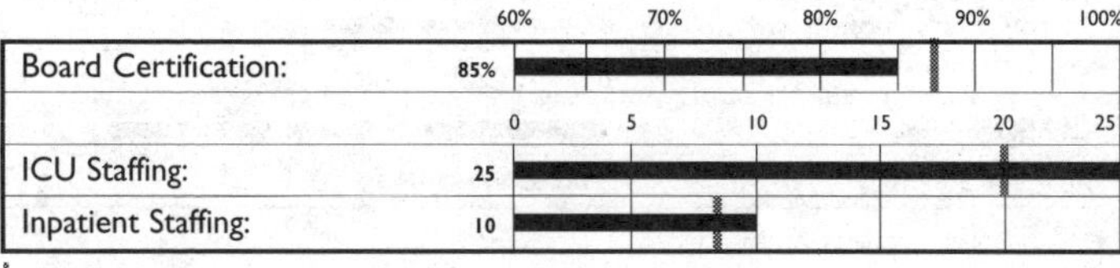

| = average for all reporting hospitals

▶ MELROSE-WAKEFIELD HOSPITAL ASSOCIATION

585 Lebanon St., Melrose 02176 (617)979-3000
Vice President of Quality Assessment: (617)979-3130
Type: Nonprofit general medical and surgical hospital
Languages: Subscribes to AT&T Language Line
Outpatient Visits: 83,720
Emergency Visits: 33,410
Maternity Service: 1,336 births in 1993
Points to Consider:

- Excelling fields are cardiology, cancer treatment, and obstetrics and maternity services (hospital-provided data).

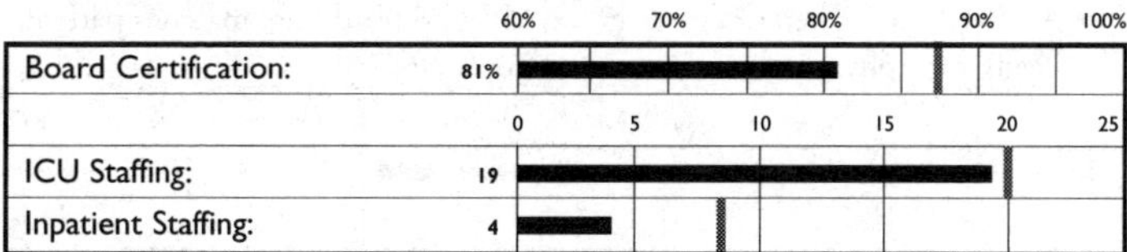

| = average for all reporting hospitals

▶ METROWEST MEDICAL CENTER

Framingham Union Campus, 115 Lincoln St., Framingham 01701
(508)383-1000
Patient Representative: (508)383-1664
Type: Nonprofit general medical and surgical hospital
Languages: N/A
Outpatient Visits: 23,923
Emergency Visits: 51,008
Maternity Service: 3,173 births in 1993
Points to Consider:

- Excelling fields are cancer care, cardiology, and behavioral medicine (hospital-provided data).
- Formed in a merger of Framingham Union and Leonard Morse Hospitals; the Leonard Morse Campus is in Natick (508)650-7000.

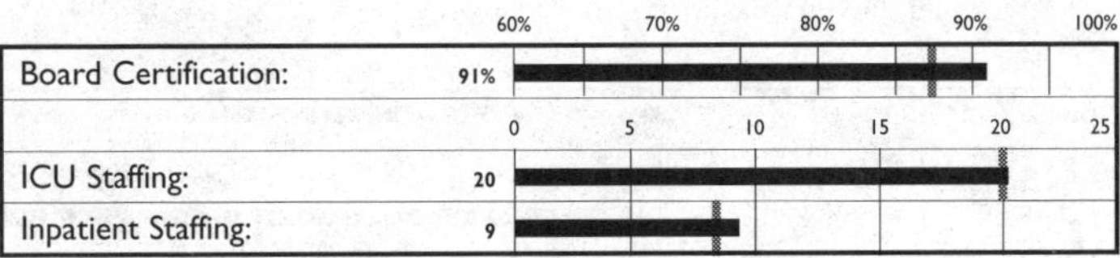

▌ = average for all reporting hospitals

▶ MILTON HOSPITAL

92 Highland St., Milton 02186 (617)696-4600
Patient Advocate Office: (617)696-4600, ext. 1360
Type: Nonprofit general medical and surgical hospital
Languages: All major languages and dialects; also subscribes to AT&T Language Line
Outpatient Visits: 3,382
Emergency Visits: 18,701
Maternity Service: None
Points to Consider:

- Excelling fields are general medical and surgical care, orthopedics, and ambulatory surgery (hospital-provided data).
- A free physician-referral service, the Milton Healthline, matches patient needs with physician specifications: (617)696-8809.

		60%	70%	80%	90%	100%
Board Certification:	75%					
		0	5	10	15	20	25
ICU Staffing:	19					
Inpatient Staffing:	7					

▌ = average for all reporting hospitals

▶ MOUNT AUBURN HOSPITAL

330 Mount Auburn St., Cambridge 02238 (617)492-3500
Patient Advocate Office: (617)492-3500 for appropriate referrals; no patient advocate
Type: Nonprofit general medical and surgical teaching hospital
Languages: Volunteer employees interpret 29 languages; subscribes to AT&T Language Line
Outpatient Visits: 74,282
Emergency Visits: 29,152
Maternity Service: 1,762 births in 1993
Points to Consider:

- Excelling fields are cardiology and cardiac surgery (hospital-provided data).
- Affiliated with Harvard Medical School.
- Performed 343 coronary artery bypass graft procedures in 1993, excluding thoracic procedures, such as pacemaker implants.
- The Center for Problem Gambling treats compulsive gamblers.

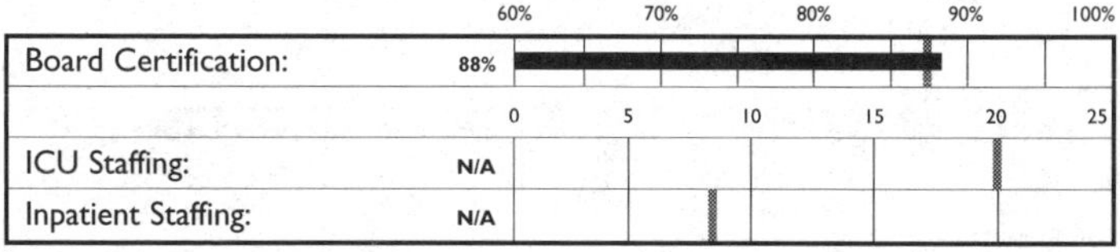

		60%	70%	80%	90%	100%
Board Certification:	88%					
		0	5	10	15	20	25
ICU Staffing:	N/A					
Inpatient Staffing:	N/A					

▌ = average for all reporting hospitals

▶ NEW ENGLAND BAPTIST HOSPITAL

125 Parker Hill Ave., Boston 02115 (617)738-5800
Administration Office: (617)738-5830, ext. 5003
Type: Nonprofit general medical and surgical hospital
Languages: Over 29 languages; subscribes to the AT&T Language Line
Outpatient Visits: 26,486
Emergency Visits: No 24-hour emergency room
Maternity Service: None
Points to Consider:

- Accreditation with commendation from JCAHO.
- Excelling fields are orthopedics and sports medicine, cardiology, and primary care services (hospital-provided data).
- The sports medicine hospital for the Boston Celtics.
- Recently came under the ownership of New England Deaconess Hospital Corp.

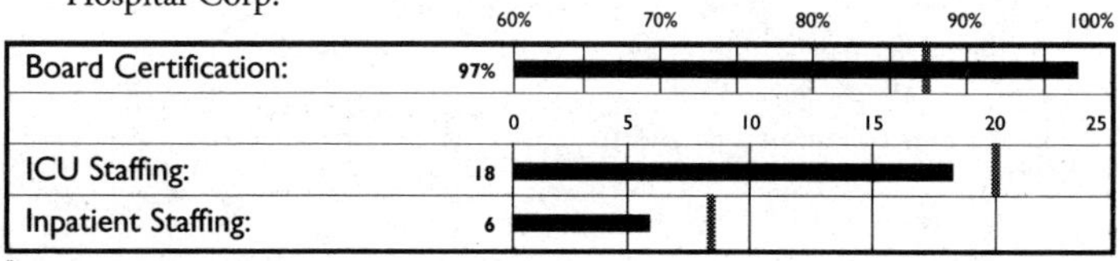

		60%	70%	80%	90%	100%
Board Certification:	97%					
		0	5	10	15	20	25
ICU Staffing:	18					
Inpatient Staffing:	6					

▌ = average for all reporting hospitals

▶ NEW ENGLAND DEACONESS HOSPITAL

185 Pilgrim Rd., Boston 02215 (617)632-8001
Quality Assessment Office: (617)632-8880
Type: Nonprofit general medical and surgical teaching hospital
Languages: Cape Verdean, French, Haitian Creole, Portuguese, Russian, Vietnamese
Outpatient Visits: 43,352
Emergency Visits: 7,702
Maternity Service: None
Points to Consider:

- Accreditation with commendation from JCAHO.
- Excelling fields are diabetes treatment, cardiovascular disease, and AIDS services (hospital-provided data).
- Affiliated with Harvard Medical School.
- Merged with Glover Memorial Hospital in 1994 (see Deaconess-Glover) and New England Baptist Hospital.
- Performed 820 coronary artery bypass graft procedures in 1993.

		60%	70%	80%	90%	100%
Board Certification:	91%					
		0	5	10	15	20	25
ICU Staffing:	N/A					
Inpatient Staffing:	N/A					

| = average for all reporting hospitals

▶ NEW ENGLAND MEDICAL CENTER

750 Washington St., Boston 02111 (617)636-5000
Patient Services: (617)636-5967
Type: Nonprofit general medical and surgical teaching hospital
Languages: American Sign, Chinese, French, Haitian Creole, Portuguese, Russian, Spanish, Vietnamese,
Outpatient Visits: 367,097
Emergency Visits: 27,567
Maternity Service: 2,000 births in 1993
Points to Consider:

- Excelling fields are cancer care, cardiac care, and pediatric services (hospital-provided data).
- Performed 471 coronary artery bypass graft procedures in 1993.
- Affiliated with Tufts University School of Medicine.
- Home of the Kiwanis Pediatric Trauma Center, the only one of its kind in the metro Boston area and the first in the country (hospital-provided data).

		60%	70%	80%	90%	100%
Board Certification:	100%					
		0 5	10	15	20	25
ICU Staffing:	21					
Inpatient Staffing:	10					

▌= average for all reporting hospitals

▶ NEW ENGLAND MEMORIAL HOSPITAL

5 Woodland Rd., Stoneham 02180 (617)979-7000

Quality Management Office: (617)979-7439

Type: Church-owned general medical and surgical hospital

Languages: Volunteer translators available, including French and Spanish interpreters

Outpatient Visits: 72,923

Emergency Visits: 21,471

Maternity Service: 911 births in 1993

Points to Consider:

- Excelling fields are maternity services, psychiatry, and elder services (hospital-provided data).
- Sole provider of child psychological care and fertility services (hospital-provided data).
- Member of the worldwide Adventist family of health care institutions.

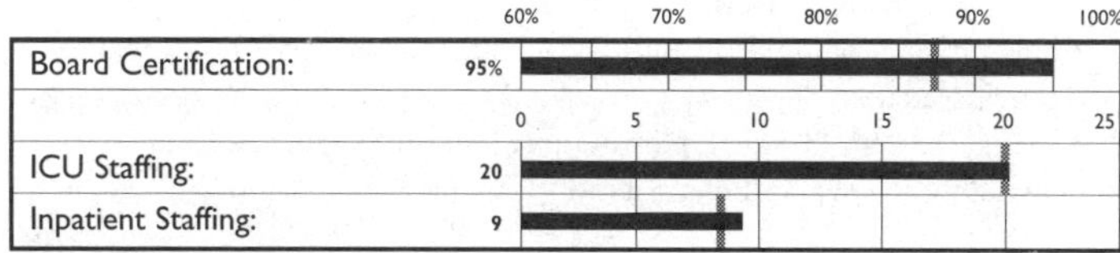

▶ NEWTON-WELLESLEY HOSPITAL

2014 Washington St., Newton 02162 (617)243-6000

Patient Representative: (617)243-6048

Type: Nonprofit general medical and surgical teaching hospital

Languages: Chinese (three dialects), German, Greek, Italian, Lithuanian, Polish, Portuguese, Russian, Spanish; subscribes to AT&T Language Line

Outpatient Visits: 93,738

Emergency Visits: 33,290

Maternity Service: 3,981 births in 1993

Points to Consider:

- Excelling fields are obstetrics, surgery such as laparoscopic surgery, and emergency medicine (hospital-provided data).
- Affiliated with Tufts University School of Medicine.

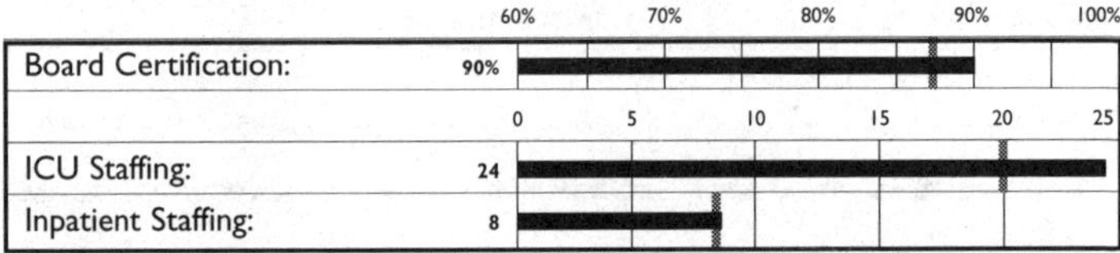

= average for all reporting hospitals

▶ NORTH SHORE MEDICAL CENTER (SALEM HOSPITAL)

81 Highland Ave., Salem 01970 (508)741-1200
Director of Customer Relations: (508)741-1200, ext. 2025
Type: Nonprofit general medical and surgical hospital
Languages: Spanish and Portuguese
Outpatient Visits: 226,750 (hospital-provided data)
Emergency Visits: 57,218 (hospital-provided data)
Maternity Service: 2,070 births in 1993
Points to Consider:

- Excelling fields are cardiology, oncology, and mental health services (hospital-provided data).
- Sole provider of a full-time cardiac catheterization service (hospital-provided data).
- Includes Salem Hospital, North Shore Children's Hospital, and Shaughnessy-Kaplan Rehabilitation Hospital.

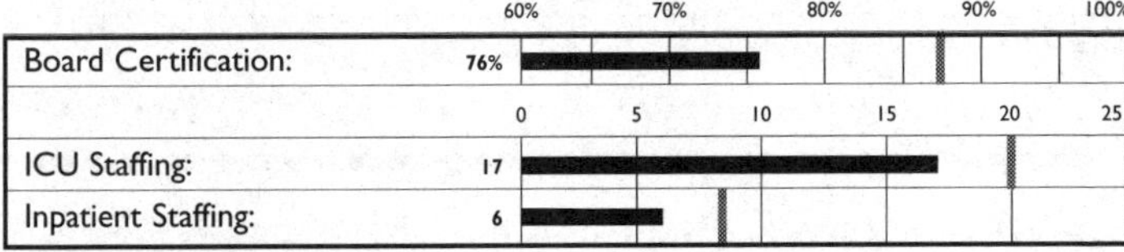

= average for all reporting hospitals

▶ NORWOOD HOSPITAL

800 Washington St., Norwood 02062 (617)769-4000
Patient Advocate Office: (617)769-4000, ext. 3626
Type: Nonprofit general medical and surgical hospital
Languages: N/A
Outpatient Visits: 43,727
Emergency Visits: 36,951
Maternity Service: N/A

Points to Consider:
- Norwood Hospital did not respond to the *Health Care Choices* questionnaire.

		60%	70%	80%	90%	100%
Board Certification:	N/A					
		0	5	10	15	20	25
ICU Staffing:	23					
Inpatient Staffing:	9					

| = average for all reporting hospitals

▶ QUINCY HOSPITAL

114 Whitwell St., Quincy 02169 (617)773-6100
Patient Advocate Office: (617)773-6100, ext. 5508
Type: City-owned general medical and surgical hospital
Languages: No full-time translators on staff; staff members fluent in Cantonese, French, German, Haitian Creole, Italian, Latvian, Mandarin, Spanish, Swedish, and Vietnamese
Outpatient Visits: 6,287
Emergency Visits: 31,626
Maternity Service: 1,228 births in 1993
Points to Consider:
- Excelling fields are cardiology, geropsychiatry (55 and older), and laparoscopic surgery (hospital-provided data).

		60%	70%	80%	90%	100%
Board Certification:	90%					
		0	5	10	15	20	25
ICU Staffing:	N/A					
Inpatient Staffing:	N/A					

| = average for all reporting hospitals

▶ ST. ELIZABETH'S HOSPITAL OF BOSTON

736 Cambridge St., Boston 02135 (617)789-3000
Patient Advocate Office: (617)789-2040
Type: Church-owned general medical and surgical hospital
Languages: Paid interpreters, oriented with nursing and trained as paraprofessionals in medical interpretation in Armenian, Cambodian, Laotian, Portuguese, Russian, Spanish, Vietnamese
Outpatient Visits: 138,313
Emergency Visits: 36,348
Maternity Service: 1,763 births in 1993

Points to Consider:

- Excelling fields are cardiovascular care, neurosciences, women's health, and oncology (hospital-provided data).
- Sole provider of prostate seed implants and gene therapy (hospital-provided data).
- Performed 295 coronary artery bypass graft procedures in 1993.

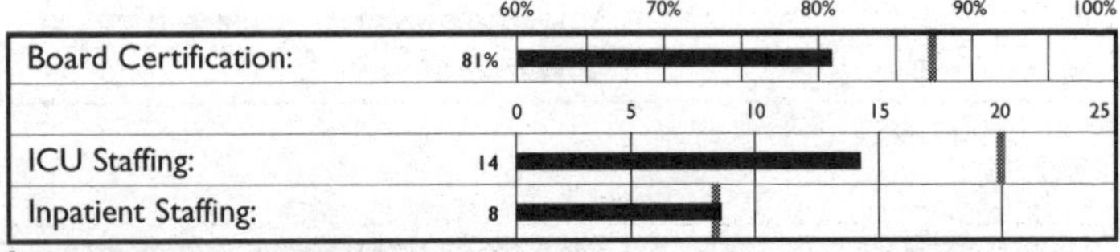

▮ = average for all reporting hospitals

▶ SOMERVILLE HOSPITAL

230 Highland Ave., Somerville 02143 (617)666-4400
Patient Advocate Office: (617)666-4400, ext. 225
Type: Nonprofit general medical and surgical hospital
Languages: Chinese, Greek, Haitian Creole, Italian, Portuguese, and Spanish
Outpatient Visits: 71,127
Emergency Visits: 21,040
Maternity Service: Prenatal and postpartum care only
Points to Consider:

- Excelling fields are primary health care, community health, and pediatrics (hospital-provided data).
- Affiliated with St. Elizabeth's Medical Center of Boston.
- Received a "distinguished recognition" honor from the Hospital Community Benefit Standards Program.
- Physician referral line: (617)776-4442.

		60%	70%	80%	90%	100%
Board Certification:	80%					
		0	5	10	15	20	25
ICU Staffing:	N/A					
Inpatient Staffing:	N/A					

▮ = average for all reporting hospitals

▶ SOUTH SHORE HOSPITAL

55 Fogg Rd., South Weymouth 02190 (617)340-8000
Patient Advocate Office: (617)340-8838
Type: Nonprofit general medical and surgical hospital
Languages: Subscribes to AT&T Language Line

Outpatient Visits: 74,486
Emergency Visits: 59,111
Maternity Service: 2,587 births in 1993
Points to Consider:

- Accreditation with commendation from JCAHO.
- Excelling fields are maternal and child health, cardiology, and outpatient rehabilitation (hospital-provided data).
- Affiliated with South Shore Visiting Nurse and Health Services, a home-care agency.
- Physician referral: (617)340-8302.

		60%	70%	80%	90%	100%
Board Certification:	95%					
		0 5	10	15	20	25
ICU Staffing:	19					
Inpatient Staffing:	8					

| = average for all reporting hospitals

▶ SYMMES HOSPITAL

Hospital Road, Arlington 02174 (617)646-1500
Patient Advocate Office: (617)646-1500
Type: Nonprofit general medical and surgical hospital
Languages: N/A
Outpatient Visits: 8,789
Emergency Visits: 14,217
Maternity Service: None
Points to Consider:

- Recently acquired by Lahey Clinic.
- Excelling fields are cardiology, geriatric care, and oncology (hospital-provided data).

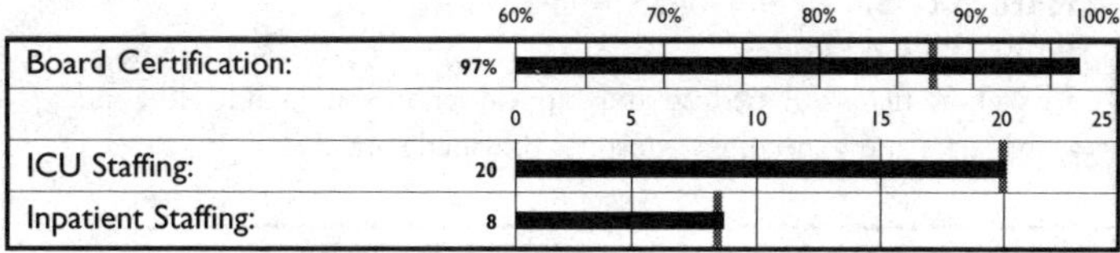

| = average for all reporting hospitals

▶ VETERANS AFFAIRS MEDICAL CENTER

150 S. Huntington Ave., Boston 02130 (617)232-9500
Patient Advocate Office: (617)232-9500, ext. 5295
Type: Federally owned general medical and surgical teaching hospital

Languages: Armenian, Asian Indian, Chinese, Finnish, French, Hungarian, Italian, Korean, Portuguese, Russian, Spanish, and Swedish
Outpatient Visits: 360,000 (hospital-provided data)
Emergency Visits: 4,400 (hospital-provided data)
Maternity Service: None
Points to Consider:
- Offers services to all veterans.
- Operates satellite outpatient clinics in Boston and Lowell.
- Affiliated with Boston University School of Medicine and Tufts University School of Medicine.
- Excelling fields are diagnostic radiology, neurology, and post-traumatic stress disorder (hospital-provided data).
- Heart patients are referred to the Veterans Affairs facility in West Roxbury.

		60%	70%	80%	90%	100%
Board Certification:	80%					
		0	5	10	15	20	25
ICU Staffing:	N/A					
Inpatient Staffing:	N/A					

| = average for all reporting hospitals

▶ WALTHAMWESTON HOSPITAL AND MEDICAL CENTER

Hope Ave., Waltham 02254 (617)647-6000
Patient Advocate Office: (617)647-6206
Type: Nonprofit general medical and surgical hospital
Languages: Spanish
Outpatient Visits: 30,915
Emergency Visits: 24,543
Maternity Service: 490 births in 1993
Points to Consider:
- Excelling fields are medical and surgical services, mental health, and obstetrics and gynecology (hospital-provided data).

		60%	70%	80%	90%	100%
Board Certification:	84%					
		0	5	10	15	20	25
ICU Staffing:	N/A					
Inpatient Staffing:	N/A					

| = average for all reporting hospitals

▶ WHIDDEN MEMORIAL HOSPITAL

103 Garland St., Everett 02149 (617)389-6270
Patient Advocate Office: (617)389-6270, ext. 2162
Type: Nonprofit general medical and surgical hospital
Languages: Many
Outpatient Visits: 101,867
Emergency Visits: 28,761
Maternity Service: None
Points to Consider:

- Excelling fields are pulmonary medicine, cardiology, home health and hospice services, and adult emergency medicine (hospital-provided data).
- Physician referral: (617)381-7104.

		60% 70% 80% 90% 100%
Board Certification:	N/A	
		0 5 10 15 20 25
ICU Staffing:	N/A	
Inpatient Staffing:	N/A	

▌ = average for all reporting hospitals

▶ WINCHESTER HOSPITAL

41 Highland Ave., Winchester 01890 (617)729-9000
Patient Advocate Office: (617)756-2190
Type: Nonprofit general medical and surgical hospital
Languages: American Sign, Armenian, Chinese, French, German, Greek, Hebrew, Indian, Italian, Lithuanian, Mandarin, Norwegian, Portuguese, Russian, Spanish, and Swedish
Outpatient Visits: 143,097
Emergency Visits: 29,236
Maternity Service: 2,059 births in 1993
Points to Consider:

- Excelling fields are obstetrics and pediatrics, cardiology, pulmonary medicine, gastroenterology, and orthopedics (hospital-provided data).

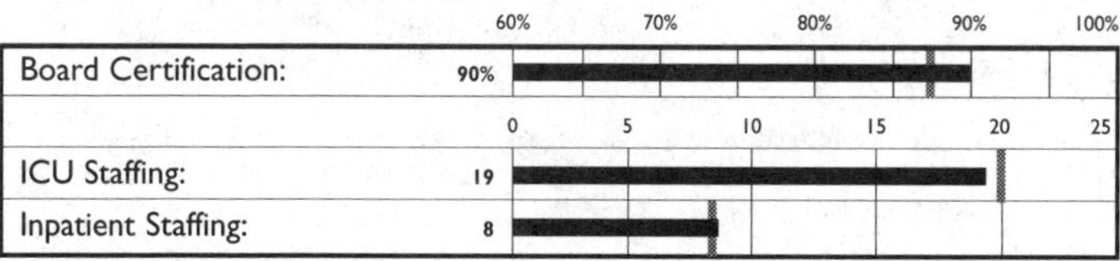

		60% 70% 80% 90% 100%
Board Certification:	90%	
		0 5 10 15 20 25
ICU Staffing:	19	
Inpatient Staffing:	8	

▌ = average for all reporting hospitals

Specialty Hospitals

Boston Specialty and Rehabilitation Hospital
249 River St., Boston 02126 (617)534-2000
Quality Management Office: (617)534-2000, ext. 250
Type: City-owned chronic disease hospital

Braintree Hospital
250 Pond St., Braintree 02184 (617)848-5353
Office of the Medical Director: (617)848-5353, ext. 2175
Type: For-profit rehabilitation hospital

Children's Hospital
300 Longwood Ave., Boston 02115 (617)735-6000
Patient Relations: (617)735-7673
Type: Nonprofit pediatric teaching hospital
Points to Consider:
- Affiliated with Harvard Medical School.

Dana-Farber Cancer Institute
44 Binney St., Boston 02115 (617)732-3000
Patient Representative: (617)632-3290
Type: Nonprofit cancer research and treatment hospital

Franciscan Children's Hospital and Rehabilitation Center
30 Warren St., Boston 02135 (617)254-3800
Patient Advocate Office: (617)254-3800, ext. 3190
Type: Church-owned children's rehabilitation hospital

Hebrew Rehabilitation Center for Aged
1200 Centre St., Roslindale 02131 (617)325-8000
Social Work Office: (617)325-8000, ext. 106
Type: Nonprofit chronic care teaching hospital

Jewish Memorial Hospital and Rehabilitation Center
59 Townsend St., Boston 02119 (617)442-8760
Patient Advocate Office: (617)442-8760, ext. 324
Type: Nonprofit rehabilitation hospital

Lawrence F. Quigley Memorial Hospital
91 Crest Ave., Chelsea 02150 (617)884-5660
Risk Management Coordinator: (617)884-5660, ext. 426
Type: State-owned long term care hospital for veterans

Lemuel Shattuck Hospital
170 Morton St., Jamaica Plain 02130 (617)522-8110
Patient Advocate Office: (617)522-8110, ext. 460
Type: State-owned general medical, rehabilitation, and long term care hospital
Points to Consider:
- Specializes in AIDS/HIV care, public health programs, specialized tuberculosis treatment, and medical/behavioral treatment.
- Services for mental health problems.
- Primary provider of ambulatory and inpatient services for the Massachusetts Department of Public Health in the Boston metro area (hospital-provided data).
- Affiliated with Tufts University Medical School.

Massachusetts Eye and Ear Infirmary
243 Charles St., Boston 02114 (617)523-7900
Patient Advocate Office: N/A
Type: Nonprofit eye, ear, nose, and throat specialty hospital
Points to Consider:
- Accreditation with commendation from JCAHO.

Massachusetts Hospital School
3 Randolph St., Canton 02021 (617)828-2440
Director of Interdisciplinary Services: (617)828-2440, ext. 338
Type: State-owned children's rehabilitation hospital

Massachusetts Respiratory Hospital
2001 Washington St., Braintree 02184 (617)848-2600
Continuing Care/Social Service: (617)848-2600, ext. 464
Type: County-owned chronic disease hospital

Middlesex County Hospital
775 Trapelo Rd., Waltham 02254 (617)895-7000
Patient Advocate Office: (617)895-7096
Type: County-owned chronic disease long term care hospital

New England Rehabilitation Hospital
Two Rehabilitation Way, Woburn 01801 (617)935-5050
Patient Advocate Office: (617)935-5050, ext. 1239
Type: For-profit rehabilitation hospital
Points to Consider:
• Accreditation with commendation from JCAHO.

New England Sinai Hospital and Rehabilitation Center
150 York St., Stoughton 02072 (617)364-4850
Social Work Services: (617)364-4850, ext. 130
Type: Nonprofit rehabilitation hospital

St. John of God Hospital
296 Allston St., Brighton 02146 (617)277-5750
Patient Advocate Office: (617)277-5750, ext. 508
Type: Church-owned chronic disease hospital

Shaughnessy-Kaplan Rehabilitation Hospital
Dove Ave., Salem 01970 (508)745-9000
Patient Advocate Office: (508)741-1200, ext. 2011
Type: Nonprofit rehabilitation hospital

Shriners Burns Institute
51 Blossom St., Boston 02114 (617)722-3000
Patient Advocate Office: (617)722-3000, ext. 110
Type: Nonprofit pediatric burns treatment hospital
Points to Consider:
• All medical care is free.

Spaulding Rehabilitation Hospital
125 Nashua St., Boston 02114 (617)720-6400
Patient Advocate Office: (617)720-6828
Type: Nonprofit rehabilitation hospital

Vencor Hospital Boston
1515 Commonwealth Ave., Brighton 02135 (617)254-1100
Patient Advocate Office: (617)254-1100, ext. 8050
Type: For-profit long-term intensive care hospital
Points to Consider:
• Formerly Hahnemann Hospital, purchased in July 1994 by Vencor Corporation.

Youville Hospital and Rehabilitation Center
1575 Cambridge St., Cambridge 02138 (617)876-4344
Patient Advocate Office: (617)876-4344, ext. 3575
Type: Church-owned rehabilitation hospital

Chapter 4 Parents

As Health Care Consumers

As a parent, no choices you make matter more than those surrounding your child's health care. From the mother's pregnancy into the child's infancy and through the teen years, you decide when to seek medical care, and you choose the people who are best qualified to provide it.

As you take these steps, you also serve as a role model for your daughters and sons. With your help—and that of their health care providers—they prepare to take over their own care and decision-making responsibilities as they reach adolescence.

> **Insurance Options for Children**
>
> The pamphlet "Finding the Health Care Coverage Your Child Needs: A Directory of Benefits for Children" clearly outlines many programs in Massachusetts that help pay for children's health care. *To order a copy, send $1 to Health Care for All, 30 Winter St., Boston 02108 (617)350-7279.*

Children and Rights

In most cases, parents make health care decisions for their daughters and sons. However, they don't have unlimited rights regarding their children's medical care. And parents usually want to involve their children as much as possible in making health care choices.

Children can consent to medical care on their own for certain conditions, such as treatments associated with drug dependency, pregnancy, and sexually transmitted diseases. In addition, an "emancipated minor"—a member of the armed forces, for example—can make medical decisions without parental permission.

▼ **FOR MORE INFORMATION**
on young women's abortion rights, turn to Chapter 5.

In most cases, any mature minor can consent to care as long as he or she can understand the nature, extent, and consequences of the medical treatment. In fact, a child can sometimes agree to treatment over the objections of parents, usually for simple procedures. By the same token, a child who legally can say yes to medical care can also say no.

Hospitals have certain rights with regard to a child. In a life-threatening emergency, they'll give treatment immediately—parental consent isn't needed. And if parents object to some types of treatment, a hospital can turn to a court for permission to treat a child whose life is in danger. If the court sides with the hospital, it will appoint a guardian, usually a member of the hospital staff, to make decisions about whether or not to proceed with a treatment.

Open Access

Hospitals can't restrict parents' right to visit hospitalized children—*at any time of day*—if the law requires them to give informed consent. Hospitals can only limit access when it would interfere with the care of other patients.

If you think a hospital is restricting access illegally, contact Children in Hospitals, 31 Wilshire Park, Needham 02192 (617)482-2915.

▼ **FOR MORE INFORMATION**
on the rights of parents and children, turn to Chapter 12.

Providers of Primary Care for Children

Every child needs a primary care provider from the day he or she is born. Parents can get this basic, ongoing care for their children from many kinds of providers:

Pediatricians are medical doctors who specialize in the care of children.

Family practitioners are medical doctors with special training to care for all members of a family, including children.

Nurse practitioners are nurses who are trained to assist doctors and can also perform a number of well-child and other routine procedures.

Depending on where you live, certain types of provider may be more available than others. Tap into a variety of sources of information to find the primary care provider who suits your needs.

Word of mouth is one excellent source: Talk to your family and friends. Who do their children see? What do your friends like—and dislike—about these providers? Ask your doctor for a recommendation. Seek referrals from local child agencies, such as day-care centers, pre-schools, schools, and early-intervention programs.

If your child has special needs, ask specific questions about a potential provider's experience with your child's condition. For example, if your child has a respiratory problem such as asthma, you might want to know how much of the responsibility for chronic care the primary care provider feels comfortable assuming. Do other children in the practice have similar special needs? What specialists, agencies, and hospitals does the provider work with on a regular basis and how does he or she communicate with them? How will you cooperate to handle emergencies?

In many cases, a pivotal factor in the choice of a child's primary care provider is your family's medical payment plan. Sometimes you can choose any provider, but some plans limit your options.

▼ **FOR A LIST**

of several hundred Boston-area primary care physicians accepting new patients, turn to Page 73.

▼ **FOR MORE INFORMATION**
on health insurance, turn to Chapter 1.

Choosing a Provider: The Factors to Consider

When you meet potential providers, weigh all criteria that matter to you. Remember, no one provider is perfect in every way. Only you can evaluate the importance of each factor.

Think about personality and style. Do you approve of the way the provider interacts with children and parents? Do you think his or her style fits the needs of you and your child? Does she or he support the right of families to be with their child for procedures and treatments? Does he or she believe in sharing all information with patients?

Keep in mind a number of other points as well:

• Do you find it easy to communicate with the provider and to ask questions? *Just as important, does your child?*

• How important is location? Can you get to the office or health center quickly if your child has an emergency? Is there a beeper number you can call? An answering service? How quickly does the doctor respond when a parent calls about a sick child?

• How do you get an appointment if your child is sick? Is this a group practice, with providers covering one another's patients when they aren't available themselves?

• Are the office hours convenient for regular appointments?

Your Role in the Partnership

Once you identify a health care provider for your son or daughter, build a partnership in which you each clearly identify your needs. From the point of view of a quality provider, you're an essential source of information about your child's development. Before you call or visit your child's provider, write down your questions or concerns. If you don't understand a reply, don't hesitate to ask again—and again. *All of your questions and opinions are legitimate and important.*

If you work days or your child is school-age, can you readily arrange evening or weekend appointments?

Immunizations

To keep your children healthy, make sure they receive all of their immunizations at the recommended times. Regional immunization information offices of the Massachusetts Department of Public Health (DPH) handle questions about local regulations, each vaccine and the diseases they prevent, and when and where to get your child immunized.

Medical providers receive vaccines for free, and they charge patients anywhere from nothing to about $50 for administrative fees for the vaccinations. If your health plan does not cover immunizations, call a DPH office to find free vaccine providers. Insurers in Massachusetts must cover all appropriate immunizations for children up to age 6 who are insured.

Every day-care program, school, and college requires proof of immunization for enrollment. (Medical and religious exemptions are allowed.) Proof includes hospital or clinic records or an immunization booklet or other official form of documentation, but not the parent's word. It is up to you to keep copies of your children's immunization records. Note the type of shot, the date, the location, and the provider. If the school has no written record, the child has to receive the shots again.

Keep Records

Build and maintain a complete record of every contact with your child's health care providers, both in person and over the phone, and write down what providers report and recommend. Include in this record a log of all immunizations, medications, and other treatments prescribed for your daughter or son. Keep your records handy at home and bring them with you to all health visits.

▼ FOR MORE INFORMATION

on vaccinations, contact your regional DPH office or your local board of health. Boston city: (617)534-5609; Metropolitan Boston: Jamaica Plain, (617)522-3700, ext. 420; Northeast: Tewksbury, (508)851-7261.

The American Academy of Pediatrics suggests this immunization schedule:

Age	Routine Vaccine
Birth	Hepatitis B
1 to 2 months	Hepatitis B
2 months	Diphtheria/tetanus/pertussis Polio Hemophilus influenza B
4 months	Diphtheria/tetanus/pertussis Polio Hemophilus influenza B
6 months	Diphtheria/tetanus/pertussis
6 to 18 months	Hemophilus influenza B Polio Hepatitis B
12 to 15 months	Hemophilus influenza B Measles/mumps/rubella (German measles)
15 to 18 months	Diphtheria/tetanus/pertussis
4 to 6 years	Diphtheria/tetanus/pertussis Polio
11 to 12 years	Measles/mumps/rubella (German measles)
14 to 16 years	Diphtheria/tetanus

Birthing Options

When you are preparing to have a child, you'll contact a specialist. The prospective mother's primary care provider also plays a central role in this event.

Couples make many decisions in the months leading up to childbirth. As you locate a primary care provider for your new child—and prepare your home and choose a name—you might also want to check on these services and options:

Childbirth Education: Parents who attend these classes gain more control over the birth and undergo fewer cesarean deliveries and other interventions. Also called birthing classes, they teach parents what to expect during labor and delivery.

Birth Arrangements: Does your hospital offer birthing rooms? Must your insurer certify admission in advance? Can siblings be present?

Obstetric Anesthesia: Does the mother want to have an epidural block to relieve the pain of childbirth? Clearly state your wishes.

Breastfeeding: Will the hospital respect your instructions about feedings and bring the newborn to you for feeding at your request? Does it offer breastfeeding instruction?

Circumcision: Once routine, this custom has joined the list of medical procedures whose necessity is being questioned. Read up on it, keep an open mind, and try to reach an informed decision.

C-Sections

Cesarean sections, when infants are delivered by an incision into the mother's abdomen and uterus, are the most frequently performed unnecessary surgery in the United States. They expose women to many health risks, often without any benefit.

When looking for an obstetrician, Public Citizen's Health Research Group suggests you ask:

- Under what conditions would the doctor perform a c-section?
- Will you have a choice?
- What is the doctor's c-section rate? Try to avoid doctors with unexplained rates above the national average, about 23 percent. Ideally, doctors dealing with high-risk pregnancies conduct c-sections in less than 17 percent of their cases, and doctors with low-risk pregnancies have rates under 10 percent.
- If you already had a baby delivered by c-section, would the doctor deliver one vaginally now? The answer may depend on the type of incision from the previous c-section.

For more information, see Unnecessary Cesarean Sections: Halting a National Epidemic. *To order a copy, send $10 to Health Research Group, Publications Department, 2000 P St., NW, Washington, DC 20036 (202)833-3000.*

Birthing Data

Massachusetts requires hospitals to disclose its maternity statistics to all registered maternity patients at preadmission on a wide variety of topics, from the rate of cesarean sections to the number of women who breastfeed upon discharge from the hospital. The hospital's maternal and child health manager should know how to get the information for you. Or call the hospital administration office directly and ask for the Maternity Disclosure Statistics.

Be wary of any hospital that doesn't offer to give the data to you. Hospital staff should also explain the statistics and their significance. If a hospital does not provide you with this data, call the Massachusetts Department of Public Health, Health Care Quality Division, 10 West St., Boston 02111 (617)727-5860. Also *A Consumer Directory of Massachusetts Hospitals* provides this and other data. To order a copy, send $5 to Children in Hospitals, 31 Wilshire Park, Needham 02192 (617)482-2915.

The maternity statistics paint a picture of all the deliveries at a hospital, but they may tell you little about your own obstetrician. Use the data to open up a discussion between you and your physician around issues of concern to you about your labor and delivery. Obstetrician practice styles vary greatly. For example, some use medical interventions more often than others. You might want to know if and when your doctor regularly uses epidurals for pain or medications to induce labor. It's important to discuss your preferences before you go into labor when there is time to think it over and discuss the options. For a further discussion of these issues, the Boston Association for Childbirth Education recommends reading *Pregnancy, Childbirth, and the Newborn*, by Penny Simkin (Simon and Schuster, 1991) $12.

▼ **FOR A LIST**

of hospitals that offer maternity services, along with the volume of births at the facility, turn to the hospital listings that begin on Page 98.

Certified Nurse-Midwife Services

Certified nurse-midwives (CNMs) are advanced practice nurses who supervise labor, perform routine deliveries, and provide gynecological exams and prenatal and postnatal care. They deliver about 4 percent of the babies in the United States. They attend births primarily in hospitals, with 11 percent in birth centers and 4 percent in homes. Besides individual practices, a number of centers offer the services of CNMs. Many of these centers also offer a variety of other women's health care services.

Boston City Hospital Midwifery Service
818 Harrison Ave.
Boston 02118
(800)982-8363
(617)534-5469 or 534-5686

Brigham and Women's Nurse-Midwifery Practice
75 Francis St.
Boston 02115
(617)732-4233

Cambridge Hospital Midwifery Service
1493 Cambridge St.
Cambridge 02139
(617)498-1660

Center for Women's Health
Quincy Hospital
114 Whitwell St.
Quincy 02169
(617)770-3033

Concord Nurse Midwifery Associates
WalthamWeston Hospital
5 Hope Ave.
Waltham 02254
(617)647-6665

Liberty Tree Nurse-Midwifery Associates
(for births at Beverly Hospital, Beverly)
140 Commonwealth Ave.
Danvers 01923
(508)777-4113

Malden Hospital Nurse-Midwife Services
Hospital Rd.
Malden 02148
(617)322-7560

Mount Auburn Hospital Midwifery Associates
330 Mount Auburn St.
Cambridge 02138
(617)499-5141

North Shore Birth Center
Beverly Hospital
85 Herrick St.
Beverly 01915-1777
(508)922-3010

North Suburban Women's Health
(for births at New England Memorial Hospital, Stoneham)
3 Woodland Rd.
Stoneham 02180
(617)665-2122

Saint Margaret's Women and Infants Center
Saint Elizabeth's Medical Center
736 Cambridge St.
Brighton 02135
(617)562-7000

Woman Care
(for births at New England Memorial Hospital, Stoneham)
180 Massachusetts Ave.
Arlington 02174
(617)648-4221

Women's Health Associates, Inc.
(for births at Newton-Wellesley Hospital)
173 Worcester St.
Wellesley 02181
(617)237-0080

2000 Washington St.
Newton 02162
(617)332-5551

Resources

Birthlink
12 Brewster Rd.
Norfolk 02056
(617)575-1089
Call or write for information on childbirth and parenting.

Boston Association for Childbirth Education Nursing Mothers' Council
P.O. Box 29
Newtonville 02160
(617)244-5102
Call or write for information and referrals on childbirth education, breastfeeding, and postpartum support services.

Boston Parent's Paper
P.O. Box 1777
Boston 02130
(617)522-1515
This monthly community publication provides parents and professionals with information, resources, and feature articles on parenting and family life. Pick up free copies at stores and public areas; subscriptions are $15 per year.

Cesarean/Support, Education and Concern (C/Sec)
22 Forest Rd.
Framingham 01701
(508)877-8266
Call or write for information and support on cesarean birth, prevention, and vaginal-births after cesarean section (V-BAC).

Children in Hospitals
31 Wilshire Park
Needham 02192
(617)482-2915
Call or write for information and advocacy for parents of hospitalized children, including supporting the rights of parents to "room-in" or stay with their children in the hospital whenever possible. Send $5 for a copy of *A Consumer Directory of Massachusetts Hospitals,* published every two years, with data on maternity, newborn, pediatric, and adult care in hospitals.

Children's Law Center of Massachusetts
P.O. Box 710
Lynn 01903
(617)581-1977
This nonprofit legal resource center provides advocacy, research, and training on issues affecting the civil rights, health, education, and welfare of young people.

Depression After Delivery
P.O. Box 706
Quincy 02269
(508)559-2229
Call or write for information on group and individual support services for women and families suffering postpartum depression and psychosis.

Family Careline
Whittier Street Health Center
20 Whittier St.
Roxbury 02120
(617)445-CARE or 445-2275
The center offers free information and referral services for pregnant and parenting women.

Federation for Children with Special Needs
95 Berkeley St.
Boston 02116
(617)482-2915
(800)331-0688
The federation advocates on behalf of children and families with special needs. Call or write for information and referrals on early intervention, special education rights and laws, issues for children with special health needs, and roles for families in programs and policies affecting children with special needs.

Fetal Alcohol Education Program
Boston University School of Medicine
7 Kent St.
Brookline 02146
(617)739-1424
Call or write for information, consultation, and referrals.

Focus Counseling and Consultation, Inc.
186 1/2 Hampshire St.
Cambridge 02139
(617)876-4488
This office offers infertility support groups for couples.

La Leche League of Massachusetts
(617)469-9423
Call for information and encouragement on breastfeeding.

Lamaze Childbirth Education, Inc.
P.O. Box 88
Belmont 02179
(617)489-4030
Call or write for information on classes on childbirth, infant care, and breastfeeding.

Massachusetts Department of Public Health Bureau of Family and Community Health
150 Tremont St.
Boston 02111
(800)882-1435
Call or write for information and referrals on such issues as genetics, Supplemental Security Income (SSI) benefits, parent groups, child disability prevention, and hearing and epilepsy evaluations. Call or write to get a free copy of *Paying the Bills: Tips for Families on Financing Health Care for Children with Special Needs.*

Massachusetts Department of Public Health Genetics Program of the Division of Family Services
150 Tremont St.
Boston 02111
(617)727-6941
Call for information on possible reproductive risks, genetic counseling, and testing facilities, as well as for information on treatment and parent support groups.

Massachusetts Department of Public Health Lead Poisoning Prevention Program
305 South St.
Jamaica Plain 02130
(800)532-9571
Call with questions about lead poisoning: prevention, treatment, testing, legal issues around lead paint and tenant's rights, and for referrals to local services.

Massachusetts Friends of Midwives
P.O. Box 3188
Boston 02130
(617)497-0124 or (508)369-1468
Send a $3.50 for the *Birthing Resources Directory,* a statewide listing of childbirth educators, labor support people, breastfeeding counselors, physicians who support home birth, and other childbirth-related services and providers.

Massachusetts Society for the Prevention of Cruelty to Children
95 Berkeley St.
Boston 02116
(617)426-1055
Call for information on support groups for families around issues of abuse and neglect.

Maternal and Child Health Center
2464 Massachusetts Ave.
Cambridge 02140
(617)864-9343
The center offers prenatal and postpartum exercise programs, physical therapy, support groups, mother and baby exercise programs, breastfeeding counseling, and a lending library.

National Birth Defects Center
40 Second Ave.
Waltham 02154
(617)466-9555
The center offers genetic counseling services and referrals for psychological counseling.

Newborn Support Service
79 Warren St.
Newton Centre 02159
(617)965-0315
This information service to new parents offers nurse home visits and advice, breast pumping rental, and support by phone.

New England SERVE
101 Tremont St.
Boston 02108
(617)574-9493
The comprehensive booklet, *Paying the Bills: Tips for Families on Financing Health Care for Children with Special Needs,* encourages families to ask questions, learn about health financing, and be persistent when seeking health services for their children. For a single copy send a self-addressed 9"x12" mailing envelope with $1.05 in postage affixed.

Parents Anonymous
140 Clarendon St.
Boston 02116
(617)267-8077
(800)882-1250
Call for information on support groups for parents who feel stressed or isolated or would like to get together with other parents to talk. Groups meet weekly; services are free.

Pregnancy/Environmental Hotline
40 Second Ave.
Waltham 02154
(617)466-8474
(800)322-5014
Call for information and referrals about chemical, environmental, medication, and infectious-disease exposures during pregnancy.

Prenatal Diagnostics
80 Hayden Ave.
Lexington 02173
(617)862-1171
This office offers genetics and birth-defects testing and counseling.

Resolve, Inc.
1310 Broadway
Somerville 02144
(617)623-0744
Call for information on infertility treatments and referrals to providers and support groups.

Chapter 5 Women

As Health Care Consumers

Metropolitan Boston hosts a wide variety of health care resources for women. Take advantage of the services these organizations and agencies offer before you make a major decision about health care, ask them to assist in your search for health care providers, and continue to consult them as your needs and situation change over the years. An informed patient is better equipped to be a strong partner in her care.

▼ **FOR RESOURCES**
on pregnancy and childbirth, turn to Chapter 4.

Finding a Provider

The first step in finding a health care provider, beginning with primary care, is to list your own requirements. What type of provider and what setting are best for you? What factors matter to you? List these in order of importance—you undoubtedly will have to compromise on some items.

Even as you search for highly skilled providers, convenience and other considerations will also significantly affect your health and your ability to actually use the services of health care professionals. Do you want a provider with an office close to your home or work? Are evening and weekend hours available for appointments? Is parking free? Do you want one provider to care for all members of your family? Do you prefer an individual practice, a group, or a clinic? Do you want a health care provider who focuses on people of your age?

These questions apply to both men and women as health care consumers, but most women want to consider additional questions. Do you prefer a female physician or nurse practitioner? Do you want specialists who focus on women? Would you prefer one clinician for all of your care or one for reproductive health plus another for general health? Does your insurance allow ob-gyns to serve as primary care physicians, if that's your preference?

To aid your search for the names of possible providers:

- Seek referrals from pediatricians, nurses, and other health care providers you know;
- Talk to friends and acquaintances about their providers;
- Contact women's health organizations listed at the end of this chapter;
- Call your local hospital's physician-referral line; *and*
- Check local newspapers and magazines for recent feature articles on women's health care and providers.

▼ FOR A LIST
of several hundred Boston-area primary care physicians accepting new patients, turn to Page 73.

Health Care Providers for Women

Your options for a primary medical provider depend partly on your age and your state of health. For example, a woman with a special health condition—say, diabetes—may see a physician who can treat it as well as provide routine care. That would probably be an internist. Or if you are nearing menopause, you may want to talk with your current primary care provider about changing to or adding a gynecologist with specialized knowledge of reproductive hormones.

Women with relatively basic health care needs can choose among several types of providers. Each has its own strengths and weaknesses. Bear in mind that any individual provider may be an exception to the rule.

• *Family practitioners:* Comprehensive training in internal medicine, pediatrics, ob/gyn, surgery, psychiatry, and public health medicine predisposes family physicians to treat the whole person, not just conditions and symptoms that relate to one specialty. Thus, they can take care of the routine health needs of your entire family, drawing on their knowledge of how the family system affects the health of each of you. Using one person for a wide range of services can also lessen the need for referrals, which usually cost you time and money. For your own care, you may want to find a family physician with special experience or interest in women's health. If your needs are more extensive—for instance, if you need obstetric care but your family physician doesn't deliver babies—you will need to see a specialist in addition to a family physician.

• *Obstetricians and Gynecologists ("Ob-Gyns"):* Ob-gyns treat only women. The typical gynecologist has in-depth knowledge of the female reproductive system, urinary system, and hormone system, and a background in screening and treating cancers particular to women. Delivering babies is the province of obstetricians. Physicians usually practice these two closely related specialties together, although many are dropping obstetrics in favor of general gynecology, with some treating mostly adolescents and others concentrating on older women. Of the physicians here, ob-gyns most consistently ensure that women receive regular Pap smears and screening mammograms. *At their best,* ob-gyns also take to heart many of the premises of primary care practice and prevention. However, the ambivalence and relative inexperience of many ob-gyns in treating other parts of the person are probably their greatest drawbacks as primary care providers. Even if you dutifully see an ob-gyn for a yearly Pap smear and pelvic and breast exams, don't assume you're getting primary care.

• *Internists:* Internists, or internal medicine specialists, are known as expert diagnosticians. They draw on training in microbiology, pharmacology, and chemistry, and have studied all the body's organs. In situations in which specialists might conduct tests or exploratory surgery to find out what's going on inside you, internists pride themselves on doing more thinking. Their ability to treat several problems at once, taking into account such factors as potential interactions among medications, makes them an excellent choice for women with complicated and chronic health problems. Within the field, your best choice is a general internist with a stated interest in preventive care and women's health, unless you have a serious problem requiring a subspecialist.

• *Advanced Practice Nurses:* Advanced practice nurses—such as nurse practitioners, clinical nurse specialists, and certified nurse-midwives—are gaining favor as an alternative to physician-centered health care for women. They have a graduate-level education or are certified in a specialty, such as women's health, children's health, gerontology, diabetes, or cardiac care. Certified nurse-midwives supervise labor, perform routine deliveries, conduct gynecological exams, and provide prenatal and postpartum care. The technical skills of advanced practice nurses tend to equal those of physicians for the services they offer, and their fees are significantly lower. Some practice independently or in conjunction with individual physicians. The main drawback of advanced practice nurses comes from legal limits on their ability to treat complicated medical conditions or prescribe medications. On the other hand, this drawback rarely will present a problem for you because advanced practice nurses almost always work in a collaborative setting with physicians and other health care providers. Most work in clinics, hospitals, and HMOs.

Ask Questions

Dr. Karen Carlson, a primary care physician with Women's Health Associates at Massachusetts General Hospital, has studied the differences between male and female patients. She found that women tend to ask more questions than men. They are also more informed and tend to exchange more information with one another. Most studies indicate that this kind of active patient involvement in care results in better health.

▼ FOR MORE INFORMATION
on primary care providers, turn to Chapter 2.

Abortion Rights and Services

Massachusetts places no legal restrictions on access to abortion services for women, except in the case of minors. The commonwealth's parental/judicial consent law requires an unmarried woman under the age of 18 to have the written consent of both parents to obtain an abortion. However, minors who prefer not to seek parental consent can ask a judge to grant their petition for an abortion—that is, issue a "judicial bypass."

For assistance with the judicial-bypass process, a minor can call Planned Parenthood's confidential counseling and referral line at (617)731-2525 or (800)682-9218. She will be connected with a volunteer from the Lawyer Referral Panel sponsored by the Women's Bar Association and the National Lawyer's Guild. More than 10,000 minors have sought judicial approval for abortions; judges have granted all but a handful of these requests.

Abortion services are provided in clinics, private physician's offices, and hospitals. The procedure costs anywhere from $250 to $1,000 if conducted in the first trimester, and from about $600 to $2,500 in the second trimester. Hospital ser-

Required Benefits

Massachusetts requires HMOs, PPOs, Blue Cross/Blue Shield, and commercial insurers to cover certain benefits. Those specifically related to women's health include pregnancy and childbirth services, annual Pap smears, baseline and annual mammograms after age 40, bone-marrow transplants for women with metastatic breast cancer, and infertility drugs and treatment, including artificial insemination, in vitro fertilization, and other non-experimental procedures. (These regulations do not apply to employers that self-insure, meaning they carry the financial risk for their employee's claims. But many companies cover the benefits anyway.)

vices tend to be much more expensive than either clinics or private physicians; clinics are generally the least expensive site. Many health plans cover abortion services.

When choosing an abortion provider, consider the experience of the physician. As with all surgical procedures, those who perform abortions more often tend to be more skilled, have fewer complications, and can recognize problems sooner than physicians who do abortions less frequently. Other areas in which providers differ significantly are the type of anesthesia used and the amount and quality of counseling and patient education they offer. Providers who take the time to involve the patient in the process by making her fully informed and aware of her options raise the quality of care and caring.

▼ FOR MORE INFORMATION

on abortion in general or for referrals to local providers, call Planned Parenthood at (617)731-2525 or (800)682-9218, the National Abortion Federation at (800)772-9100, or Ask-a-Nurse at (800)544-2424, which offers referrals to providers associated with the 15 hospitals sponsoring the service.

Mammograms

The Jacobs Institute of Women's Health asked American women why they get screening mammograms less often than they should. The most frequent reason: their doctors had never recommended it! Second was the erroneous assumption that they were not at risk if no breast cancer existed in their family.

All women run the risk of breast cancer as they grow older. One out of every eight U.S. women will develop it in her lifetime. In four out of five cases, age is the only known risk factor.

Most breast cancer can be treated if discovered early enough. Mammograms detect breast lumps when they are mere specks on film—up to two years before you can feel them by hand. The American Cancer Society recommends an initial mammogram by age 40, repeat mammograms every year or two to age 49, and every year after age 50. Examine your own breasts every month.

Beginning October 1, 1994, all mammography facilities must be federally certified annually and prominently display a certificate of Food and Drug Administration (FDA) accreditation. Some facilities may have provisional accreditation until April 1, 1995. In the meantime, look for accreditation from the American College of Radiology.

As of April 1, 1995, every facility must have full FDA accreditation. To receive a certificate, a facility must ensure that:

- Those who perform or interpret mammograms are properly trained and experienced;
- It uses only up-to-date machines;
- Women with suspicious results receive notification and follow-up care; *and*
- FDA-trained inspectors conduct an inspection every year.

For the complete guidelines, call the federal Agency for Health Care Policy and Research at (800)358-9295 and ask for a free copy of "Things to Know About Quality

Free Mammograms and Pap Smears

Government-funded sites provide free mammograms and Pap smears for women over 40 who have no health insurance or whose insurance does not cover such tests.

Medicare pays for mammograms every two years. Women can get free tests at these same sites in the off years.

Boston City Hospital (617)534-4627
Cambridge Hospital (617)498-1859
Dimock Community Health Center (617)442-8800, ext. 533
Dorchester House Health Center (617)288-3230, ext. 420
East Boston Neighborhood Health Center (617)568-4708
Fenway Community Health Center (617)267-0900, ext. 296
Mass. General Hospital/Chelsea Health Center (617)889-8525
Melrose-Wakefield Hospital (617)979-3101
Roxbury Community Health Center (617)442-7400, ext. 327
Joseph M. Smith Community Health Center (617)783-0500
Somerville Hospital (617)666-4400, ext. 688
South Cove Health Center (617)521-6716
Upham's Corner Health Center (617)287-8000, ext. 17
WalthamWeston Hospital and Medical Center (617)647-6680

Mammograms." To find a certified facility, ask your provider or call the National Cancer Institute's Cancer Information Service at (800)4-CANCER. The Massachusetts Department of Public Health Radiation Control Program also inspects and licenses facilities; call (617)727-6214 to check on a facility's status.

Mammography facilities conducting the most tests usually offer the best quality at the lowest price. Get referrals from your physician or call a local hospital. Be sure to check under what conditions your insurance policy will cover mammograms. The cost of a screening mammogram ranges from $50 to $275. If possible, ask that two radiologists from the same center look at your X-ray.

Some Typical Charges

Mammograms
Boston: $131
U.S. Average: $123

Routine Gynecological Exam and Pap Smear
Boston: $157
U.S. Average: $110

Source: Medirisk, Inc.

Ask any facility you are considering using:

- *Does the facility have FDA certification?* Make sure the certificate is prominently displayed.
- *How will you get results?* You should be told directly, in lay language, and ideally before you leave or within 10 days otherwise. You and your doctor should get a written report. If the exam is abnormal, your doctor should be called.
- *What happens if the results of the exam are abnormal?* The facility should explain what steps to take next.

If a facility doesn't answer these questions to your satisfaction, go elsewhere.

Resources

General Resources

American Medical Women's Association
Massachusetts Branch
P.O. Box 620299
Newton 02162
(617)332-3293
Call for referrals to female physicians.

Anorexia and Bulimia Care, Inc.
P.O. Box 213
Lincoln Center 01773
(617)259-9767
Call for support and referrals.

Boston Women's Health Book Collective
240A Elm St.
Somerville 02144
(617)625-0271
Call for a literature list of information on a wide variety of subjects. Call or visit the Women's Health Information Center, Tuesdays 2 p.m.-8 p.m. or Thursdays 10 a.m.-4 p.m. Send questions and messages through e-mail to: bwhbc@igc.apc.org. The collective or its members are the authors of *The New Our Bodies, Ourselves* (Simon & Schuster, 1992—$20) and *The New Ourselves, Growing Older: Women Aging with Knowledge and Power* (Touchstone Books, 1994–$18).

Massachusetts Breast Cancer Coalition
2 Boylston St.
Boston 02116
(617)423-6222 or (800)649-MBCC
Call for information on breast cancer and treatment or to reach your local chapter.

New England Eating Disorders
119 Braintree St.
Boston 02134
(617)254-0054
Call or write for information on reaching or organizing a support group.

Osteoporosis Awareness Program
Massachusetts Department of Public Health
(800)95-BONES
Call with questions about osteoporosis or to order a free information packet.

Planned Parenthood League of Massachusetts Counseling and Referral Hotline
1031 Beacon St.
Brookline 02146
(617)731-2525 or (800)682-9218
Call with any questions relating to reproductive health, such as contraception, abortion, sexually transmitted diseases, pregnancy, prenatal care, and breastfeeding. Also call for referrals to social-service and health-access programs.

Project on Women and Disability
One Ashburton Pl.
Boston 02108
(617)727-7440 (voice, TDD) or (800)322-2020
The project organizes women with disabilities for empowerment and social change, conducting campaigns around such issues as reproductive rights. It provides information and referrals to women with disabilities and offers discussion groups and social events.

Women's Center
46 Pleasant St.
Cambridge 02139
(617)354-8807
Visit, call, or write for information on the Women's Community Cancer Project, the Battered Women's Directory, and many other services and programs.

Women's Health Resource Center
Brigham and Women's Ambulatory Care Center
850 Boylston St.
Chestnut Hill 02167
(800)522-8765
A bookstore is open to the public. Call or visit for recommendations on books and publications and referrals to women's health providers.

Women's Mental Health Collective
61 Roseland St.
Somerville 02143
(617)354-6270
Call for mental health referrals. The collective can refer women for a range of needs, such as therapy for families and individuals, adolescents, women with eating disorders, adult children of alcoholics, and lesbian couples.

Reproductive Health Care Services

The following independent clinics and health centers offer a variety of services and several types of providers. Many hospitals also house women's health centers and group practices primarily serving women. Call your local hospital for information. The list of primary care physicians that begins on Page 73 includes some ob-gyns as well. All community health centers offer reproductive health services; these are listed beginning on Page 73 as well.

Crittenton Hastings House
10 Perthshire Rd.
Brighton 02135
(617)782-7600
Women's reproductive health services, including contraceptive and abortion services and screening and treatment for sexually transmitted diseases

Gynecare
177 Tremont St.
Boston 02111
(617)426-4700
Women's reproductive health services, including abortion services

Healthquarters
Four sites offering complete women's reproductive health services, provided by nurse practitioners

19 Broadway St.
Beverly 01915
(508)927-9824

65 Munroe St.
Lynn 01901
(617)593-1115

Riverview Business Park
300 Commercial St., Suite 31
Malden 02148
(617)397-9389

xFantasia Building
274 Main St.
Reading 01867
(617)944-8325

North Shore Women's Care
125 Main St.
Reading 01867
(617)942-0743
Reproductive health care services provided by nurse practitioners

Nurse Practitioner Associates
2464 Massachusetts Ave.
Cambridge 02140
(617)354-6028
Specializes in women's health care

Planned Parenthood Clinic of Greater Boston
1031 Beacon St.
Brookline 02146
(800)682-9218
(617)738-1370
Women's reproductive health services, including contraceptive and abortion services and screening and treatment for sexually transmitted diseases

Preterm
1842 Beacon St.
Brookline 02146
(617)738-6210
(617)739-6639 TDD
Women's reproductive health services, including contraceptive and abortion services and screening and treatment for sexually transmitted diseases

Women's Health Services
Reservoir Office Park
822 Boylston St.
Chestnut Hill 02167
(617)277-0009
(800)675-5550
Women's reproductive health services, including abortion services

Chapter 6 Elders

As Health Care Consumers

Some of the health care challenges elders face mirror those that other consumers encounter: choosing the right services, forming partnerships with health care providers, investing limited financial resources wisely.

At the same time, elders have special concerns and needs. It's important for you, your health care providers, and your family to recognize that:

- Older people respond in distinctive ways to drugs, foods, stress, infections, and wounds.
- Elders are more likely to have a wide variety of both single and combined health problems.
- Elders are far more likely to need long term care, which represents their largest out-of-pocket health care expense.
- A federal insurance system (Medicare) pays for a significant part of the health care of almost all people 65 and older; on the other hand, elders spend more out of their own pockets today for health care than they did before Medicare, and they also devote far more of their income to health care than do younger adults.

Medicare and Medicaid

Medicare is the federal health insurance program for older Americans and for certain younger adults who are disabled. If you are eligible for Social Security or Railroad Retirement benefits and are 65 or older, you automatically qualify for Medicare, as does your spouse when she or he reaches 65. Medicare pays for a significant part of *all* the health care needs of almost all elders. Coupled with supplemental insurance, it also pays a significant portion of the bills for *acute medical care* for 95 percent of older Americans.

Medicare applications are handled through your local Social Security office. If you are eligible, you should receive Medicare automatically, effective the month you turn 65.

Medicare has two parts:

- *Part A,* hospital insurance, applies to hospital costs, skilled nursing facilities, psychiatric hospitals, and hospice care. Part A is "free" if you qualify for Medicare: you've paid for it already in payroll taxes. Even if you are not automatically eligible for Medicare, anyone over 65 can buy Part A: in 1995 it costs $183 to $261 per month, depending on your Social Security benefits.
- *Part B,* medical insurance, is automatically yours the

Provider Shortage

If you are over 60, the most disturbing aspect of the health care system may well be the lack of providers with training specific to your needs. Older people aren't middle-aged adults, just as children aren't small adults. For example, you react to diseases differently from the way you did as a young adult, and diseases may take different courses.

With far too few people fully trained in geriatrics, a lack of such credentials won't eliminate a candidate for providing your care. But look more favorably on a person who has a certificate for completing a geriatrics course, participates in a group practice with access to a geriatrician, or belongs to a relevant professional group, such as the American Geriatrics Society or the Gerontological Society of America.

month you turn 65 unless you decline it. It covers certain doctor's fees, laboratory tests, X-rays, many outpatient services, some ambulance facilities, home health care, and in-home use of durable medical equipment. For Part B coverage in 1995, the government deducts $46.10 from your monthly Social Security check.

All doctors in Massachusetts must accept the Medicare-approved amount as payment in full for Medicare-covered services. However, Medicare won't pay for *all* of your health care expenses. In particular, Medicare *doesn't* cover most nursing-home care unless it is in a skilled nursing facility (designated a Level I facility in Massachusetts), certain long term care in the home, prescription drugs outside a hospital, eyeglasses, dental care, or hearing aides. Even though disability, frailty, and memory loss may heighten your need for services, such chronic conditions don't normally require a hos-

Medicare and Your Family

Medicare only covers one individual, not dependents. Many younger spouses lose their health insurance as dependents when the working spouse turns 65 and switches to Medicare. A spouse covered through his or her former employer usually has the right to buy the group insurance for three years.

For Low Income Seniors

Medicare offers two programs for low-income people over age 65 and for the disabled.

The *Qualified Medicare Beneficiaries Program* applies to people with incomes at or below the federal poverty level. Massachusetts picks up the cost of the standard Medicare Part B premiums, as well as Part A hospital deductibles and coinsurance.

The *Specified Low-Income Medicare Beneficiary Program* assists people with incomes just above the poverty level. Massachusetts pays the Part B premium.

For more information, contact the Medicare Advocacy Project at (800)323-3205 or (617)536-0400.

1995 Medicare Deductibles and Coinsurance Amounts

Part A, Hospital Insurance

Deductible	You pay $716 per benefit period
Hospital Coinsurance	
61st through 90th day	You pay $179/day
91st through 150th day	You pay $358/day
Skilled Nursing Facility Coinsurance	
21st through 100th day	You pay $89.50/day

Part B, Medical Insurance

Deductible	You pay $100/year

The deductible is the amount you must pay before Medicare starts paying the bill. The coinsurance is the amount you must pay for services after the deductible is satisfied.

pital stay or the daily attention of a doctor or skilled nurse. If a medical problem isn't acute, Medicare may not pay for it.

If you are enrolled in Medicare and require skilled care, this is the preferred way to finance home care. Medicare will pay the *Medicare-approved amount* for skilled health services delivered at home under certain circumstances. You must be homebound, under the care of a physician who signs a plan of care, *and* in need of only part-time or intermittent home health services. Medicare home health care can be provided over a long period of time; it is not just for a recovery period. For information and referrals on Medicare-covered home care, consult the Home and Health Care Association of Massachusetts at (800)332-3500.

Medicaid, also known as MassHealth, can be a viable option to help pay for acute care, home care, and nursing-home and long term care (in facilities designated as Level I, II, or III in Massachusetts). To qualify for coverage, you must meet strict income and asset requirements. Medicaid potentially covers part or all of the copayment for some home health services covered by Medicare, some other home health services not covered by Medicare, private nursing care, and other services. In addition, Supplemental Security Income (SSI) can help pay for care in rest homes.

▼ **FOR MORE INFORMATION**
on Medicaid, turn to Chapter 1. For more information on SSI, contact your local Social Security office.

Medicare Oversight: Ask the PROs

The federal government contracts with MassPRO, the Massachusetts Peer Review Organization, to ensure that Medicare beneficiaries receive care that is reasonable, medically necessary, provided in the most appropriate setting, and meets professionally accepted standards of quality. A subsidiary of the Massachusetts Medical Society and staffed by physicians and other health care professionals, MassPRO reviews all written complaints from beneficiaries and their representatives concerning quality of care. It also reviews bills and records to determine when Medicare shouldn't pay.

If you're admitted to a hospital, you'll receive a notice explaining your rights under Medicare and how to contact MassPRO if the need arises.

If you are a Medicare beneficiary, you have the right to:

• Receive all of the hospital care necessary for the proper treatment of your illness and injury. Your discharge should be determined solely by your medical needs.

Emergency Aid to the Elderly, Disabled and Children Program

Elders who qualify for cash assistance under the Emergency Aid to the Elderly, Disabled and Children Program are also eligible for medical assistance. This assistance covers physician services, all services provided by community health centers, prescription drugs, and the cost of care related to substance abuse. EDC beneficiaries are eligible for hospital care under the Free Care Pool.

Application for EDC medical assistance is automatic when you apply for the EDC program—there is no way to apply separately. For more information, contact the Public Assistance Information number, (800)249-2007. You can also call a local legal-services office for information.

Hospital Discharge Rights

If you are receiving hospital care through Medicare, Massachusetts requires hospitals to provide you with a written discharge plan 24 hours before discharging you. If you don't receive one, contact the Medicare Advocacy Office of the Department of Public Health, Division of Health Care Quality, 10 West St., Boston 02111 (800)462-5540. Call this same office to complain about abuse or neglect in facilities the department licenses, which includes most hospitals, nursing homes, rest homes, and clinics.

• Be fully informed about decisions affecting your Medicare coverage or payment for your hospital stay.

• Request a review, reconsideration, and ultimately an appeal of any written notice stating that Medicare will no longer pay for your hospital stay.

If you have a concern regarding the quality of Medicare-financed care provided to you by a hospital, skilled nursing facility, home health agency, HMO, or ambulatory surgery center, you can submit a complaint to MassPRO for review and correction if necessary.

If you receive a "notice of non-coverage" from a hospital or other Medicare facility (indicating you should be discharged) and you believe you still need hospital care:

• First, speak with your physician about your condition and medical care needs.

• If that doesn't resolve your concern, ask the facility to issue a written notice of non-coverage.

• Contact MassPRO and ask it to review your case. *If you choose to appeal a discharge, do so as soon as possible.*

As long as you request an appeal by noon of the business day following your receipt of the notice, you cannot be discharged against your wishes or be held liable for any charges until noon of the day following the MassPRO decision. MassPRO will issue its decision on whether your stay still meets Medicare requirements within two working days. About 75 percent of the time, MassPRO upholds the hospital's original decision.

▼ **FOR MORE INFORMATION**
or to register a complaint, call MassPRO's toll-free number for Medicare beneficiaries (800)252-5533.

Medicare and HMOs

Medicare usually operates on a fee-for-service basis: you are billed for each visit to a health care provider. HMOs and similar forms of *prepaid* health care are also available to Medicare enrollees. For just a copayment, HMO members sometimes receive certain services not generally covered by Medicare, such as prescriptions and preventive eye exams. HMOs in the Medicare program can't deny enrollment to Medicare beneficiaries.

Two types of HMO offer Medicare coverage in Massachusetts:

Medicare Advocacy Project

For assistance with a wide variety of Medicare-related problems, contact the Medicare Advocacy Project. MAP provides free advice and representation for elderly and disabled Massachusetts residents who have been denied Medicare coverage for health care or home care services.

Contact MAP at Greater Boston Elderly Legal Services, 102 Norway St., Boston 02115 (617)536-0400 or (800)323-3205.

• *Risk-contract HMOs* are most common. Medicare pays the HMO a monthly sum to provide your full Medicare-covered health care. Depending on the plan, you may have to pay a monthly premium, deductibles, and copayments or coinsurance for certain services. The name "risk contract" comes from the fact that the plan assumes the financial risk for providing your health care.

If you join a risk-contract HMO, follow the plan's rules. If you don't use plan-affiliated providers, you—not Medicare—pay the bills.

In metropolitan Boston, Fallon, Harvard Community Health Plan, Pilgrim, Tufts, and U.S. Healthcare enroll Medicare beneficiaries in risk-contract HMOs.

• With *health care prepayment plans*, Medicare pays the plan to provide physician visits, X-rays, lab tests, and other diagnostic tests that are part of Medicare Part B. Other medical services may be included. You can go outside the plan and still have Medicare benefits. HMO Blue and Neighborhood Health Plan offer such plans to Medicare beneficiaries in the Boston area.

As a Massachusetts Medicare enrollee in an HMO, you have the right: to receive appropriate health care for your condition; to have access to health care when needed; to receive quality care; *and* to be discharged only when you are medically ready to leave the hospital.

If you think your rights have been denied, first contact your HMO to try to resolve the problems. If the HMO doesn't address the problem to your satisfaction, contact MassPRO at (800)252-5533.

Beyond Medicare: Medigap

A variety of private insurance policies can help you pay for medical expenses that Medicare covers only partly or not at all. By far the most important one is Medigap insurance. Most Medigap policies cover Medicare's coinsurance; some also pay the deductibles. And some pay for health services not covered by Medicare at all. Consider buying Medigap insurance if you need and can afford private insurance to meet health care costs that Medicare doesn't cover *and* you aren't covered by a former employer's health insurance plan. Blue Cross/Blue Shield of Massachusetts, most Massachusetts HMOs, and some commercial insurers issue Medigap policies.

As of January 1, 1995, all insurers offering new Medigap

One Is Enough

Don't purchase more than one Medigap policy. It's illegal for insurance agents to use scare tactics to frighten consumers into dropping existing policies or purchasing policies they don't need or can't afford. If you suspect a violation of this law, contact the Massachusetts Division of Insurance at (617)521-7794.

> **HMO Medigap Coverage**
>
> All HMOs in Massachusetts currently offer some form of Medigap coverage. This coverage is available to people who carry Medicare Parts A and B and do not have end-stage renal disease. Coverage may be offered on an individual basis or as part of a group. All contracts must offer an open-enrollment period during February and March of each year and must offer coverage effective within 90 days from the date of enrollment.

polices in Massachusetts must:

- Charge all subscribers the same premium;
- Guarantee policies to be renewable;
- Offer plans that conform to one of three standard benefit packages;
- Offer policies to all applicants within six months of their date of Medicare eligibility and annually thereafter during an open-enrollment period; after 1997, a surcharge may be imposed for later enrollment or upgrading of coverage;
- Offer at least one policy with a mandated level of drug coverage;
- Not deny coverage to an applicant based on age or health experience or status;
- Not offer policies with waiting periods or that exclude people with preexisting conditions; *and*
- Not raise the cost of premiums by more than 10 percent without the prior approval of the Insurance Commissioner. (This does not apply to HMO risk contracts.)

A policy issued before 1995 can stay in effect even if it does not conform to these rules.

Long Term Care and Home Care

Long term care is just that: care provided over a long period of time to people who can't take care of themselves without assistance. This means services that help you with activities you must do every day. Though they relate to health, these services don't necessarily require a physician or a skilled nurse. Services are provided in the home, in the community, or in a variety of residential settings, including nursing homes.

Most long term care expenses are paid out-of-pocket or by Medicaid. Also, the insurance industry has developed products in response to public alarm over skyrocketing costs for long term care, but most financial experts advise against purchasing such policies unless you have substantial assets.

Before *considering* a purchase, ask your insurance agent or insurance company to give you a copy of "A Shopper's Guide to Long-Term Care Insurance," published by the National Association of Insurance Commissioners. And before you buy insurance for long term care, you may wish to seek the advice of a lawyer familiar with Medicaid law and estate planning.

Nursing Home Ombudsman

If you or a loved one lives in a nursing home, contact the Ombudsman Program of the Massachusetts Executive Office of Elder Affairs to report patient-care complaints such as dietary issues, abuse, visitation problems, and lost or stolen personal items. You can reach the Ombudsman Office at (617)727-7750. In addition, every nursing home in Massachusetts has a weekly visit from an ombudsperson under the program.

▼ **FOR MORE INFORMATION**

on long term care insurance, including consumer tips and a list of policies approved for sale in Massachusetts, call Mass Home Care's ElderLine at (800)AGE-INFO.

Determining What You Need

Given the choice, most people choose to live at home even if they require ongoing, around-the-clock services and can no longer care for themselves. About one-third of older Americans—mostly women—live alone. If no family member is immediately available to provide care, qualified home care providers are available in almost every community in Massachusetts, often at affordable prices or with fees set according to a sliding scale.

Home care can mean anything from help with the everyday tasks of living to advanced medical care. The goal is to main-

Guide to Long Term Care

The Women's Educational and Industrial Union, in cooperation with the Massachusetts Department of Public Health, publishes *The Guide to Long Term Care Alternatives in Massachusetts*. Updated annually, it contains a wealth of up-to-date information on facilities, government programs, and much more. Facility listings are also available on computer diskette; ask the WEIU nursing home guide coordinator for details.

To obtain a copy, contact WEIU, Home Care & Support Services, 356 Boylston St., Boston 02116 (617)536-8210. $19.95 each, plus $3 for shipping and handling and $1 for state tax.

tain or restore your ability to function well enough to continue living at home. As many as seven million elders, plus millions of disabled people of all ages, need help with at least one of the five "activities of daily living"—bathing, dressing, walking, eating, or using the toilet. Even more people need occasional assistance with other routine tasks, such as grocery shopping, getting to the doctor, managing chores, and paying bills.

It can be difficult and expensive to arrange a complete set of home care services, especially if you don't have support from family members. As a result, people who live alone and have major care needs are more likely to move into assisted-living facilities or a nursing home. Advanced planning is usually essential. You, your family, and health professionals collaborate in developing a plan of care.

The planning process rests on a geriatric assessment. Ideally, this looks at your environment, functional and mental status, socioeconomic position, and physical condition. Together with professionals, you'll assemble an individualized plan of care that:

- *Integrates* acute care and long term care;
- *Provides* services for mental health, rehabilitation, and prevention;
- *Integrates* medical care with other services;
- *Coordinates* paid and unpaid—and formal and informal—caregivers; *and*

• *Assures* the quality of the system and its direct services.

Specialists trained to help elders and others conduct a geriatrics assessment and develop plans for long term care and home care are available through local home care corporations. Mass Home Care and the Massachusetts Executive Office of Elder Affairs can refer you to local agencies for assistance. The Alzheimer's Federation of Eastern Massachusetts can also refer you to people who conduct geriatric assessments. Contact Mass Home Care's ElderLine at (800)AGE-INFO; the Office of Elder Affairs at (800)882-2003; or the Alzheimer's Federation at (617)494-5150.

The ElderLine—(800)AGE-INFO—serves as a clearinghouse for reaching home care corporations and can "direct-connect" you with any home care corporation in Massachusetts. These local home care agencies provide various social, supportive, and care services to elders on a free, reduced-fee, or sliding-scale basis. Services include: care management, chore services, companionship and escort, emergency services, home-delivered meals, homemaker services, personal-care attendants, information and referral services, legal services, respite care, social day care, and transportation.

The SHINE Program

To assist you with any questions about health insurance, the Massachusetts Executive Office of Elder Affairs operates the Senior Health Information Needs for Elders (SHINE) Program. Call to talk with a counselor for benefits information and free assistance with many different topics and programs, including Medicare, HMOs for Medicare beneficiaries, long term care insurance, Medicaid, Medigap, referrals, nursing home placements, and general information and complaints. Call (617)727-7750 or (800)882-2003 to find the location of the SHINE program office nearest you.

Local Councils on Aging also provide community-based services and are usually appointed by city or town governments to serve elders. Services may include health information and screening, referrals, meal programs, multi-service and drop-in senior centers, transportation, and other programs.

▼ **FOR MORE INFORMATION**
on ways to finance home care and long term care, contact the Massachusetts Executive Office of Elder Affairs at (800)882-2003 or call the ElderLine at (800)AGE-INFO for referral to one of the 27 agencies around the state that act as focal points for getting services.

Services in the Community

Most cities and towns provide a variety of community-based programs to serve senior citizens and help people continue to live at home. Many programs offer services to people in need of care and to their families—services such as meals, counseling, and referrals. In most case, you can begin your search for these services by calling the ElderLine at (800)AGE-INFO. Here are some of the most important services:

Adult day care covers a variety of health, social, and related support services for adults who have functional impairments and need supervision. Adult day-care centers often employ staff skilled in responding to the special needs of people with Alzheimer's.

Adult day health centers offer skilled health services, generally rehabilitation therapy or other services specifically related to health care. These centers may also help with specific tasks that are especially hard for a family to manage, such as bathing.

Congregate meal programs provide nutritious hot meals to older people in senior centers, schools, churches, and other community settings. Congregate meal programs provide at least one-third of the recommended daily diet, as do Meals on Wheels programs.

Senior centers, sometimes called multipurpose senior centers,

Congregate Housing

For many seniors who don't require constant supervision, congregate housing offers a long-term alternative to a nursing home. These residences integrate a cooperative living environment with supportive services on site or nearby. In part because people share certain facilities—kitchens, for example—congregate housing encourages residents to socialize and support one another.

are community or neighborhood facilities offering older people social and recreational opportunities and a broad spectrum of supportive services. Senior centers may provide health, educational, counseling, and legal services along with congregate meals.

Hospice programs assist people with terminal illnesses by offering comfort and controlling pain.

▼ FOR MORE INFORMATION
on hospices, turn to Page 159.

Legal-assistance programs have elder-law attorneys on staff or available by referral to handle such legal matters as reverse mortgages, estate planning, Medicaid planning, and nursing home insurance.

Assisted living units serve people who need daily assistance but not constant care. Most facilities for assisted living only admit residents who are not confined to a bed. Accommodations vary from single or double rooms to suites or apartments. Typical services include reminders about or physical assistance with meals, bathing, dressing, eating, medication, transportation, shopping, housekeeping, and other activities.

For Adults with Disabilities

Several state agencies offer services for adults with disabilities. Older adults are often unaware of these programs unless they have had a disability since early childhood.

• *The Massachusetts Rehabilitation Commission* offers information and referrals on vocational rehabilitation, personal-care assistance (no new referrals), and determination of eligibility for Social Security Disability Income (SSDI). For more information, call (617)727-2183 or (800)245-6543. For informal and referrals on home-care assistance, call (617)727-1595.

• *The Massachusetts Office on Disability* offers assistance and advocacy for gaining access to services. For more information, call (617)727-7440.

• *The Massachusetts Assistive Technology Partnership* provides information on assistive-technology products and services. "Assistive technology" refers to devices that ease life for a person with a disability. MATEP also has regional offices, an electronic bulletin board, and a newsletter. For more information call (800)848-8867 (voice or TDD) or (617)735-7153 (voice only).

• *The Massachusetts Commission for the Blind* offers a wide range of services to vision-impaired people, including support and education *in the home* for people who need help adapting to a vision loss and adapting their home for safe living. For more information, call (617)727-5550 (voice) or (800)392-6556 (voice or TDD).

• *The Massachusetts Commission for Deaf and Hard of Hearing* provides information, referrals, interpreter services, and some assistance with case management. For more information, call (617)727-5106 (voice) or (800)822-1155 (voice or TDD).

• *The Medicaid Personal Care Attendant Program* serves people who receive Medicaid, have permanent or chronic disabilities, *and* require physical assistance with any of the daily activities of daily living. The program enables you to hire and train your own personal-care worker in your home. For more information, contact your Medicaid social worker.

Elder Abuse

Elder abuse takes several basic forms, including neglect, physical or emotional injury, and financial exploitation. To report suspected abuse, call the Massachusetts Executive Office of Elder Affairs' elder-abuse hotline at (800)922-2275, 24 hours a day.

In most cases, your local home care corporation investigates reports of abuse and provides services to help end abusive situations. For example, Mass Home Care's Money Management Program helps prevent financial exploitation by offering one-on-one help in dealing with household expenses. Call the ElderLine: (800)AGE-INFO.

Elder Service Plans

In 1990, the East Boston Neighborhood Health Center opened the first Elder Service Plan in Massachusetts, modeled after a program started in 1988 in San Francisco. As an alternative to nursing-home care, these plans target elders who would be eligible for a nursing home, with the goal of enabling them to live at home with supportive services.

The Elder Service Plan consolidates care and financing in one local program. While it is not an HMO, it has some similar qualities. It works through primary care doctors who manage each person's care. And rather than providing one piece in a fragmented care system, the plan deals with many components, such as meals, home care, and day-care centers that meet many of the elder's social and medical needs.

There is no extra charge for those eligible for both Medicaid and Medicare. Those eligible for Medicare (and not Medicaid) and who have assets pay about $2,000 per month, compared to the $3,500-$4,000 that seniors usually pay out-of-pocket for nursing home care.

The Urban Medical Group opened the second Elder Service Plan on December 1, 1994, to serve residents of Allston, Back Bay, Brighton, Brookline, Jamaica Plain, Kenmore/Fenway, Roslindale, and West Roxbury. By early 1995, Elder Service Plans will open in Cambridge (operated by Cambridge City Hospital), Dorchester (Uphams Corner Health Center and Dimock Community Health Center together), Lynn (Lynn Community Health Center and Greater Lynn Senior Services together), Quincy (Manet Community Health Center), South Boston (Harbor Health Services and South Boston Community Health Center together), and Worcester (Fallon Community Health Plan).

▼ FOR MORE INFORMATION

on the Urban Medical Group Elder Service Plan, call (617)734-5198. For information on other Elder Service Plans, *turn to the listings for the community health centers that begin on Page 95.*

Hospice Care

As a culture, we often try to deny death. But dying patients usually know better. Even more than death, they fear isolation and pain. Probably the first and foremost need, and right, of dying patients is to know the truth about their situation. The "ignorance is bliss" attitude deprives a dying person of his or her last opportunity to accomplish goals and say things they would want to. We can make our deaths a bit easier—for our families and ourselves—by planning and by requiring health care professionals to take our humanity, our needs, and our rights seriously.

Hospice care is designed for people with a terminal illness who will probably die within six months. The hospice movement is built around the principle that people should be able to die at home and free from pain but without complex medical invasions of their bodies. Hospice care treats the physical as well as the emotional and spiritual needs of the patient, supports family members as an essential part of the mission, and values quality of life to be as much as length of life.

Medicare Hospices

To locate Medicare-approved hospice care in your area, contact the Hospice Federation of Massachusetts, 1420 Providence Hwy., Norwood 02062 (617)255-7077.

When a Medicare-eligible patient receives care from a Medicare-approved hospice, Medicare pays almost the entire cost for services and supplies for six months or more. In general, this coverage includes physician services, nursing care, counseling, medical equipment and supplies, drugs for managing symptoms and relieving pain, short-term inpatient and respite care, homemaker services and home health aides, and physical and other therapy. About three-quarters of U.S. hospice programs are either Medicare-certified or have certification pending. Hospice coverage replaces your usual hospital coverage under Medicare Part A. You can revoke the hospice benefit at any time to revert to the usual Part A benefits.

Even if you don't qualify for Medicare's hospice benefit, the health insurance of more than 80 percent of employees in medium and large companies covers hospice care. It's also covered under Medicaid/MassHealth. Most hospice patients receive their care under Medicare or Medicaid.

Hospices will assist families lacking insurance to explore other options for coverage. And most hospices will provide for anyone who can't pay, using money raised from the community or other donations.

FOR MORE INFORMATION
on death with dignity and preparing for when you can no longer make your own decisions about health care, turn to Chapter 12.

Resources

Alzheimer's Association of Eastern Massachusetts
1 Kendall Sq.
Cambridge 02139
(617)494-5150
Call for information on the symptoms and patterns of Alzheimer's disease, diagnostic evaluations, medical care, legal assistance, patient management and care, family and patient support groups, home care, day centers, respite care, and nursing homes.

American Association of Retired Persons New England Office
116 Huntington Ave.
Boston 02116-5739
(617)424-0400
AARP is the largest organization for Americans age 50 and over. It offers a wide range of benefits, including *Modern Maturity* magazine and the monthly "Bulletin." Call or write for membership information and a catalogue of publications and audio-visual materials. For legal assistance, contact AARP's Legal Council for the Elderly at (202)434-2120.

Boston Commission on Affairs of the Elderly
One City Hall Plaza
Boston 02201
(617)635-4000
Hotline: (617)635-4646
For general information, call 635-4000. Call 635-3000 for information about free transportation to medical appointments, food shopping, and social/recreational events. Call 635-3993 for information on retirement and government benefit programs. Call 635-4050 for information on blood pressure screening, vision screening, hearing screening, dental screening, pharmacist's advice, and health promotion. Call 635-3988 for the retired senior volunteer program, senior aides program, and senior companion program. Call 635-4877 for information, referral, and direct assistance for elder tenants and homeowners in all housing issues.

Home and Health Care Association of Massachusetts
20 Park Plaza
Boston 02116
(800)332-3500
Call for information and referrals on Medicare-covered home care.

Hospice Federation of Massachusetts
1420 Providence Hwy.
Norwood 02062
(617)255-7077
Call or write for information on hospice care, referrals, and the contact for hospice care in each community in Massachusetts.

Lifeline Foundation of Massachusetts
175 Paramount Dr.
Raynham 02767
(800)328-8824
Call for information about emergency notification systems.

Mass Home Care
24 Third Ave.
Burlington 01803
(617)272-7177
ElderLine: (800)AGE-INFO
Call the ElderLine for free information and referrals on a variety of elder-care topics, including home care, nursing homes, legal resources, medical-benefits programs, long term care insurance, smoking cessation, and more. The ElderLine will connect you for free with any Home Care Corporation/ Area Agency on Aging in Massachusetts. Also available is a free pamphlet, "Free Prescription Drug Programs for the Elderly," listing 51 national programs that offer reduced prices on 263 brand-name drugs.

Massachusetts Assisted Living Facility Association
139 Main St.
Cambridge 02142
(617)252-6511
Call or write for information on assisted-living options and availability. To order the *Guide to Assisted Living in Massachusetts*, send $15 plus $2 postage and handling.

Massachusetts Association of Older Americans
110 Arlington St.
Boston 02116
(617)426-0805
MAOA provides resources and information to bring knowledge and empowerment to elders in the areas of health, housing, and economic security. Health promotion services include free workshops and other services to educate women over age 60 about what they can do to protect themselves from breast cancer and cervical cancer and education programs for elders about the dangers of smoking and the benefits of quitting at any age.

Massachusetts Council for Home Care Aide Services
34 1/2 Beacon St.
Boston 02108
(617)523-6400
Contact the council for information and referrals for homemaker and home health aides.

Massachusetts Department of Public Health Division of Health Care Quality
10 West St.
Boston 02111
(617)727-5860
(800)462-5540
Call with complaints about quality of care by home health agencies, nursing homes, hospitals, and clinics in Massachusetts. Also use this number to report fraud and elder abuse.

Massachusetts Department of Public Welfare
600 Washington St.
Boston 02111
(617)348-8500 General information
(617)292-8900 Client services
(800)841-2900 for information on Medicaid eligibility and benefits.
(800)249-2007 Public Assistance Information Number for eligibility information on AFDC, food stamps, and EAEDC programs.
The division administers several medical assistance programs: Medicaid, the Specified Low-Income Medicare Beneficiary Program (SLMB), the Qualified Medicare Beneficiary Program (QMB), CommonHealth, and Emergency Aid to the Elderly, Disabled and Children (EAEDC).

Massachusetts Division of Insurance Consumer Services Section
470 Atlantic Ave.
Boston 02210
(617)521-7794
Consumer HelpLine: (617)521-7777
Call the Helpline with complaints about insurance claims, delays in payment, or denial of coverage. Ask for

free information packets on long term care, Medigap, and other topics, as well as a list of insurance carriers licensed in the state.

Massachusetts Division of Medical Assistance
600 Washington St.
Boston 02111
(617)348-5500
Call or write for information Medicaid/MassHealth, providers of adult foster care and adult day health care, home health agencies, hospitals, home care corporations, housing organizations, and other community agencies.

Massachusetts Executive Office of Elder Affairs
One Ashburton Pl.
Boston 02108
(617)727-7750
(800)882-2003
Elder Abuse Hotline: (800)922-2275 (24 hours).
Information and Referrals: (800)882-2003 (9 a.m.-5 p.m.)
Ombudsman Program: (617)727-7750
Office of Alzheimer's Information: (617)727-7750; (800)351-2299; (800)872-0166 TDD
Call or write for information about the Home Care Program for Elders in the Commonwealth of Massachusetts or for a list of Home Care Corporations/ Area Agencies on Aging.

Call the Ombudsman Program to report patient-care complaints such as dietary issues, abuse, visitation problems, and lost or stolen personal items. Every nursing home in the state of Massachusetts has a weekly visitor, usually a retired health care professional.

Call or write for a free copy of "Alzheimer's Disease: Principles of Caregiving and Resources for Caregivers," "A Consumer's Guide to Nursing Homes and Rest Homes," "Consumer's Guide to Long Term Care," "Continuing Care Retirement Communities," "Directory of Long Term Care Facilities," "Legal Handbook for Massachusetts Elders," "Medicare and Managed Care Plans," "Prescription Drug Assistance Programs: How to Apply," and "Retirement Housing in Massachusetts."

Massachusetts Federation of Nursing Homes
990 Washington St.
Dedham 02026
(800)227-3367
Call or write for an Assisted Living Directory or Nursing Home Directory to locate these services in your area.

Massachusetts Office of the Attorney General Medicaid Fraud Control Unit
131 Tremont St.
Boston 02111-1317
(617)727-2200
Contact the office to report patient abuse, neglect, and mistreatment in nursing facilities and acute and chronic care settings.

Massachusetts Senior Action Council
277 Broadway
Somerville 02145
(617)776-3100
Boston office: 90 South St., Jamaica Plain 02130 (617)524-8088
MSAC, the Massachusetts chapter of the National Council of Senior Citizens, uses organizing, advocacy, and public education to promote social justice for all. Contact MSAC if you have any problems related to health care. Members can also receive legal assistance on Medicare and other matters through the Law Plan benefit, which offers a panel of attorneys at reduced fees. MSAC's *Source Book for Seniors* ($5.95) contains information on health, housing, income assistance, insurance, legal services, nutrition, personal care, and transportation. In addition, MSAC has published *Knowing Your Rights as a Medicare Patient* ($3) and *What You Should Know About Medigap Insurance Options* ($3).

MassPRO
Massachusetts Peer Review Organization
235 Wyman St.
Waltham 02154-1231
Information Line: (800)252-5533
(617)890-0011
Medicare beneficiaries can call MassPRO for information about coverage, to ask questions about hospital care, and to pursue rights to care in hospital. Call if you have questions about hospital benefits, concerns over hospital bills or the quality of care, or want to appeal a hospital-issued Notice of Non-Coverage from a hospital.

National Association of Area Agencies on Aging
1112 16th St., NW
Washington, DC 20036
(202)296-8130
The association runs the Eldercare Locator for identifying information and referral services provided by state and local Agencies on Aging. Call (800)677-1116 to get free referrals to elder services in your area and to order a copy of *The National Directory for Eldercare Information and Referral.*

National Association of Private Geriatric Care Managers
655 N. Alvernon Way
Tucson, AZ 85711
(602)881-8008
Call or write for referrals to geriatric care managers. You can also order a national directory for $35.

National Council on the Aging
409 Third St., SW
Washington, DC 20024
(202)479-1200
Call or write for publications and information on elder services, independent living, and other forms of long term care.

U.S. Department of Health and Human Services
Social Security Administration
Baltimore, MD 21235
(800)772-1213
Call with questions about eligibility, coverage, and costs for Medicare, Social Security, and Supplemental Security Income. Free pamphlets include "The Medicare Handbook," "SSI," and "Understanding Social Security."

Visiting Nurse Association of Eastern Massachusetts
162 Highland Ave.
Somerville 02143
(617)623-3600
(800)696-6666
Call to arrange for nurses and home health aides for home health care, including care for elders, infants, children, people needing therapy, people with HIV home care, and hospice.

Legal Assistance

Boston College Legal Assistance Bureau
24 Crescent St.
Waltham 02154
(617)893-4793
Free legal counseling for Medicare recipients in Belmont, Brookline, Needham, Newton, Waltham, Watertown, Wellesley, and Weston.

Cambridge and Somerville Legal Services
432 Columbia St.
Cambridge 02141
(617)494-1800
Free legal counseling and referral for Medicare recipients in Acton, Arlington, Belmont, Boxborough, Cambridge, Concord, Littleton, Maynard, Somerville, Stow, Wilmington, Winchester, and Woburn.

Greater Boston Elderly Legal Services
102 Norway St.
Boston 02115
(617)536-0400
(800)323-3205
The statewide Medicare Advocacy Project operates out of this office, providing free advice and representation for elderly and disabled Massachusetts residents who have been denied Medicare coverage for health care or home care services. For other issues, call your local legal services office. This office serves Boston, Braintree, Chelsea, Cohasset, Everett, Hingham, Holbrook, Hull, Malden, Medford, Melrose, Milton, Norwell, Quincy, Randolph, North Reading, Reading, Revere, Scituate, Stoneham, Wakefield, Weymouth, Winthrop, and Wollaston. For residents in these areas, it provides free or low-cost advice and representation for issues of income entitlements of all sorts, including Medicare and Medicaid, as well as advice and representation for all nursing home residents on questions of resident rights.

Neighborhood Legal Services
37 Friend St.
Lynn 01902
(617)599-7730
(800)747-5056
Free legal counseling for Medicare recipients in Beverly, Beverly Farms, Danvers, Essex, Gloucester, Hamilton, South Hamilton, Ipswich, Lynn, Lynnfield, Magnolia, Manchester, Marblehead, Middleton, Nahant, Peabody, Pride's Crossing, Rockport, Salem, Saugus, Swampscott, Topsfield, and Wenham.

South Middlesex Legal Services Senior Citizens' Project
354 Waverly St.
Framingham 01701
(508)620-1830
(617)235-7428
(800)696-1501
Free legal counseling for Medicare recipients in Ashland, Canton, Dedham, Dover, Foxborough, Framingham, Holliston, Hopkinton, Hudson, Marlborough, Medfield, Millis, Natick, Norfolk, Northborough, Norwood, Plainville, Sharon, Sherborn, Sudbury, Walpole, Wayland, Westborough, Westwood, and Wrentham.

Chapter 7 Mental Health

Mental illness encompasses a variety of disorders that range in severity. That is, they result in greater and lesser degrees of mental well-being. Furthermore, mental well-being is dynamic: some people experience severe short-term problems, while others have long-term conditions with symptoms that occur only intermittently.

Most people receiving mental health care live at home and visit providers for appointments. In the private sector, you'll generally receive care in practitioners' offices. In addition, many public outpatient mental health clinics and organizations provide services. Community mental health centers, in particular, are prime providers of mental health care. Also, some psychiatric clinics operate under the auspices of general hospitals, mental hospitals, Veterans Affairs medical centers, and family-service agencies, and hospitals provide psychiatric or psychological treatment in emergency rooms.

To find out about the appropriate mental health services for you, you can begin by checking the listings that follow or consulting:

- The Massachusetts Department of Mental Health;
- The Massachusetts Department of Social Services;

- The Massachusetts Department of Public Health;
- Religious social-services agencies;
- Your priest, rabbi, or minister;
- Neighborhood service centers; *and*
- Local hospitals and health clinics.

▼ **FOR MORE INFORMATION**
about the rights of people receiving mental health services in Massachusetts, turn to chapter 12.

Money Matters

All Massachusetts insurance policies that cover mental health must reimburse mental health services provided by comprehensive health service organizations, licensed or accredited hospitals, community mental health centers, other mental health clinics, and day-care centers that furnish mental health services. Policies must cover consultations by psychotherapists, psychologists, licensed independent clinical social workers, and clinical specialists in psychiatric or mental health nursing.

When assessing the mental health coverage of an insurance plan, ask:

- What services does it cover, such as family counseling, substance-abuse counseling, children's mental health?
- How do you get care? Do you need a referral? Must you use a provider on a restricted list?

Mistreatment in the Mental Health System

The federal government funds Protection and Advocacy for Individuals with Mental Illness (PAIMI) programs in every state. These programs offer referrals and information on the rights of people with mental and developmental disabilities, answer questions about discrimination in housing or employment, and handle complaints of abuse or neglect in mental health facilities.

The Massachusetts PAIMI office is the Center for Public Representation, 22 Green St., Northampton 01060 (413)584-1644, with a Boston office at 246 Walnut St., Newton 02160 (617)965-0776.

• What criteria does it use to exclude people from mental health benefits?

• What is the extra premium for mental health coverage, if there is one?

• What portion of mental health bills will you have to pay?

• What are the annual or lifetime limits on the quantity of treatment?

• Does an outside company contract with the insurer to provide the mental health benefits? If so, who decides what mental health services are covered in each case?

If your insurance doesn't cover mental health, several federal and state programs can pay for some treatment for some people. In Massachusetts, Medicaid covers mental health services as well as related services such as physician services, community health center services, inpatient and outpatient care, prescription drugs and non-prescription drugs necessary for life and safety, rehabilitative care and therapies, home health care and personal care attendants, adult day health services, and drug treatment. If you receive Aid to Families with Dependent Children, Supplemental Security Income, or Refugee Resettlement Program assistance, you are automatically eligible for Medicaid. Otherwise, you must meet the basic, categorical, and financial eligibility criteria.

The Department of Medical Security of the Massachusetts Department of Health and Human Services administers three programs that provide for some mental health coverage. The Medical Security Plan covers psychiatric care and substance-abuse services for people receiving unemployment benefits. You should receive infor-

Sliding Scales

If you are not eligible for Medicaid, the Massachusetts Department of Mental Health offers some services through its clinics with charges based on your ability to pay. The Boston area also benefits from a strong network of community mental health centers that offer many services with sliding-scale fees. *For more information on DMH-operated facilities in your area, turn to Page 170. For more information on community health centers, turn to Page 95 and the listings at the end of this chapter.*

mation and an application for this program with your first unemployment check; if you don't, call Blue Cross/Blue Shield of Massachusetts at (800)914-4455 for information. The Children's Medical Security Plan covers outpatient mental health care for children if recommended by a physician. It pays for up to 13 visits per child per year for a nominal copayment of $1 to $5, depending on income. The CenterCare program offers free care at some health centers. For information about these programs, contact the Department of Medical Security, One Ashburton Pl., Rm. 1105, Boston 02108, (800)238-0990.

▼ FOR MORE INFORMATION
about insurance, turn to Chapter 1.

Credentials and Certification

A number of different agencies license mental health facilities and providers. You can contact these agencies to inquire whether a facility or practitioner is licensed or to file a complaint related to your care.

The Massachusetts Department of Mental Health licenses psychiatric hospitals and psychiatric units in general hospitals which admit patients on an involuntary basis. Call (617)727-5600.

The Massachusetts Department of Public Health licenses independent mental health clinics, which should display this certification prominently. No facility can operate without this certification. Call (617)727-5860.

The Massachusetts Board of Registration in Medicine licenses psychiatrists, who are medical doctors. Call (617)727-3086.

The Massachusetts Division of Registration licenses most other mental health professionals. Within the division, the Board of Psychologists licenses clinical psychologists (617)727-9925; the Board of Allied Mental Health licenses mental health counselors, marriage and family therapists, rehabilitation counselors, and educational psychologists (617)727-1716; and the Board of Social Workers licenses clinical social workers (617)727-3073. Massachusetts does not license psychotherapists per se.

Resources

Alliance for the Mentally Ill of Massachusetts
295 Devonshire St.
Boston 02111
(617)426-2299
The Massachusetts affiliate of the National Alliance for the Mentally Ill, AMI provides support, information, referrals, education, and advocacy for consumers and families affected by severe mental illness. Membership of $25 per year includes the newsletter.

Disabled Person's Protection Commission
99 Bedford St.
Boston 02111
(617)727-6465
(800)426-9009, 24-hour abuse hotline
The commission provide services to help prevent physical, mental, or sexual abuse of disabled people (including mentally and developmentally disabled) aged 18-59 by any public or private caretaker. Call or write for free copies of their brochures "Indicators of Abuse" and "A Guide to the Investigational Process of DPPC."

Family Services of Greater Boston
Center for Counseling
Local centers offer family counseling, home-based substance-abuse counseling, and counseling and support programs for elders and victims of sexual abuse. There are three centers in the Boston area:

34 1/2 Beacon St.
Boston 02108
(617)523-6400

389 Main St.
Malden 02148
(617)324-8181

20 Whitney Rd.
Quincy 02169
(617)471-0630

Massachusetts Department of Mental Health
25 Staniford St.
Boston 02114
(617)727-5600, ext. 436
Call or write for a free copy of the *Resource Guide to the Department of Mental Health*, which contains local contacts for comprehensive mental-health services, or the pamphlet, "Understanding People with Mental Illnesses: What You Should Know."

Massachusetts Department of Mental Health
Office of Consumer and Ex-Patient Relations
(800)221-0053
Call for referrals to specialists, to register a complaint, and to receive information about mental health services and peer support. All calls are confidential.

Massachusetts Department of Mental Health Area Offices
Contact your area office for comprehensive services, including acute care (emergency and crisis intervention), supportive mental health and rehabilitation services, and community-based services. Ask for information about sliding-scale fees.

Metro-Boston
Department of Mental Heath
20 Vining St.
Boston 02115
(617)727-4923
Emergency line: (800)981-HELP
Serves Boston, Brookline, Cambridge, Chelsea, Revere, Somerville, and Winthrop.

Metro South
Medfield State Hospital
45 Hospital Rd.
Medfield 02052
(508)359-7312, ext. 600
(617)727-9830
Serves Braintree, Canton, Cohasset, Dedham, Foxborough, Hingham, Hull, Medfield, Millis, Milton, Needham,

Newton, Norfolk, Norwell, Norwood, Plainville, Quincy, Randolph, Scituate, Sharon, Walpole, Wellesley, Weston, Westwood, Weymouth, and Wrentham.

Metro West
Westborough State Hospital
P.O. Box 288 Lyman St.
Westborough 01581
(508)792-7400, ext. 2073
Serves Acton, Arlington, Ashland, Bedford, Belmont, Boxborough, Burlington, Carlisle, Concord, Dover, Framingham, Holliston, Hopkinton, Hudson, Lexington, Lincoln, Littleton, Maynard, Marlborough, Natick, Northborough, Sherborn, Southborough, Stow, Sudbury, Waltham, Watertown, Wayland, Westborough, Wilmington, Winchester, and Woburn.

Emergency Hotlines

Al-Anon/Alateen
639 Granite St.
Braintree 02184
(617)843-5300
Call to find out about meetings for people affected by a loved one's alcoholism.

Alcohol and Drug Hotline
(617)445-1500
(800)327-5050
Call for referrals to halfway houses, outpatient counselors, battered women's shelters, and facilities for detoxification, rehabilitation, and urinalysis. Information on AIDS/HIV is also available.

Alcoholics Anonymous Eastern Massachusetts Office
368 Congress St.
Boston 02210
(617)426-9444

Bridge Over Troubled Waters
147 Tremont St.
Boston 02108
(617)423-9575
This suicide hotline works with runaway and homeless adolescents and provides shelter, education, counseling, and medical services.

Contact
P.O. Box 287
Newtonville 02160
(617)244-4350
For youths: (617)244-1155
Call this personal-crisis and suicide hotline for resolving any kind of problem.

The Samaritans
500 Commonwealth Ave.
Boston 02215
(617)247-0220
73 Union St.
Framingham 01701
(508)875-4500
Call or visit for confidential help if you are suicidal or despairing.

The Samariteens
500 Commonwealth Ave.
Boston 02215
(617)247-8050
536-6262
Call or visit for counseling by and for teenagers

Substance Abuse Services Hotline
Massachusetts Department of Public Health
(617)727-1960

Massachusetts Psychiatric Society
40 Washington St.
Wellesley 02181
(617)237-8100
(800)831-3134
Call for referrals to psychiatrists and for certification information on a psychiatrist you are considering.

Massachusetts Psychological Association
14 Beacon St.
Boston 02108
(617)720-1546
Call for referrals to psychologists.

Massachusetts Division of Registration
Board of Psychologists
100 Cambridge St.
Boston 02202
(617)727-9925
Call for information on certification of psychologists.

National Association of Social Workers
Massachusetts Affiliate
14 Beacon St.
Boston 02108
(617)720-2828
(800)242-9794
Call or write for confidential referrals to licensed social workers for mental-health counseling. Information available on providers about specialties, skills, location, fees, groups, licensing, and other information.

Northeastern Society for Group Psychotherapy
P.O. Box 356
Belmont 02178
(617)484-4994
Call for referrals to a variety of group psychotherapists.

Community Mental Health Centers

Community mental health centers provide a range of services, usually with sliding-fee scales. In addition to the facilities listed below, most community health centers also provide a variety of mental health services. *For those addresses and phone numbers, turn to the listings that begin on Page 95.*

The Dr. Solomon Fuller Carter Mental Health Center
85 E. Newton St.
Boston 02118
(617)266-8800 or 727-7510

Center House
81 Bowker St.
Boston 02114
(617)723-6300

Beacon Hill Multicultural Psychological Associates
14 Beacon St.
Boston 02108
(617)720-3413

Brighton/Allston Mental Health Clinic
77 Warren St.
Brighton 02135
(617)787-1901

Dorchester Counseling Center
622 Washington St.
Dorchester 02124
(617)282-1511

East Boston/Winthrop Counseling Center
14 Porter St.
East Boston 02128
(617)569-3189

Bay Cove Mental Health Center
Shattuck Hospital
170 Morton St.
Jamaica Plain 02130
(617)522-8110 ext. 488

West Roslindale Park Mental Health Center
1295 River St.
Hyde Park 02136
(617)364-6380

Boston Community Services
780 American Legion Highway
Roslindale 02131
(617)325-6700
TDD: (617)325-3533

Roxbury Multi Service Center
Family Life Center
317 Blue Hill Ave.
Roxbury 02121
(617)427-4470

Arlington Youth
Consultation Center
1670 Rear Massachusetts Ave.
Arlington 02174
(617)641-5478
Serves Arlington residents only

Center for Mental Health Retardation Services
742 Massachusetts Ave.
Arlington 02174
(617)646-7300

Appleton Outpatient Clinic/
Higginson House
McLean Clinic
115 Mill St.
Belmont 02178
(617)855-3361

Brookline Community
Mental Health Center
43 Garrison Rd.
Brookline 02146
(617)277-8107

Cambridge/Somerville
Mental Health Center
12 Maple Ave.
Cambridge 02139
(617)491-0600

Cambridge Mental
Health Association
5 Sacramento St.
Cambridge 02139
(617)354-2275

Malden Center for Counseling
389 Main St.
Malden 02148
(617)324-8181

Marblehead Community
Counseling Center
66 Clifton Ave.
Marblehead 01945
(617)631-8273

Needham Guidance Clinic
46 Hillside Ave.
Needham 02194
(617)449-1884

Newton Guidance Clinic
64 Eldredge St.
Newton 02158
(617)969-4925

Cutler Center
Norfolk Mental Health Association
Outpatient Service Center
886 Washington St.
Norwood 02062
(617)762-6592

Riverside Community Mental Health and Retardation Center
190 Lenox St.
Norwood 02062
(617)769-8670 or 769-8674

Sexual Abuse Treatment Unit
20 Whitney Rd.
Quincy 02169
(617)471-0630

Quincy Mental Health Center
460 Quincy Ave.
Quincy 02169
(617)727-1250 or 770-4000

Revere Mental Health Center
265 Beach St.
Revere 02151
(617)289-9331

Somerville Mental Health Center
63 College Ave.
Somerville
(617)623-3278

Eastern Middlesex Human Services
338 Main St.
Wakefield 01884
(617)246-2010 or 245-0344

Beaverbrook Guidance Center
118 Central St.
Waltham 02154
(617)891-0555

Beaverbrook Guidance Center
127 N. Beacon St.
Watertown 02172
(617)926-4055

Psychiatric Hospitals

Psychiatric hospitals provide inpatient and outpatient care for mental illnesses. The hospitals listed here are accredited by the Joint Commission on Accreditation of Healthcare Organizations.

McLean Hospital, Belmont
(617)855-2000
Arbour Hospital, Jamaica Plain
(617)522-4400
Dorchester Mental Health Center, Dorchester (617)436-6000
Bournewood Hospital, Brookline
(617)469-0300
Human Resource Institute, Brookline
(617)731-3200
Edith Nourse Rogers Memorial Veterans Hospital, Bedford
(617)275-7500
Medfield State Hospital, Medfield
(508)359-7312
Heritage Hospital, Somerville
(617)625-8900
Charles River Hospital, Wellesley
(617)235-8400
Westwood Lodge Hospital, Westwood
(617)762-7764
Choate Health System, Woburn
(617)933-6700
West Roxbury Veterans Affairs Medical Center, West Roxbury
(617)323-7700

General Hospitals with Psychiatric Facilities

Many general hospitals provide care for mental health crises, as well as a variety of inpatient and outpatient services related to mental health. In addition, in case of a crisis—when a person is violent or suicidal, for example—the emergency room of your local hospital can be the appropriate place to go.

The following hospitals all provide some mental health services. For addresses, phone numbers, and other information, turn to the hospital listings that begin on Page 98:

Atlanticare Medical Center
Beverly Hospital
Beth Israel Hospital
Boston City Hospital
Boston University Medical Center
Brigham and Women's Hospital
Cambridge Hospital
Carney Hospital
Children's Hospital
Emerson Hospital
Faulkner Hospital
Massachusetts General Hospital
Malden Hospital
Melrose-Wakefield Hospital
Mount Auburn Hospital
New England Deaconess Hospital
New England Medical Center
New England Memorial Hospital
Newton-Wellesley Hospital
North Shore Medical Center
Norwood Hospital
Quincy Hospital
St. Elizabeth's Hospital of Boston
Somerville Hospital
Veterans Affairs Medical Center
Whidden Memorial Hospital
WalthamWeston Hospital

Chapter 8 Dental Care

More important than anything a dentist can do for you is what you do for yourself. Thus, you want a dentist or dental hygienist who thoroughly explains proper brushing and flossing and advises you on selecting the best type of brush, floss, fluoride toothpaste, and other supplies. Equally important, the dentist or hygienist should have you demonstrate your technique periodically so she or he can suggest improvements. If your dentist doesn't do this automatically, ask him or her to do so.

The Qualities to Seek

While the most important steps you can take to promote dental health can be done within your own home, it's also essential to get regular professional care and maintain a good relationship with your dentist and dental hygienist.

Many aspects of prevention require regular office visits, so you want a dentist who notifies you when you need to come in for regular checkups and care. For example, one key to prevention is regular "scaling" by a dentist or hygienist to remove the calculus (hardened plaque) that accumulates on your teeth.

Another is diagnosis and treatment of decay and gum disease at an early stage.

In addition, a good dentist:

• Takes a thorough medical history at the first exam and updates the history at each subsequent visit;

• Gives you complete, up-to-date instructions on how to care for your teeth;

• Asks you questions and carefully inspects your mouth during each exam;

• Explains your options and provides a written treatment plan before major procedures;

• Shows concern for your safety and comfort by wearing gloves to prevent the spread of infection and using lead aprons to protect you during X-rays;

• Works efficiently and gently;

Finding a Dentist

The best way to start looking for a dentist is to consult friends, especially those with dental-care needs similar to yours. When you identify a few dentists who seem right, press your friends for more details and check out the dentists yourself.

Ask your friends:

- Does the dentist discuss any symptoms you have, such as loose teeth, bleeding gums, pain when eating, or a continual bad taste in your mouth?
- Does the dentist check your technique in flossing and brushing?
- Does the dentist explain diagnosis, treatment plans, and costs?
- Does the dentist offer alternatives?
- Does the dentist encourage second opinions in complex cases?
- Does the dentist have a pleasant, clean office and a pleasant staff?
- How long do you wait in the waiting room? In the dental chair?
- Does the dentist arrange an appointment quickly when needed?

Typical Charges

Health Care Choices surveyed dentists in the Boston area about their fees. Presented here are the range of prices quoted for several standard services:

Initial Exam, including cleaning, a consultation, and, occasionally, X-rays and fluoride treatment
High: $60
Low: $15
Most Common: $35-$40

Adult cleaning, sometimes including fluoride treatment
High: $80
Low: $40
Most Common: $55-$60

Full set of X-rays: 14-20 films or a panoramic film, to be done every 3-5 years
High: $93
Low: $45
Most Common: $60-$80

4 bite-wing X-rays: most common of the X-ray procedures
High: $80
Low: $20
Most Common: $25-$35

2 bite-wing X-rays
High: $55
Low: $15
Most Common: $15-$20

Fluoride treatment
High: $77
Low: $15
Most Common: $15-$30

Simple extraction
High: $100
Low: $50
Most Common: $60-$85

• Leaves you with a comfortable bite and nicely finished tooth surfaces; *and*

• Tailors care to each individual—for example, by scheduling different intervals between visits depending on each patient's risk for dental disease.

Dentists often vary on these and other items of concern to consumers, although this variation doesn't necessarily translate directly into important differences in quality. Most consumers consider their dentists adequate or better. In all cases, the relationship between you and your dentist is very personal, and a dentist others don't like might be just right for you. Nonetheless, asking questions may prove useful as you begin your search.

Reduced-Fee Dental Clinics

Several clinics below offer dental services at a substantial discount. Much of the work at these clinics is performed by dental and dental hygiene students supervised by dentists. Besides price, another advantage of schools is that you often receive more comprehensive care during a routine visit so that students can get thorough training.

These clinics have drawbacks. Because students are learning, your visits will be longer—and your mouth will be open longer. This means some additional discomfort. And you run a small risk if a new student treats you. For more complicated problems, you might prefer a more advanced student—but then your dentist might graduate before you get follow-up care. In sum, they are a good resource for a person on a limited income and with the time to spend at the clinic.

A Low-Cost Alternative

Many community health centers have dental facilities and charge for care on a sliding-scale basis. For information on which centers provide dental care, contact the Massachusetts League of Community Health Centers at (617)426-2225 or the Boston Community Dental Program at (617)534-4717.

- Boston University, Goldman School of Graduate Dentistry, 100 East Newton St., Boston 02118 (617)638-4700;
- Brookline Public Health Department, 11 Pierce St., Brookline 02146 (617)730-2326—serving income-eligible Brookline children up to age 18;
- Forsyth Dental Clinic, 140 The Fenway St., Boston 02115 (617)262-5200;
- Harvard Dental Clinic, 188 Longwood Ave., Boston 02115 (617)432-1416;
- Massachusetts Dental Society, Dentistry for All Program, 83 Speen St., Natick 01760 (800)342-8747—for patients on a fixed income and lacking dental insurance;
- Middlesex Community College, Dental Hygiene Program, Springs Rd., Bedford 01730 (617)275-2383;
- Tufts Dental Clinic, One Kneeland St., Boston 02111 (617)956-6828.

This chapter is adapted from Checkbook *Magazine, published by the Center for the Study of Services.*

Resources

Massachusetts Dental Society
83 Speen St.
Natick 01760
(508)651-7511
(800)342-8747
Call or write about the Dental Referral Program to receive a list of dentists in your area, the Dentistry for All Program for low-income individuals and families without dental insurance, the Council on Dental Care for handicap and special-needs referrals, and the Peer Review Committee to file a complaint about a dentist or practice.

Massachusetts Board of Registration in Dentistry
100 Cambridge St.
Boston 02202
(617)727-9928
Call or write to get background and licensing information on specific dentists.

Department of Public Health Office of Oral Health
150 Tremont St.
Boston 02111
(617)727-0732
Call for referrals to dentists specializing in care for people with disabilities and for listings of dentists who accept sliding-scale fees. Also available are pamphlets on oral hygiene.

Boston Department of Health and Hospitals Community Dental Program
1010 Massachusetts Ave.
Boston 02118
(617)534-4717
Call or write for information on access to dental care for Boston residents or for assistance with consumer complaints about dental care. An HIV Dental Ombudsperson handles complaints about discrimination in dentistry against people with HIV and educates dentists and the public about HIV. The office also helps HIV-infected people in Greater Boston locate dental care.

Chapter 9
Eye Care

Over half the people in the United States wear eyeglasses or contact lenses. Unfortunately, many forms of medical insurance don't cover eyeglasses or contact lenses, so price is a critical factor. Moreover, the differences in both quality and cost among the different types of eye-care providers, let alone the providers of a single variety, are difficult to determine. To a large extent, you must rely on your own initiative as you seek the best place to buy your eyeglasses or contact lenses.

The Three Os

In general, you can seek eye care from three types of provider.

Ophthalmologists are physicians who specialize in eye disorders. They check eyes for vision problems, diseases, abnormalities, and symptoms of such general bodily disorders as diabetes and hypertension. They treat eyes with drugs, surgery, and other means, and they prescribe corrective glasses and contact lenses. Most ophthalmologists expect you to get eyeglasses elsewhere, but quite a few dispense contacts.

Optometrists are not physicians but are called doctors. Like ophthalmologists, they give eye exams, looking for a wide range of eye problems as well as symptoms of general health problems. They are limited in the range of drugs they can prescribe. Some use visual therapy to counter certain eye problems, and most prescribe and dispense eyeglasses and contact lenses.

Opticians have less training than ophthalmologists or optometrists. Opticians can't write prescriptions. Using a prescription from an ophthalmologist or optometrist, they fit, supply, and adjust glasses and sometimes contacts. A few opticians grind eyeglass lenses to the correct prescription, but most buy the lenses from a wholesaler and fit them into a frame.

The Eye Exam

Get your eyes checked every one to two years; less often if you have no eye problems. A thorough vision exam takes 30 to 60 minutes.

The exam should include:

- A complete health history taken at the start of the examination;
- An inspection of the exterior and interior of your eyes for signs of disease;
- A test of your ability to see sharply and clearly at all distances;
- A test of your eye's ability to focus light rays exactly on the retina;
- A check of eye coordination and eye muscle control;
- A test of your eyes' ability to change focus; *and*
- A glaucoma test.

The exam may also include special tests for color perception, depth perception, field of vision, and other vision skills.

The Choice: Glasses or Contacts

If you have a recent prescription from an ophthalmologist or optometrist, your next step may be determined largely by your preference: do you want eyeglasses or contact lenses?

If you prefer glasses, you can go to any optician or optometrist. Many opticians and optometrists dispense contact lenses as well, as do many ophthalmologists.

Although most practitioners dispense contact lenses based on a recent prescription you've gotten elsewhere, some insist on doing their own exam. They argue that providing contact lenses is a professional service in which the exam, the supplying of lenses, and follow-up care must go together to produce a consistently safe and satisfactory result. Other practitioners dispute this view—especially opticians, who can't do exams.

If you do take a prescription to a different location to be filled, a prescription from the past year is usually considered new enough; some practitioners let you go back further, particularly for glasses, depending on your age and eye-care history.

If you don't have a current prescription, you can get one at many places. While opticians can't give an exam, you can get one at some optician practices and chain outlets if an optometrist works in the office or an affiliated office nearby.

This chapter is adapted from Checkbook *Magazine, published by the Center for the Study of Services.*

Typical Charges

Health Care Choices surveyed eye-care providers in the Boston area about their fees. Presented here are the ranges of prices quoted for several standard services:

Eye exam for glasses
High: $90
Low: $34
Most common: $40-$50

Eyeglass lenses without frames
High: $99
Low: $45
Most common: $60-$70
Note: Frames range from $30-$300 depending on style.

Eye exam for contact lenses
High: $99
Low: $50
Most common: $70-$75

Daily-wear soft contact lenses
High: $200
Low: $25
Most common: $60-$90

Three-month supply of disposable contact lenses
High: $190
Low: $45
Most common: $100-$130

Resources

Massachusetts Society of Optometrists
101 Tremont St.
Boston 02108
(617)542-9200
Call or write for referrals, general information, and information on vision therapy.

Massachusetts Society of Eye Physicians and Surgeons
38 Willard Grant Rd.
Sudbury 01776
(617)426-2020
Call or write for referrals and for pamphlets on medical eye care.

New England Eye Institute
1255 Boylston St.
Boston 02215
(617)262-2020
Call for information on reduced-fee services and on the Home Eye Care Service for elderly and home-bound patients.

Massachusetts Board of Registration in Optometry
100 Cambridge St.
Boston 02202
(617)727-1818
Call or write for licensing and background information on a specific optometrist.

National Eye Care Project
P.O. Box 429098
San Francisco, CA 94142
(800)222-EYES
Operated by the American Academy of Ophthalmology, the NECP is a nationwide program to provide medical eye care to disadvantaged senior citizens. The project refers people 65 or older to participating ophthalmologists for diagnosis and follow-up care. Qualifying patients receive treatment at no out-of-pocket expense.

Chapter 10 Workplace Illness and Injury

Work can endanger your health. Every day, about 200 Massachusetts workers are injured severely enough to lose at least five days of work. Every week in the commonwealth, about two people die from acute on-the-job injuries. Every month, more than 100 workers are diagnosed with cancer related to their jobs. And workplace illness and injury are occurring more and more frequently due to the rapid pace and repetitive nature of many of today's jobs, as well as the widespread use of toxic chemicals.

You *don't* have to endure unhealthy conditions. Working to support yourself and your family doesn't have to mean compromising your health.

The causes of many workplace *injuries* are usually obvious—and almost always preventable. Proper guards and maintenance for machinery, adequate rest periods, and good training programs go a long way toward preventing calamities.

Unfortunately, it's usually much harder to recognize when *illnesses* result from work. In the first place, most occupational illnesses closely resemble those that result from other causes. A bakery worker with occupational asthma may wheeze and cough pretty much the same as another asthma victim. In addition, symptoms can show up long after a person is exposed to hazardous materials. Cancers and other diseases may appear many years later, perhaps well after the victim has left the job. Even the patient can easily fail to connect his or her illness to workplace origins.

Fortunately, many organizations and agencies can help you identify harmful workplace conditions, find assistance when you confront risks to your health and safety, and actively work with your health care providers to get the best treatment.

Workers Compensation

Workers compensation provides insurance for job-related injuries or illnesses. It can pay doctor and hospital bills, part of your salary if you can't work, and benefits to your family if you are killed on the job. Most employers must buy this insurance for their employees.

To file a claim, contact the Massachusetts Department of Industrial Accidents, 600 Washington St., Boston 02111 (617)727-4900.

To learn more about workers compensation, call (800)338-6004 to receive a free guide, *The Massachusetts Workers' Compensation Act*, by Robert M. Schwartz. In

Massachusetts Coalition for Occupational Safety and Health

Established by unions and health care professionals, MassCOSH provides information and training to workers and unions on occupational health and safety hazards, develops strategies to control hazards, and offers workers information about their legal rights. It also provides written and audiovisual materials in English and Spanish and has special expertise in the area of reproductive hazards. MassCOSH can refer workers to occupational medicine clinics, relevant state and federal agencies, and attorneys who handle workers compensation and other cases related to workplace health and safety. For more information, contact MassCOSH, 555 Amory St., Jamaica Plain 02130 (617)524-6686.

addition, the Western Massachusetts Committee on Occupational Safety and Health will publish a guide to workers compensation in mid-1995, with English and Spanish editions. For more information, contact Western MassCOSH at (413)731-0760.

Occupational Health Services

To locate a clinic that offers occupational health services, contact:

- Association of Occupational and Environmental Clinics, 1010 Vermont Ave., NW, Washington, DC 20005 (202)347-4976;
- MassCOSH, 555 Amory St., Jamaica Plain 02130 (617)525-6686;
- New England College of Occupational and Environmental Medicine, Harvard School of Public Health, 665 Huntington Ave., Boston 02115 (617)432-3314; *or*
- Any other university-based occupational health program. The Boston University School of Public Health and the Tufts University School of Medicine both have such programs.

Resources

Bowdoin Street Health Center
Worker's Health Clinic
200 Bowdoin St.
Dorchester 02122
(617)825-9800
Staffed by occupational health doctors and nurses, the clinic offers care for occupational illness and injury. Fees are based on ability to pay.

Injured Workers United
P.O. Box 4357
Fall River 02723-0304
(508)822-7564
IWU serves as an education and referral resource for injured workers, provides medical and legal referrals, and offers a support network for injured workers and their families.

Massachusetts Coalition for Occupational Safety and Health
555 Amory St.
Jamaica Plain 02130
(617)524-6686
Contact MassCOSH for information on workplace hazards and your legal rights to a safe workplace and for referrals to occupational medicine clinics, labor attorneys, workers compensation attorneys, and state and federal agencies.

Massachusetts Commission Against Discrimination
One Ashburton Pl.
Boston 02108
(617)727-3990
MCAD receives and investigates complaints of discrimination. It also responds to questions regarding the rights of disabled workers and acts on behalf of people who have been wrongfully refused employment or fired from a job due to injury or illness.

Massachusetts Department of Industrial Accidents
600 Washington St.
Boston 02111
(617)727-4900
Contact DIA to file a claim for workers compensation.

Massachusetts Department of Labor and Industries
Division of Industrial Safety
100 Cambridge St.
Boston 02202
(617)727-3460
Contact DIS to report suspected violations of state health and safety laws, including child-labor safety laws, deleading and asbestos regulations, and the state Worker Right to Know law regarding hazards in the workplace.

Massachusetts Department of Labor and Industries
Division of Occupational Hygiene
1001 Watertown St.
West Newton 02165
(617)969-7177
DOH responds to worker and physician complaints about workplace hazards and to requests from employers for recommendations on reducing hazards. The Occupational Lead Registry offers educational materials and information on workplace lead hazards.

Massachusetts Department of Public Health
Occupational Health Surveillance Program
150 Tremont St.
Boston 02111
(617)727-2735
OHSP provides information to the public and health care providers on occupational health and medicine. An occupational medicine physician is available for consultation to physicians. Call for a free pamphlet, "Resource Guide to Occupational Health Information and Services in Massachusetts."

Massachusetts Occupational Health Nurses Association
c/o Judy Manchester, Manager of Nursing and Health Services
GTE EPG HQ Health Services
100 Endicott St.
Danvers 01923
(508)750-2380
Call for referrals to registered nurses who provide care in the workplace, offer information on workers compensation, assess health hazards, and promote workplace health.

Office Technology Education Project
One Summer St.
Somerville 02143
(617)776-2777
OTEP educates computer users about the risk of injuries from repetitive strain and the hazards of video display terminals. It also provides ergonomic, medical, and legal referrals and houses a resource library. Call or write for information on the relation of health to the office environment.

Pregnancy and Environmental Hotline
National Birth Defects Center
30 Warren St.
Brighton 02135
(617)787-4957
(800)322-5014
Call for confidential, free phone consultations, written information on potential risks to pregnancy from workplace or environmental exposure, and referrals to occupational health agencies and clinics.

U.S. Department of Labor Occupational Safety and Health Administration
New England Regional Office
133 Portland St.
Boston 02114
(617)565-7164
(800)321-OSHA Hotline
OSHA establishes and enforces federal occupational health and safety standards. It conducts regular worksite inspections as well as investigations in response to worker and physician complaints. Call the hotline to report on-the-job hazards, without fear of reprisal.

University of Massachusetts Medical Center
Occupational and Environmental Reproductive Hazards Clinic and Education Center
55 Lake Ave., North
Worcester 01655
(508)856-6162
Staffed by an obstetrician and occupational health physician, the clinic provides confidential consultations regarding the effects of environmental and occupational exposures on pregnancy, breastfeeding, and male and female fertility. It also offers educational sessions for workers and health care providers.

University of Massachusetts Medical Center
Occupational Health Program
55 Lake Ave., North
Worcester 01655
(508)856-2734
An occupational medicine clinic, staffed by board-certified occupational physicians, evaluates patients with a wide variety of work-related illnesses and injuries. Areas of special interest include reproductive and toxic hazards, cumulative trauma disorders, and implementation of the Americans with Disabilities Act.

Chapter 11 Alternative Providers

A growing number of people in the United States seek alternative ways to address their health concerns. Many of these practices fall under the broad category of holistic medicine—a range of healing philosophies that view a patient as a whole person, not just as a disease or a collection of symptoms. Holistic practitioners often address their clients' emotional and spiritual dimensions, as well as nutritional, environmental, and lifestyle factors that may contribute to illness. Many combine natural or alternative techniques with conventional ones like medication and surgery.

On the other hand, many Americans regard alternative healers with suspicion even as they have learned to doubt the infallibility of conventional medicine and its practitioners. And their suspicion may often be justified, given the fragmentation of, and minimal opportunities for, clinical training in alternative healing. As a result, the consumer's task of finding trustworthy, well-trained practitioners is especially important—and challenging.

Before you begin treatment, make sure you understand what the practitioner says will happen. Know your treatment plan.

Discuss what to expect in terms of best-case and worst-case scenarios.

If you think you are seriously ill, consult your primary care provider first if at all possible. No matter who you see for treatment, someone with through clinical training should diagnose your problem, and you should keep your primary care provider informed about all of your health care.

Who Does What?

It's impossible to do justice in a short space to every system of alternative medicine, or even to any one approach. The depth and variety of the field are tremendous. Some techniques are geared to the long term and others to a few office visits. Some might form your primary medical care; others you'd consider if you had a specific problem, such as a chronic headache. Some people seek all their health care from alternative providers, but just as often conventional and alternative practices can complement one another beneficially. Here are a few of the most common forms of alternative medicine:

- *Acupuncture:* Acupuncture is perhaps the best known and most popular of a variety of Chinese healing techniques. Acupuncturists insert very thin needles into patients' skin to treat illness and improve overall well-being. In Massachusetts, acupuncturists are licensed by the Board of Registration in Medicine and practice under the supervision of a physician.
- *Chiropractic:* Chiropractic rests on the premise that the spine is a fundamental conduit and support: misaligned vertebrae press on the spinal cord and lead to illness. A chiropractic doctor (DC) seeks to analyze and correct these misalignments, as well as prescribing diet modification and exercise to promote wellness. Chiropractors are licensed to practice in Massachusetts by the Board of Registration of Chiropractors but not to provide primary care or deliver medical care.
- *Homeopathy:* Homeopathy addresses illness by administering infinitesimal amounts of natural substances that in larger amounts would cause the same illness to occur in a healthy person. Only health care professionals who are licensed to prescribe medicine—medical doctors, for example—can legally practice homeopathy. However, many people who have no

formal medical training claim to be homeopaths.

• *Naturopathy:* Naturopathic medicine, which traces its origin to Hippocrates, builds on the concept of the healing power of nature and the body itself. A naturopathic physician (ND) may use a combination of nutrition, herbal medicine, homeopathy, acupuncture, exercise therapy, lifestyle counseling, and psychotherapy to treat disease and restore health. Naturopaths cannot practice medicine in Massachusetts.

• *Osteopathy:* Osteopathic medicine considers the entire body when treating disease, with particular attention to the joints, bones, muscles, and nerves. An osteopathic physician (DO) provides comprehensive medical care, including preventive medicine, diagnosis, surgery, and prescriptions. One major difference between osteopathy and conventional medicine is the use of manipulative therapy—using hands to diagnose, treat, and prevent illness. Osteopaths are licensed by the Massachusetts Board of Registration in Medicine.

Resources

American Association of Naturopathic Physicians
2366 Eastlake Ave.
Seattle, WA 98102
(206)323-7610
Call or write for information on naturopathy.

Massachusetts Acupuncture Society
319 Arlington St.
Watertown 02172
(800)729-0071
Call or write for information and referrals for Chinese medicine or acupuncture.

Massachusetts Chiropractic Society
76 Woodland St.
Methuen 01844
(508)682-8242
(800)442-6155
Call or write for information or referrals.

Massachusetts Osteopathic Society
100 Concord St.
Framingham 01701
(508)872-8900
Call or write for information or referrals.

National Center for Homeopathy
801 North Fairfax St.
Alexandria, VA 22314
(703)548-7790
Call or write for information on homeopathy, including a directory of licensed homeopathic doctors and pharmacists.

Chapter 12 Health Care Rights

Know your rights when you see health care providers and make decisions about your care. Most important is your *right to decide* about treatment. You also have the *right to information* about all reasonable alternatives and the *right to choose* among all the options available, although you may have to go outside your health plan if you choose certain ones.

No one can treat or even touch you until you make an educated decision to accept or reject treatment unless you are legally declared incompetent. Health care providers must supply the information you need, and they must do so in language you can understand.

If you have a medical emergency or are in labor, any hospital with emergency facilities must treat you if it can. If it can't, it must refer you elsewhere. An emergency is an injury or acute medical condition likely to cause death, disability, or serious illness if not attended to very quickly.

If you are under age 18, your parent or legal guardian usually makes decisions about your medical care. Some minors may legally make health care decisions on their own.

▼ FOR MORE INFORMATION

on the rights of children, turn to Chapter 4, Parents As Health Care Consumers.

▼ FOR MORE INFORMATION

on abortion rights in Massachusetts, turn to Chapter 5, Women As Health Care Consumers.

The Rights of Patients

All hospitals and mental health institutions in Massachusetts need a license to operate. All licensed health facilities—hospitals, clinics, nursing homes, psychiatric hospitals, etc.—must provide patients and residents with written notice of their legal rights upon admittance. HMOs must provide this notice at the time a member enrolls and post it conspicuously in all their facilities.

As a patient or resident of a Massachusetts health facility, you have the right:

- To receive an itemized bill reflecting laboratory charges, pharmaceutical charges, and third-party credits;
- To receive and examine an explanation of your bill; this information is also available to your attending physician;
- To prompt responses to all reasonable requests;
- To prompt lifesaving treatment, with no attention to your

Rights Guides

Two worthwhile books summarize your legal rights to health care under federal law. These are:

- *The Rights of Patients,* by George J. Annas (Southern Illinois University Press, 1989). $8.95.
- *The Consumer's Legal Guide to Today's Health Care: Your Medical Rights and How to Assert Them,* by Stephen Isaacs and Ava Swartz (Houghton Mifflin, 1992). $12.70.

In addition, consult *Health Care Choices for Today's Consumer,* with chapters by George J. Annas on health care rights and death with dignity.

economic status or how you will pay any bills;

• To know the name and specialty of the person responsible for your care;

• To confidentiality of all records and communications about your medical history and treatment to the extent provided by law;

• To privacy during medical treatment to the extent reasonably possible;

• To informed consent to the extent provided by law;

• To designate a person to make medical decisions for you in the event that you can't communicate your wishes;

• To refuse to serve as a research subject;

• To refuse any care or examination when the primary purpose is educational or informational rather than therapeutic;

• To refuse to be observed, examined, or treated by students or any other staff without jeopardizing your access to care;

• To receive information about financial assistance and free health care;

• To receive a description of the relationship of the facility and your doctor to any other facility or institution if the relationship relates to your care; *and*

• To obtain complete information on all alternative treatments that are medically viable if you are suffering from breast cancer.

If you are refused treatment because you can't pay for it, you have the right to prompt and safe transfer to a facility that agrees to receive and treat you. The facility refusing to treat you is responsible for:

• Ascertaining that you can be safely transferred;

Saying No

All competent adults have the *right to refuse* any treatment, even if that means you will likely get sicker or even die. The decision about what treatment options *exist* is medical, but the decision to *undergo* treatment is personal—only you can make it.

Physicians *can* treat you in an emergency without consent, but if the emergency can be anticipated and you refuse to consent in advance, no one has the legal or ethical right to impose any procedure on you.

- Contacting a facility willing to treat you;
- Arranging transportation;
- Providing accompaniment appropriate for your safety and comfort;
- Assuring that the receiving facility assumes the necessary care promptly;
- Providing pertinent medical information about your condition; *and*
- Maintaining records of this process.

Your Right to Your Medical Records

The information in your medical record is *your* information. You may need the information to decide on treatment, prepare for your future, and determine if and when to change physicians or health plans.

In Massachusetts, you have the right to scrutinize your records upon request and to receive a copy for a reasonable fee (determined by the copying expenses). Whether you get to see a summary or the complete record is up to the physician.

> **Rights Exception**
>
> Massachusetts laws on patient rights make an exception for institutions operated by the First Church of Christ, Scientist, in Boston, as well as for other patients whose religious beliefs limit the forms and qualities of treatment to which they may submit.

Physicians may withhold the record from you if providing it would damage your health; this applies particularly in cases involving psychotherapy. In such cases, he or she must make the record available to a responsible person whom you designate. Health care providers can't require you to pay outstanding charges for medical services as a condition for examining your medical record.

Despite the law, obtaining your records is often a long and difficult process. The New England Patients' Rights Group suggests you request records as your treatment progresses, rather than at the end of your illness or when you change doctors. It's also important to specify which records you want to see, such as operation reports, lab reports, X-rays, prescriptions, and other technical information. Keep a file at home with your own copy of all your records.

Medical Records and Insurance

Health insurance companies often report the contents of medical records to national databanks, such as the Medical Information Bureau. The largest such private databank in the United States, MIB holds records on more than 12 million Americans and Canadians. It releases data to its members—mostly insurance companies—to control fraud.

Check with the MIB to see if it has a file on you. Because it affects your insurance claims, make sure that any information about you in the databank is accurate. The bureau will answer your request and correct errors you report at no charge.

Read It or Refuse It

If you are in a hospital and want to see your record, don't consent to any treatment or testing until you can review it. If you are denied access, complain to the hospital's patient representative, the hospital administrator, or the ethics committee.

▼ FOR MORE INFORMATION

and a free brochure, contact the MIB, P.O. Box 105, Essex Station, Boston 02112 (617)426-3660.

Mental Health and Your Rights

The rights of mental health patients in psychiatric hospitals, general hospitals, and mental health clinics in Massachusetts include all those listed above, with some variations and exceptions. Specifically, people receiving mental health services have:

- *The Right to Refuse Treatment:* Except in limited circumstances, adults can refuse any mental health treatment.
- *The Right to Treatment:* Institutionalized mental patients have a right to treatment. This includes the right to an individualized treatment plan that meets professionally accepted standards in the least restrictive setting possible.

• *The Right to Decide on Your Treatment:* Before administering *any* type of treatment, including medication, your physician must obtain your informed consent, except in cases of emergency or incompetence (which must be proven in court).

• *The Right to Protection* from intrusive and hazardous procedures, such as forced sterilization, and from harm, such as corporal punishment or unsanitary conditions.

• *The Right to be Free from Restraint:* A hospital may not physically, mechanically, or chemically restrain a patient except in an emergency, and only with a written order by the superintendent or an authorized physician.

Getting Your Medical Records

Medical Records: Getting Yours, by Bruce Samuels and Sidney M. Wolfe, is a comprehensive guide to state-by-state rules. To order the rules for Massachusetts, send $10 ($20 for businesses) plus $2 for postage and handling to Public Citizen, Publications Dept., 2000 P St., NW, Washington, DC 20036.

You can also contact the American Health Information Management Association, 919 N. Michigan Ave., Chicago, IL 60611 (800)335-5535. Send $1.35 for the pamphlet, "Your Health Information Belongs to You."

• *The Right to Communicate with Relatives, Friends, and Counsel.*

• *The Right to Confidentiality and Access to Records:* As medical records, psychiatric records are confidential. Conversely, you are entitled to know the content of your records. Inpatients in private facilities and state hospitals and outpatients at any facility have an absolute right to their record. This also applies to patients who would have received care in Department of Mental Health facilities but instead receive it in private hospitals under contract with the department to replace closed state facilities. Inpatients in DMH facilities must demonstrate to the hospital that it is in their *best interest* to acquire the record.

• *The Right to Control Your Own Assets:* Mental patients are presumed to be capable of handling their own funds—unless the hospital determines that you can't sufficiently understand how to manage money. You have a right to keep and use your personal possessions, including clothes and toiletries.

Your rights regarding admission to and discharge from a mental health facility depend on your legal status. If you are a *voluntary* patient, you may leave whenever you choose or when the hospital determines that it is appropriate to discharge you. Hospitals rarely offer voluntary admissions. You may apply for *conditional voluntary* admission status, in which you remain hospitalized until the hospital decides to discharge you or you ask to leave by filing a "three-day notice."

A hospital may petition the district court for your *involuntary civil commitment*, which is valid initially for six months; subsequent commitments are valid for 12 months. The hospital must prove that you pose a danger to yourself or others and that no less restrictive alternative is appropriate. If you are involuntarily committed, you must go through a court or the hospital administration to be discharged.

Physicians, qualified clinicians, police officers, and district court justices may *involuntarily* commit you for a 10-day emergency hospitalization if there is a likelihood of serious

Mental Health Legal Assistance

For information, advice, and referrals about mental health law and for help if you encounter discrimination, you can contact two organizations, both located at 11 Beacon St., Suite 925, Boston 02108:

- The Mental Health Legal Advisors Committee, a state agency within the Supreme Judicial Court, takes calls Mondays and Wednesdays, 1 p.m.-3 p.m. (617)723-9130.
- The Disability Law Center offers free legal assistance to disabled people in Massachusetts. (617)723-8455.

For a copy of the handbook, "Your Rights as a Mental Patient in Massachusetts," send $5 to the Ruby Rogers Advocacy and Drop-In Center, One Davis Sq., Somerville 02144 (617)625-9935.

harm. This is called a "Section 12 Admission" or "the Pink Paper." You may change your status to that of a *conditional voluntary* patient at any time during the 10 days. A hospital may discharge you or petition for involuntary commitment during that time as well.

If you feel your rights have been violated, speak with the human-rights officer or patient representative of your facility. You may also file a written complaint with the Area Director of the Department of Mental Health if the violation occurred in a department facility or with the superintendent of the hospital if it was in a private non-DMH hospital. Send a copy of the complaint to the Licensing Unit of the Department of Mental Health.

▼ **FOR MORE INFORMATION**
on contacting the Department of Mental Health, turn to Chapter 7.

Rights of Nursing Home Residents

All residents of facilities for long term care (including nursing homes, convalescent or rest homes, residential care facilities, and homes for the aged) have the same health care rights as everyone else in Massachusetts. The following regulations also apply:

- The facility must post conspicuously a copy of the residents' rights and the facility's written policies, and furnish a copy to each new resident upon admission. This means at least posting a copy of the state regulations.
- A facility can't require residents to pay any non-refundable deposit or to deposit their personal funds with the facility.
- A facility can't require a third party to guarantee payment or be responsible for giving consent on behalf of the resident.
- Residents may choose their physician and pharmacy.
- The facility must make clear which services the daily rate includes and excludes and must specify the charges for each additional service. It may not provide and charge for additional services (except emergency medical services) without a prior written request from the resident or her or his legal representative.

• The facility must give 60 days notice before increasing the basic daily rate.

• A resident must have privacy during medical examinations and treatment and during care for personal needs, such as bathing, dressing, and using the bathrooms.

• Married residents in the same facility may share a room, and residents must have privacy during visits by their spouse.

• Except in an emergency, a facility must notify a resident 48 hours in advance if it wants to change his or her roommate.

• A facility must permit immediate access to a resident by anyone visiting with her or his consent.

• Residents may participate in social, religious, and community activities at their discretion.

• Residents have the right to private written and telephone communications.

Advocates for Nursing Home Residents

Ombudsmen from the Massachusetts Executive Office of Elder Affairs visit all nursing homes in Massachusetts once a week. If a nursing-home resident feels her or his rights have been violated, he or she may contact one of the ombudsmen by calling (617)727-7750.

• Residents have the right to interact with other residents or people outside the facility.

• Residents have the right to present grievances free from interference or coercion.

• Residents have the right to manage their personal finances. If a resident authorizes a facility in writing to manage his or her personal funds, the facility must keep the funds in a separate account and provide records of all transactions.

• Residents can keep and use personal possessions.

• Facilities must ensure residents' access to their medical records within 24 hours.

• Residents can refuse treatment or have an advance directive followed.

• A facility must fully inform residents in advance about care and treatment that will affect them.

• Residents have the right to be free from any physical or chemical restraint.

• Residents have the right to be free from verbal, sexual, physical, and mental abuse, as well as corporal punishment and involuntary seclusion.

• Residents are entitled to 30 days' notice of transfers or discharges.

• Facilities can't move residents to different living quarters except for health or safety reasons.

Filing a Complaint About a Health Care Practitioner

The best way to express an initial complaint about a physician or other health care professional is with that person. Everyone makes mistakes and deserves a chance to learn from and correct them. If you complain in writing, keep a copy.

To pursue a problem further with the provider, send that person a certified letter and ask for a reply within 10 days. For a billing dispute, include a copy of the bill, keeping the original in your file. Address more serious, recurrent, or unresolved grievances to your insurance company or HMO.

All physicians and nurses, and most other health care providers, are licensed by a state agency, usually a licensing board or board of registration. If you believe your health care provider has acted unethically or negligently in your care, you can *and should* file a

The Mediation Option

Mediation is growing in popularity as an alternative to lawsuits in health care, including malpractice cases. In mediation, a neutral third party helps disputants discover mutually beneficial resolutions to their conflict.

The Center for Health Care Negotiation began working with the Massachusetts Board of Registration in Medicine recently to resolve patient complaints. After the board decides to act on a complaint, it may refer the case to the center, which contacts the parties involved. If they decide to try mediation, the center handles the arrangements.

For more information on this and other center activities, contact the Center for Health Care Negotiation, 1085 Commonwealth Ave., Boston 02215 (617)277-9494.

written complaint with this board. You should receive a written response, which is likely to include a request to see your relevant medical records.

To find which board licenses your health care provider, see the chapter in this book covering that type of care or contact the Board of Registration in Medicine, 10 West St., Boston 02111 (617)727-1788. The board should investigate your complaint and decide whether to dismiss it, close it, or take action. The board could reprimand the health care provider, suspend her or his license to practice, or even revoke the license.

Even if the board supports your complaint, you won't get money. However, you'll help other patients by alerting the health care practitioner and those responsible for licensing him or her. This may also help prevent future injury.

Use legal action only as a last resort or in more serious cases of negligence or harm. Many lawyers will take a serious malpractice claim on a contingency basis—that is, the lawyer takes a fee out of any settlement you win; you pay nothing otherwise.

Advance Directives

While few people look forward to their own death, we should all make at least some provision for it. Through a document called an "advance directive," you can designate someone *now* to make health care decisions for you when you can't decide for yourself.

The term advance directive generally applies to two kinds of legal documents: a living will and a durable power of attorney for health care, also called a health care proxy. In a living will, you state your wishes concerning treatment if you are incapacitated, specifying the kinds of treatment you refuse and the conditions under which this refusal applies. With a durable power of attorney, you formally designate a friend or relative to make decisions on your behalf if you can't make them for yourself. A health care proxy is better than a living will because it's impossible to anticipate every circumstance.

The Massachusetts Health Care Proxy by Individuals Act of 1990 defines standard practices for executing a proxy.

If You *Don't* Have a Health Care Proxy

You don't have to complete a health care proxy to receive medical care. You have the right to the same type and quality of health care whether or not you complete a proxy.

If you haven't completed a proxy, your family may be asked to make decisions based on what they believe you would want done. If you have no family, or if the members of your family disagree about what treatment you would want, a court may appoint a guardian to make those decisions on your behalf.

Even without signing a formal proxy, you can still write down specific instructions about how you wish to be treated if you can't make your own decisions. These instructions can help other people know your wishes.

However, Massachusetts is one of only three states without a living-will law. Still, most lawyers and health care practitioners recognize a living will as legal, and many states are changing their laws regarding both living wills and health care proxies.

Any competent person 18 years or older may execute a health care proxy. In your proxy, you designate a health care agent to act for you if, *and only if,* your doctor determines *in writing* that you can't make or communicate your own health care decisions—if you are in a coma, for example. Your agent would then have the legal authority to make all such decisions, including those about life-sustaining treatment. Your proxy can put specific limits on your agent's authority.

If you have completed a proxy, give copies to your doctor and health care facilities. If you haven't completed one, ask a health care provider for information and a form.

▼ FOR MORE INFORMATION

on advance directives, end-of-life medical care, and one free set of the most up-to-date advance directives for Massachusetts, call Choice In Dying at (800)989-WILL.

Organ Donation

Any competent person 18 years or older can donate any part of his or her body for transplantation, therapy, education, or research. Obtain a donor card through the New England Organ Bank, the Massachusetts Registry of Motor Vehicles, or any hospital. Fill out the card in the presence of two witnesses and carry it with you at all times.

Because the legal next of kin also needs to give permission for any organ donation, it is especially important to discuss your wishes with your family now. If a family member dies and you would like to donate his or her organs, discuss it with your physician.

▼ **FOR MORE INFORMATION**

contact the New England Organ Bank, 1 Gateway Center, Newton 02158 (617)244-8000 or (800)446-6362.

Resources

Choice In Dying, Inc.
200 Varick St.
New York, NY 10014
(212)366-5540
(800)989-9455 (989-WILL)
Call or write for information on recent state or federal legislation or to obtain forms for advance directives.

Disability Law Center
11 Beacon St.
Boston 02108
(617)723-8455
Call or write for information and referrals on disability-related government benefits, special education, or discrimination. The center offers free legal assistance to disabled people in Massachusetts. Also available is a handbook on discrimination ($10).

Health Care For All
30 Winter St.
Boston 02108
Helpline: (617)350-7279 or (800)272-4232
Call with any problems related to access to health care.

Massachusetts Health Decisions
P.O. Box 417
Sharon 02067
(617)784-1966
Call or write for information on advance directives.

Mental Health Legal Advisors Committee
11 Beacon St.
Boston 02108
(617)723-9130
(800)342-9092
MHLAC provides informational services, advocates on behalf of adults and children with mental illness, and monitors access to mental health services. Publications include the "Mental Health Law Packet," "Minors' Rights Handbook," "Handbook on Guardianship and the Alternatives," and the semiannual newsletter "Advisor." Each is available for a suggested donation of $10–35.

Resources continued on page 207 ▶

Sample Health Care Proxy

MASSACHUSETTS HEALTH CARE PROXY

(1) I, ______________________________, hereby appoint

____

(name, home address and telephone number of agent)

as my health care agent to make any and all health care decisions for me, except to the extent that I state otherwise below. This Health Care Proxy shall take effect in the event I become unable to make or communicate my own health care decisions.

(2) I direct my agent to make health care decisions in accord with my wishes and limitations as may be stated below, or as he or she otherwise knows. If my wishes are unknown, I direct my agent to make health care decisions in accord with what he or she determines to be in my best interest.

(3) Other directions (optional):

____

____

(4) Name of alternate agent if the person I appoint above is unable, unwilling or unavailable to act as my health care agent (optional):

____

____

(name, home address, and telephone number of alternate agent)

(5) Signature: ______________________ Date: __________

Address: ______________________________________

Statement by Witnesses

I declare that the person who signed this document appears to be at least 18 years of age, of sound mind, and under no constraint or undue influence. He or she signed (or asked another to sign for him or her) this document in my presence. I am not the person appointed as agent or alternate agent by this document.

Witness 1: ____________________________________

Address: ______________________________________

Date: ______________

Witness 2: ____________________________________

Address: ______________________________________

Date: ______________

Reprinted by permission of Choice In Dying

Sample Living Will

In the absence of a statury form for Massachusetts, you can use this generic document.

LIVING WILL

I, ________________________________, being of sound mind, make this statement as a directive to be followed if I become permanently unable to participate in decisions regarding my medical care. These instructions reflect my firm and settled commitment to decline medical treatment under the circumstances indicated below:

I direct my attending physician to withhold or withdraw treatment if I should be in an incurable or irreversible mental or physical condition with no reasonable expectation of recovery.

These instructions apply if I am a) in a terminal condition; b) permanently unconscious; or c) if I am minimally conscious but have irreversible brain damage and will never regain the ability to make decisions and express my wishes.

I direct that treatment be limited to measures to keep me comfortable and to relieve pain, including any pain that might occur by withholding or withdrawing treatment.

While I understand that I am not legally required to be specific about future treatments, if I am in the condition(s) described above I feel especially strongly about the following forms of treatment:

__ I do not want cardiac resuscitation (CPR).

__ I do not want mechanical respiration.

__ I do not want tube feeding.

__ I do not want antibiotics.

However, I do want maximum pain relief, even if it may hasten my death.

Other directions (insert personal instructions):

____

____

These directions express my legal right to refuse treatment, under federal and state law. I intend my instructions to be carried out, unless I have rescinded them in a new writing or by clearly indicating that I have changed my mind.

Signed: ______________________________ Date: __________

Address: ____

I declare that the person who signed this document is personally known to me and appears to be of sound mind and acting of his or her own free will. He or she signed (or asked another to sign for him or her) this document in my presence.

Witness: ______________________________

Address: ______________________________

Witness: ______________________________

Address: ______________________________

Reprinted by permission of Choice In Dying

Massachusetts Office of the Attorney General
See Chapter 1 (Insurance) and Chapter 6 (Elders).

Massachusetts Office of Handicapped Affairs
One Ashburton Pl.
Boston 02108
(617)727-7440
(800)322-2020
The Client Assistance Program oversees federally funded vocational rehabilitation and personal-care-attendant services. It also provides referrals and direct advocacy on issues of civil rights, housing, and health.

National Center for Patient Rights Massachusetts Chapter
10 Windsor Dr.
Foxboro 02025
(508)543-6379
The center offers advocacy and support to victims of malpractice. It answers questions on filing complaints, getting medical records and physician-malpractice information, and finding attorneys.

New England Patients' Rights Group
P.O. Box 141
Norwood 02062-0002
(617)769-5720
Call or write for information and assistance concerning patients' rights, as well as for support and networking with other advocacy groups, to arrange for a speaker, or to receive a newsletter. Related issues include quality of care, informed consent, accurate information, and insurance.

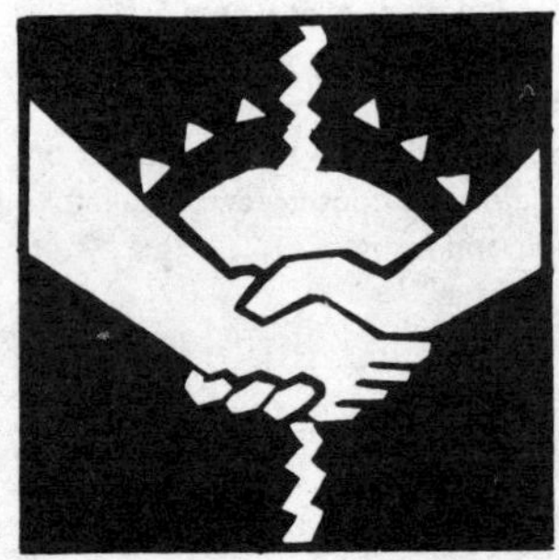

Chapter 13 Partners in Health:

Mutual Aid and General Resources

When faced with a personal health care crisis, thousands of people in Massachusetts every year turn to a support group composed of others in similar situations. Members of such self-help or mutual-aid groups provide one another with emotional support and practical information far beyond what a physician or professional therapist can offer. These informal groups are made up of 10 to 20 people who face a common problem—such as addiction, illness, or a handicap—or provide care for someone else with such a problem. Members offer mutual support and advice based on the vast experiential knowledge and practical coping skills each person has acquired. The groups are voluntary, member-run, and nonprofit, and dues are minimal.

▼ FOR MORE INFORMATION

on self-help groups in Massachusetts, contact the Massachusetts Clearinghouse of Mutual Help Groups, 113 Skinner Hall, University of Massachusetts, Amherst 01003 (413)545-2313. The clearinghouse sells the "Directory of Mutual Help Groups in Massachusetts" for $10.

Self-Help Sources

A good way to find a mutual-help group is to call the national office or hotline of an organization related to your health concern to get referrals to their local chapter or affiliate. Look in the phone book. Ask your health care provider for suggestions or contact a hospital social-service department, mental health department, or United Way office.

Two national clearinghouses have information on groups all over the country. Contact the American Self-Help Clearinghouse, St. Clares-Riverside Medical Center, 25 Pocono Rd., Denville, NJ 07834 (201)625-7101 or the National Self-Help Clearinghouse, CUNY Graduate School and University Center, 25 W. 43rd St., Rm. 620, New York, NY 10036 (212)354-8525.

Advocacy: Health Care for All

Some organizations form not around one issue but around a variety of health concerns that affect diverse individuals. One of the nation's largest and most effective of these groups is Health Care For All (HCFA) in Massachusetts. Its experience illustrates the benefits that can result when health care consumers unite around a common goal.

HCFA reaches people through problems close to their own lives. For example, one person came to HCFA because he has post-polio syndrome and needs reliable, affordable care; he wanted to know how health care reform might affect him personally. He joined HCFA's Community Leaders Project and met people with similar concerns. Together, they have come to recognize that their health care questions relate to the fragmentation and chaos of the system as a whole. And they are determined to change that system for themselves and others.

In the past year, HCFA has:

• Helped over 4,000 callers get needed health care;

• Launched the Boston Health Access Project to push government agencies and health care providers to allocate more health resources for community-based services;

• Informed over 2,700 people of their rights to free hospital care; *and*

• Cofounded the Massachusetts Women's Health Care Coalition to ensure that health care reforms respond to the needs of women.

HCFA serves many victims of the health care crisis through an "intake and referral" process that centers on the Health Care Access Helpline. Trained volunteers assist people who call with a wide variety of needs—from finding out about low-cost prescription drugs to advice on applying for free health care to keeping their insurance coverage after losing a job.

In addition, people served by established health care programs and institutions generally want to protect their access to care and will fight for a program that provides it. HCFA reaches them through direct mail, organizational networks, leafleting at unemployment offices, and radio ads and newspaper articles.

HCFA also produces a variety of materials and publications that explain changes in health care policies and services, translating difficult subjects into language understood by the lay person. These educational and outreach materials keep consumers informed of their rights to health care and help them better understand the issues and contribute to the debate.

▼ FOR MORE INFORMATION

contact Health Care For All, 30 Winter St., Boston 02108 (617)350-7279 or call the Helpline at (800)272-4232.

General Resources

AIDS Action Committee
131 Clarendon St.
Boston 02116
(617)437-6200
Hotline: (800)235-2331, (617)536-7733, (617)437-1672 (TTY)
Call or write for information and referrals about HIV testing, risk reduction, treatment, support, and legal, financial, and housing issues. AAC offers free legal representation for people with HIV/AIDS.

American Cancer Society
Massachusetts Division
247 Commonwealth Ave.
Boston 02116
(617)267-6250
Call for information on cancer prevention and treatment and for referrals to support groups.

American Diabetes Association
Massachusetts Affiliate
P.O. Box 968
Framingham 01701
(508)879-1776

The ADA offers information, educational materials, and referrals from a nationwide network of attorneys for people with diabetes who face discrimination.

Ask-A-Nurse
(800)544-2424
Registered nurses staff this 24-hour hotline, sponsored by 15 Boston-area hospitals. Call for health information on any illness or injury, advice in an emergency, and referrals to local physicians. All calls are confidential.

Boston Mayor's Health Line
(617)534-5050
(800)847-0710
Call for information on such health issues as screening programs, flu shots, breast cancer, pregnancy programs, community health centers, hospitals, and programs for the uninsured.

Boston Self Help Center
18 Williston Rd.
Brookline 02146
(617)277-0080
The center offers mutual-help groups for people with such disabilities or chronic illnesses as cerebral palsy, muscular dystrophy, blindness, multiple sclerosis, chronic fatigue syndrome, and HIV/AIDS.

Epilepsy Association of Massachusetts
59 Temple Pl.
Boston 02111
(617)542-2292
Call or write for information on controlling, treating, preventing, and living with epilepsy. The advocacy program assists people who are discriminated against on the basis of epilepsy.

Health Care For All
30 Winter St.
Boston 02108
Helpline: (617)350-7279 or (800)272-4232
Call with any problems related to access to health care.

Human Service Yellow Pages of Massachusetts and Rhode Island, 1993-1994
George D. Hall Co.
50 Congress St.
Boston 02109
(617)523-3745
This comprehensive listing is available for $19.95, or in many libraries.

Parents Anonymous of Massachusetts
140 Clarendon St.
Boston 02116
(617)267-8077
(800)882-1250
PA is a treatment and prevention program for child abuse and neglect. For example, consider contacting PA if your kids are driving you crazy, you feel like you're always yelling and still no one listens, or the pain of your own childhood gets in the way of caring for your children.

People's Medical Society
462 Walnut St.
Allentown, PA 18102
(215)770-1670
(800)624-8773
Call or write this national organization for information on a variety of patient-rights issues, including the publications *Your Medical Rights: How to Be an Empowered Consumer* ($14.95; $12.95 for members) and *Your Complete Medical Record* ($12.95; $11.95 for members).

Public Citizen Health Research Group
2000 P St., NW
Washington, DC 20036
(202)872-0320
This consumer advocacy group provides information about medical care, drug safety, medical-device safety, physician competence, and health issues in general. It prepares many publications, offers testimony before Congress and regulatory agencies, participates in lawsuits on patient-rights issues, and publishes "Health Letter" monthly.

About the Editors

Marc S. Miller is project director for the Health Care Choices series. An award-winning writer and editor, Dr. Miller's works include *State of the Peoples: A Global Human Rights Report on Societies in Danger* (Beacon Press, 1993), *The Irony of Victory: Lowell During World War II* (University of Illinois Press, 1988), and *Working Lives: The* Southern Exposure *History of Labor in the South* (Pantheon, 1981).

Martha S. Grover is project associate for the Health Care Choices series. She has a master's degree in public health and has worked with the Massachusetts Department of Public Health, the American Public Health Association, and the Planned Parenthood Clinic of Greater Boston.

Philippe Villers is president of Families USA, founder of three high-technology companies, philanthropist, and human-rights activist. He and his wife Katherine S. Villers founded Families USA in 1981.

About Families USA

Families USA is the national consumer advocacy organization working for comprehensive reform of America's health and long term care systems. Families USA issues reports and analyses designed to educate the public, opinion leaders, and policymakers on issues of critical importance to health care reform.

Yes! I want to make the best possible decisions about health care!

Please send me:

TOTAL

____ copies of *Health Care Choices for Today's Consumer* ($14.95 each) $ __________

____ copies of *Health Care Choices for the BOSTON Area* ($10.95 each) $ __________

____ copies of *Health Care Choices for the WASHINGTON Area* ($10.95 each) $ __________

Order the two-volume set: *Health Care Choices for Today's Consumer* plus a companion guide and get a deal! —Both for just $23.95.

____ set(s) including the BOSTON Area companion ($23.95 per set) $ __________

____ set(s) including the WASHINGTON Area companion ($23.95 per set) $ __________

☐ I'd like to place an advance order for the 1996 edition of *Health Care Choices for Today's Consumer* at 10% off this year's price! ($13.45 each) $ __________

Members of Families USA subtract 10% from your book order: less $__________ *Subtotal:* $ __________

☐ I'd like to join Families USA for $25 (or more!)

____ *Families USA tax-exempt Donation:* $ __________

Add $3 for shipping and handling of the first book or set; $1 for each additional book or set. *Shipping:* $ __________

____ ***Total:*** $ __________

Payment can be made with a credit card or by mailing a check, payable to Families USA Foundation, to Health Care Choices, Families USA, 30 Winter St., Boston, MA 02108. Allow 3-4 weeks for delivery.

Name____

Mailing Address __________________________________

City ________________________ State ______ Zip__________

Telephone ______________________________________

☐ Please send me information about Families USA Foundation

☐ Charge to (check one): ☐ MasterCard ☐ Visa

Account No.__________________________ Exp. Date __________

Signature ______________________________________

Copy or clip this form and mail to:

Families USA, Health Care Choices, 30 Winter St., Boston, MA 02108
Or call (800)699-6960